# REPLENISH
# THE EARTH

# REPLENISH
# THE EARTH

*A History
of Organized Religion's Treatment
of Animals and Nature—
Including the Bible's Message
of Conservation and Kindness
toward Animals*

## LEWIS G. REGENSTEIN

Foreword by John A. Hoyt

CROSSROAD • NEW YORK

1991

The Crossroad Publishing Company
370 Lexington Avenue, New York, NY 10017

Printed in the United States of America
Typesetting output: TEXSource, Houston

This book is printed on recycled paper.

**Library of Congress Cataloging-in-Publication Data**

Regenstein, Lewis.
    Replenish the earth : a history of organized religion's treatment
of animals and nature—including the Bible's message of conservation
and kindness toward animals / Lewis G. Regenstein ; foreword by John A.
Hoyt.
      p.    cm.
    Includes index.
    ISBN 0-8245-1075-5 (pbk.)
    1. Nature—Religious aspects. 2. Animal welfare—Religious
aspects. 3. Human ecology—Religious aspects. 4. Nature—Biblical
teaching. 5. Animal welfare—Biblical teaching. 6. Human ecology-
-Biblical teaching.  I. Title.
BL435.R44 1991
291.5'691'09—dc20                      90-2667
                                        CIP

*The earth is the Lord's,*
*and the fullness thereof;*
*the world, and they that dwell therein.*
*–Psalm 24*

*For that which befalleth*
*the sons of men befalleth beasts . . .*
*as the one dieth, so dieth the other . . .*
*a man hath no preeminence above a beast.*
*–Ecclesiastes 3:19*

*A righteous man has regard*
*for the life of his beast.*
*–Proverbs 12:10*

*Are not five sparrows sold for two pennies?*
*And not one of them is forgotten before God.*
*–Luke 12:6*

84127

# Contents

**Part Three**
**Religions of the East**

# Foreword

As I write these words, and as you read them, acres of rainforests are being levelled every second; entire species of plants and animals are being killed off; the earth is becoming dangerously overheated; and the atmosphere's protective layer, which is essential for all life on earth, is being depleted.

Given these and the other severe threats to the survival of our environment and indeed our civilization, one would have thought that our religious institutions would have taken the lead in speaking out against these abuses that represent a direct assault on "God's Creation." But with the planet's future now in question, these fundamental issues must at last be faced. Most knowledgeable scientists agree that human abuse of the environment is causing severe problems that place in jeopardy the continued well-being of the Earth and its inhabitants. And most theologians and religious authorities agree that the Lord cares about the Creation, the earth, and its forests, its rivers, its wildlife — and its people.

Given these facts, doesn't this situation compel the conclusion that the world's religions should be in the forefront of the movement to save the planet?

There is little doubt that Christian theology is partly to blame for the churches' apathy, for some aspects of it have traditionally regarded this world as something less than a place to be desired or affirmed. Indeed, to leave this world meant for the "true believer" an escape from a place that is corrupting and full of sin. And, though this view is perhaps expressed a bit more eloquently in present-day theology, it is still fundamental to the doctrine perpetuated by various religious groups. As a former Presbyterian minister, I am well aware that the religious orientation of most of us has had a major influence on how we view ourselves in relation to other creatures and to nature in general. We have all too often accepted the notion that we are superior to everything else and that the world was made expressly for the benefit of us human beings. As a consequence, we have exploited other creatures for every imaginable purpose (and for some that were pretty unimaginable), and have carelessly plundered and damaged the Earth to no end to satisfy our own needs and whims.

But now we are coming to realize that the Earth and its resources are not without limits and that the creatures we so wantonly exploit can become extinct — as could we ourselves. We are also recognizing, however slowly, that the Earth's biosphere can withstand only so much harm and that we may very well be on the verge — pray we are not over it — of making our planet so terribly ill that full recovery may be impossible.

Finally, we are beginning to acknowledge, however reluctantly, that other creatures are, like ourselves, capable of intelligently experiencing pain and misery and are, therefore, deserving of some consideration that would spare them, as much as possible, undue abuse and suffering.

There is thus the possibility of hope that people are being awakened to these threats to our survival and are beginning to petition that these dangers be addressed and changes made.

And wherein lies the hope that we can turn the tide? It lies, I think, among those persons who, at least in their better moments, are able to view themselves and humans in general as only one part of a very complex and marvelous world, rather than its master. It lies with those who have chosen to accept the proposition that all life has intrinsic value and is, therefore, deserving of some of those same considerations we generally reserve for humankind. It lies with those whose vision for a better world is not restricted to a better life for themselves, but also for their fellow inhabitants of the globe. It lies with those who understand that being truly human means being truly humane and that the wanton and needless destruction of other creatures destroys ourselves as human beings.

The Humane Society of the United States has been most gratified by our collaborative efforts with the religious community over the last few years in promoting a spiritually based humane and conservation ethic and in bringing theological perspectives to bear in fighting abuse of animals and the environment. The fact that so many church groups and individuals have recently become involved in these areas of concern bodes well for both our environment and our religious institutions. And we look forward to the day when all mainstream religious groups will give ecological issues the priority they deserve, so that our "dominion" — our stewardship — over the Creation will "let justice run down as waters, and righteousness as a mighty stream" (Amos 5:24).

In order to support effectively the humane and conservation movements, churches have only to return to the roots of our Judaic-Christian religious heritage, which has a remarkably strong ethic of reverence for nature and the myriad life forms with which we share this fragile planet. There are many millions of people in the United States and around the world who would be more concerned about conservation and animal protection issues if they were helped to realize that the underlying tenets of their faiths teach the sanctity of the Creation, of the Earth, of the land, of the "swarms of living creatures" all around us.

This book provides those concerned with ecological issues the tools, the documentation, and the biblical and spiritual references to reach out to the religious community and bring it into the fight to save our planet.

It is my hope that every minister, priest, and rabbi in the country could read this book, begin to speak out on these issues, and spread the "good news" that the Lord cares about the Earth and wants us to preserve and care for the Creation. Only then will our religious institutions be truly fulfilling their missions.

JOHN A. HOYT
*President*
*The Humane Society of the United States*
*Washington, D.C.*

# Acknowledgments

I would like to express my deep appreciation to several people and organizations without whom this book could not have been written and who have made extremely valuable contributions to it.

The assistance of the Humane Society of the United States in Washington, D.C., and especially its president, John A. Hoyt, and its executive vice president, Paul G. Irwin, has been invaluable in making possible the publication of this book and in supporting its creation. HSUS's efforts to bring the religious community into the humane and conservation movements has made a major contribution toward increasing public support for protecting animals and the environment, and I hope that this book will be useful in furthering this project.

The Fund for Animals, especially its president, Cleveland Amory, and director, Marian Probst, has been very generous and helpful over the years, as has the New England Anti-Vivisection Society, and I am most grateful to all of them.

Doris Dixon, of the Interfaith Council for the Protection of Animals and Nature (ICPAN) and the Fund for Animals, has for over twenty years worked tirelessly on behalf of animals, and research by her has provided valuable data for this book and the others I have written.

Other distinguished individuals who have been most helpful in providing information, guidance, and help include Larry Allison; Debbie Berger of ICPAN; Virginia Bourquardez of the International Network for Religion and Animals; Glenn Chase; Donald Conroy of the North American Conference on Religion and Ecology: J.J. Ebaugh of Turner Broadcasting System; Michael Fox of the Center for Respect of Life and Environment; Jan Hartke, director of the Global Tomorrow Coalition; Ed King; Diane King; Roberta Kalechofsky; Michael Leach of Crossroad Publishing; Joanie Martin-Brown of the United Nations Environment Program, who helped inspire the title of the book; Aaron Medlock; Veronica de Mello; Nina Natelson of Concern for Helping Animals in Israel (CHAI); Patricia Olvera, who typed the entire manuscript for this book and was even able to read my handwriting; John Robbins, author of *Diet for a New America*; Dr. Joel Saper; Judy Scherff; Scott Smith; Christine Stevens of the Animal Welfare Institute; Lucille Stewart, my mother-in-law; Susie and Craig Van Note of the Monitor Consortium; and Eloise and Delbert Wells.

I hope that this book will be worthy of the time, attention, and hard work that these people have donated to it.

# Author's Note

Unless otherwise noted, the source for the biblical verses cited is the King James Authorized Version, except in the chapter on Judaism, where a 1917 translation of the Masoretic text was used.

# Introduction

All the major religions of the world have, until relatively recent times, taught conservation, respect for nature and the environment, and kindness to animals. Protestant, Catholic, Jewish, Moslem, Hindu, and Buddhist scriptures all have at least some tradition recognizing a doctrine of God's love for creation and for *all* the creatures of the world. The obligation of humans to respect and protect the natural environment appears throughout the Bible and the writings of the prophets and leaders of these great religions.

The early founders and followers of monotheism were filled with a sense of wonder, delight, and awe by the greatness of God's creation. Indeed, nature and wildlife were sources of inspiration for many of the prophets of the Bible, and one cannot fully understand the scriptures, their teachings and symbolism, without an appreciation for the natural environment that inspired so much of what appears therein.

Although this is rarely preached from the pulpit, the Bible contains a message of conservation, respect for nature, and kindness to animals.

It is a reverence for life, if you will, for "God's creation," over which we were given stewardship responsibilities to care for and cherish and protect. The Bible clearly teaches that in despoiling nature we are destroying the Lord's handiwork and violating our sacred trust as caretakers of the land, over which we were given "dominion," or stewardship.

There is nothing in the Bible that would justify our modern-day policies and programs that despoil the land, desecrate the environment, and destroy entire species of wildlife. Such actions clearly violate God's commands to humans to "replenish the earth," conserve natural resources, and treat animals with kindness, as well as suborning God's instructions to the animals to "be fruitful and multiply" and fill the earth.

We are now paying a price for our disregard for nature. Humanity is today facing about a dozen potentially catastrophic environmental crises. Any *one* of these could seriously affect the stability of our civilization — and *all* are becoming increasingly severe and damaging.

These problems include the so-called greenhouse effect, in which pollution is causing a steady and perhaps irreversible warming of the earth's atmosphere; the resulting drastic change in climate (exacerbated by worldwide deforestation), which will dry out and ruin our best agricultural areas; the depletion of the world's protective ozone layer, a stratum that, by filtering out ultraviolet radiation, makes life on earth possible, and the impending extinction of literally hundreds of thousands of species of plants and animals.

Environmentalists have been warning about these and other dangers for years. But what makes the situation different today is that the government's top scientists are now confirming that finding solutions to these problems may be critical to our survival.

Indeed, these environmental problems are threatening to overwhelm the earth's ability to support life and could soon endanger the existence of our civilization.

Today, some theologians are asking what greater sin could there be than destroying the earth and making it unsuitable for sustaining the variety of life forms inhabiting it, including humans.

When I began this book in the late 1970s, I wrote that Western religions had remained strangely silent in the face of these ecological threats to the survival of our planet. But this is no longer true.

In the last decade of the twentieth century, we are well on the way to coming full circle in religion's attitude toward the natural world. The largely indifferent or negative role organized religion has played for the last few centuries in influencing humankind's relationship to the natural world is changing. Many religious leaders and institutions are attempting to make the earth sacred again.

Religion is beginning to enter the battle to save our planet earth — a fight we are now losing. But it is one we must win — because, as someone once said, a good planet is hard to find.

With its vast power, resources, and influence, organized religion now has the opportunity to accomplish its greatest feat — the literal salvation of humankind, of the planet, of God's creation.

The handbook for what needs to be done could be the Bible and the teachings of the world's other great religions, for they contain much wisdom that we would do well to heed if we wish to guarantee a future for ourselves, and for our children.

The teachings discussed in the following pages show us the path we must follow if we are to preserve our earthly home for generations to come. Only then will our future be secure and the habitat of humanity safe from destruction.

L. G. R.

# PART ONE _____

# *The Impact of the Judaic-Christian Ethic*

# The Bible's Message of Conservation and Kindness to Animals

### The Bible's Conservation Message

The theme of humankind's obligation to respect and protect the natural environment appears throughout the Bible. Trees and forests are accorded a special reverence; and one of the world's first and strongest nature protection regulations is found in the Mosaic law (Deut. 20:19), which forbids the destruction of fruit-bearing trees even when waging war against a city. The verse concludes that "thou shalt not cut them down (for the tree of the field is man's life) to employ them in the siege."

Elsewhere in the Mosaic law, strict and detailed rules are set forth on caring for trees. For example, Genesis (19:23–25) orders that fruit trees be left wild and unpruned for the first few years in order to give them strength and increase their yield.

Throughout the Old Testament, in stressing the reverence humans should have toward the land, the scriptures impart a strong conservation message, warning against overutilizing and wearing out natural resources. In Leviticus (25:2–4), the Lord commands that "the land shall keep a Sabbath unto the Lord ... in the seventh year shall be a Sabbath for the Lord; thou shalt neither sow thy field, nor prune thy vineyard."

In Leviticus (26:3–6), the Lord's appreciation for the land is made clear when the Lord promises the Israelites that if they obey the commandments, the land will reward them: "If ye walk in my statutes, and keep my commandments, and do them; then I will give your rains in their season, and the land shall yield her produce, and the trees of the field shall yield their fruit.... And I will give peace in the land."

And in verses 31–35, the Lord warns the Israelites of what will happen to them if they disobey the commandments and stresses the importance of allowing the land to rest and recover:

And I will make your cities waste, and bring your sanctuaries unto desolation ... and I will bring the land into desolation ... and I will scatter you among the heathen ... and your land shall be desolate, and your cities waste. Then shall the land enjoy her sabbaths, as long as it lieth desolate, and ye be in your enemies' land; even then shall the land rest, and enjoy her sabbaths. As long as it lieth desolate it shall rest; because it did not rest in your sabbaths, when ye dwelt upon it.

And the Book of Numbers suggests that the land itself is sacred and should not be polluted or defiled, since it is the habitation of the Lord. As the Lord puts it in Numbers 35:33–34: "So ye shall not pollute the land wherein ye are ... defile not therefore the land which ye shall inhabit, wherein I dwell."

And Isaiah 5:8 has a word of admonition to real estate developers, farmers and others who build homes and fields too close together and leave no room for nature and the solitude people so often need: "Woe unto them that join house to house, that lay field to field, till there be no place, that they may be placed alone in the midst of the earth!"

Indeed, Numbers 35:2–5 requires that cities in Israel be surrounded by a natural area, or greenbelt, of "open land round about the cities ... a thousand cubits round about," to be used for the cities' public enjoyment, cattle grazing, and "for all their beasts."

There is even a suggestion that practicing conservation and kind treatment of animals may ensure one of a long life. Deuteronomy 22:6–7 says that if one chances upon a bird's nest with the mother sitting upon eggs or the young, and one takes the latter, one must let the mother go "that it may go well with you" and that you may live a long life ("prolong thy days.") Besides the humane ethic enunciated here, which is remarkable for a food-gathering society, the early Hebrews understood the conservation principle of preserving breeding stock.

## Kindness to Animals

In telling the story of the creation, the Bible tells us that the Lord created the animals to be companions to humans. Genesis 2:18 states that the animals were formed by the Lord "out of the earth" or "the ground," the same substance from which man was formed, in order to be man's "help mate":

And the Lord God said, It is not good that the man should be alone; I will make him an help meet for him. And out of the ground the Lord God formed every beast of the field, and every fowl of the air; and brought them unto Adam to see what he would call them: and whatsoever Adam called every living creature, that was the name thereof.

The Mosaic law laid down in the Books of Exodus and Deuteronomy clearly teaches compassion and kindness toward animals. Numerous passages forbid the overworking of animals and require that stray and lost creatures be helped. The law handed down by God makes it clear that these injunctions to help animals were intended for the sake of these creatures, and not that of the owner. One was required to help animals that belonged to enemies to whom no obligation was owned, as well as those of friends; one could not "pass by" an animal in distress.

Even the most holy of the laws — the Ten Commandments — specifically mentioned that livestock must not be worked on the Sabbath.

Outlawing the working of animals on the Sabbath first appears in Exodus 20:10 and is repeated in Exodus 23:12 and Deuteronomy 5:13–14: "Six days thou shalt labor, and do all the work. But the seventh day is the sabbath of the Lord thy God: in it, thou shalt not do any work, thou, nor thy son, nor thy daughter, nor thy manservant, nor thy maidservant, nor thy ox, nor thy ass, nor any of thy cattle."

In Exodus 23, the following animal protection statutes are given by the Lord to Moses:

> Six days thou shalt do thy work, and on the seventh day thou shalt rest: that thine ox and thine ass may rest...
>
> If thou meet thine enemy's ox or his ass going astray, thou shalt surely bring it back to him again. If thou see the ass of him that hateth thee lying under his burden...thou shalt surely help with him.

In this chapter, the Lord also commands that farmers share their bounty with wildlife. Every seventh year the land, the vineyards, and the olive groves must not be sown or harvested but be allowed to "rest and lie still; that the poor of thy people may eat: and what they leave the beasts of the field shall eat." Similarly, in Leviticus 25:4–7, the Lord commands that what grows naturally in the fields left fallow in the seventh year shall be for one's servants "and for thy cattle, and for the beasts that are in thy land."

And the ox, we are also told, is entitled to the fruit of its labor, for "thou shalt not muzzle the ox when he treadeth out the corn" (Deut. 25:4). In his first letter to Timothy, Paul approvingly quotes this passage. Moreover, Deuteronomy 22:10 tells us, "Thou shalt not plow with an ox and an ass together," suggesting that pairing animals of different sizes and strengths would cause a conflict and would place a strain on the weaker of them, or perhaps on both.

The Bible makes clear that God condemns and harshly punishes cruelty to animals. When Jacob called together his twelve sons — representing the twelve tribes of Israel — to say what fate would befall them, only two were castigated and chastised, Simeon and Levi, among other things for crippling oxen (Gen. 49:6–7).

Proverbs 6:16–17 tells us that among the "six things which the Lord hates" are "hands that shed innocent blood." Proverbs 12:10 goes on to say that a righteous person cares for his animals: "A righteous man has regard for the life of his beast, but the tender mercies of the wicked are cruel." This important verse suggests a biblical division of people into two distinct types: those who are "righteous" and just and who are kind to their animals, and those who are "wicked" and are cruel to creatures under their control.

The Book of Hosea (2:18–20) suggests that God would make a pact with the animals to give them safety from being hunted and persecuted by abolishing the instruments of their destruction: "And in that day, will I make a covenant for them with the beasts of the field, and with the fowls of heaven, and with the creeping things of the ground; and I will break the bow and the sword, and the battle out of the earth; and I will make them to lie down safely."

The fifth chapter of Job also prophesies a day when people will be at peace with nature: "Neither shalt thou be afraid of the beasts of the earth. For thou shalt be in league with the stones of the field; and the beasts of the field shall be at peace with thee."

Isaiah 11:6–9 eloquently describes how the animal kingdom will be included in the blessings of peace on earth when it is achieved:

> The wolf shall dwell with the lamb, and the leopard shall lie down with the kid, and the calf and the young lion . . . and the lion shall eat straw like the ox. . . . They shall not hurt nor destroy in all my holy mountain: for the earth shall be full of the knowledge of the Lord.

The Book of Psalms makes it clear that God's goodness and compassion are not reserved just for humans, but extend to all of God's creatures. In Psalm 36:6, David praises the Deity, saying that animals as well as humans are subject to God's protection: "Thy righteousness is like the great mountains. . . . O Lord, thou preservest man and beast. How excellent is thy loving kindness, O God! Therefore the children of men put their trust under the shadow of thy wings." Psalm 145:9 reiterates this theme of God's concern for all creatures: "The Lord is good to all, and his tender mercies are over all his works. . . . thou satisfiest the desire of every living thing."

Although animal sacrifices are common early in the Old Testament (originally as a substitute for human sacrifice), they are harshly and repeatedly condemned by the later prophets, especially Jeremiah, Hosea, Isaiah, and Amos (see pp. 50–53).

In fact, in Isaiah 66:2–3, the Lord goes so far as to equate the sacrifice of an animal with the murder of a human, saying: "He that killeth an ox is as if he slew a man."

## Humane Lessons in the Bible

The Bible contains several important incidents and anecdotes stressing the importance to one's character of a kind disposition toward animals.

The story of Rebekah at the well recounts how the patriarch Abraham, seeking a wife for his son Isaac, had his trusted servant and ten camels go to the well at the city of Nahor. There, the servant (presumably Eliezer, though he is not named) set up a test to find a woman with a favorable disposition and a kind attitude toward animals. Rebekah was chosen when, after giving water to the servant, she said, "I will draw for thy camels also, until they have done drinking" (Gen. 24:19).

Moreover, after the servant accompanied Rebekah to her home, he fed, watered, and ungirded his camels *before* going into the house to wash himself and eat (Gen. 24:31–33), an act of compassion to which biblical scholars attach great significance (see p. 190).

Moses obtained his wife, Zepporah, under similar circumstances. After he killed an Egyptian who was beating a Hebrew, Moses fled from the Pharaoh and became "a stranger in a strange land." One day, he sat down by a well in the land of Midian; and when the seven daughters of the priest of Midian came to water their father's flock, they were driven away by some shepherds. "But Moses stood up and helped them, and watered their flock." And when the daughters returned home and told their father what happened and that Moses "drew water for us; and watered the flock," the priest sent for him and later gave him one of his daughters for his wife (Exod. 2:11–21).

When the Lord wanted to teach King David a lesson and show him the error of his ways, the Lord used an example concerning abuse of a pet lamb. This story clearly demonstrates the kind feeling toward pet animals that the Bible exemplifies as a virtue.

As recounted in the 2 Samuel 12, God sent the prophet Nathan to David to reprimand him for abuse of power. As commander of Israel's army, David had sinned by ordering one of his men, Uriah, to be sent to almost certain death because David wanted his wife.

Nathan told David a story of two men, one of whom was rich and had many flocks of sheep. The other was poor, with "nothing, save one little ewe lamb, which he had bought and reared; and it grew up together with him, and with his children, it did eat of his own morsel, and drank of his own cup, and lay in his bosom, and was unto him as a daughter." But when a traveler came to visit the rich man, instead of taking one of his own lambs, the wealthy man took the poor man's and prepared it for dinner.

After hearing the tale, "David's anger was greatly kindled against the man; and he said to Nathan: 'As the Lord liveth, the man that hath done this deserveth to die; and he shall restore the lamb fourfold because he did this thing, and because he had no pity.' "

Nathan responded to David, "Thou art the man," explaining that God had given David many blessings, but David had Uriah killed and took his wife to be his own.

And in the Book of Jonah (4:11), God reproves Jonah for failing to show compassion not only to the people, but also the cattle, of Nineveh: "And should not I have pity on Nineveh, that great city, wherein are more than sixscore thousand persons . . . and also much cattle?" It should also be noted that the animals of Nineveh helped save the city. After the "great fish" that had swallowed Jonah (popularly believed to be a whale) vomited him out (2:11), he traveled to Nineveh to proclaim that in forty days the city would be overthrown (3:4). In order to avoid this, the people prepared a fast, and the king and nobles decreed (3:7–8): "Let neither man nor beast, herd nor flock, taste any thing; let them not feed, nor drink water, but let them be covered with sackcloth, both man and beast, and let them cry mightily unto God." As a result, "God saw their works, that they turned from their evil way; and God repented of the evil, which he said he would do unto them" (3:10).

And the Book of Numbers (22:22–35), in recounting the story of Balaam and his faithful donkey, contains a moving and eloquent plea on behalf of beasts of burden everywhere who are abused by their owners (see p. 36).

### Preserving Wildlife: "Into Your Hand Are They Delivered"

The Bible also contains numerous strictures against the wanton or cruel killing of wildlife and domestic animals. The ancient Israelites in many ways had a greater appreciation for the interdependent relationship between people and wildlife than does our modern society. The view that our own fate depends on protecting and preserving the earth's life support systems — the environment — can be found in Ecclesiastes 3:19, which stresses that if the wildlife perishes, humans will not long survive: "For that which befalleth the sons of men befalleth beasts; even one thing befalleth them: as the one dieth, so dieth the other, yea, they have all one breath; so that a man hath no preeminence above a beast."

This conservation message, the ethic of respect for animals and nature, is repeated throughout the Old Testament: if we do not protect animals, if we kill them off and destroy our environment, we too shall perish.

Interestingly, in numerous places in the Bible, the Lord acts toward humans and animals in an equitable way. When God saved Noah and his family from destruction, God treated the animals in a similar manner:

"And God remembered Noah and every living thing, and all the cattle that were with him in the ark" (Gen. 8:1). Genesis 9:8–10 also points out at some length that after the waters of the great flood receded, God promised there would never again be a flood to destroy the earth. Saying, "I have set my bow in the cloud," the Lord used the rainbow to symbolize the divine promise. Significantly, God made this covenant not only with Noah and his descendants, but also with "every living creature that is with you, the fowl, the cattle, and every beast of the earth with you; of all that go out of the ark, even every beast of the earth." Indeed, God makes no distinction between people and animals in establishing this covenant "between me and the earth" (Gen. 9:13):

> " ... which I make between me and you and every living creature that is with you, for perpetual generations ... and I will remember my covenant, which is between me and you and every living creature of all flesh ... the everlasting covenant between God and every living creature of all flesh that is upon the earth." And God said unto Noah, "This is the token of the covenant, which I have established between me and all flesh that is upon the earth."
>
> (Genesis 9:12, 15–17)

The book of Genesis clearly spells out the stewardship responsibilities humans assumed toward the animals delivered into their care after the Great Flood. Genesis 9 begins with the Lord commanding Noah and his sons to "be fruitful and multiply, and replenish the earth," adding that "the fear of you and the dread of you shall be upon every beast of the earth, and upon every fowl of the air, and upon all that moveth upon the earth, and upon all the fishes of the sea: into your hand are they delivered."

## God's Love for Nature

Odes to nature and wildlife appear throughout the Bible. In the Book of Genesis, God looks with special favor on "the swarms of living creatures" that God created, blessing them, commanding them to "be fruitful and multiply," and repeatedly characterizing their creation as "good." Some biblical scholars see significance in the fact that God pronounced each created thing — the whales, birds, cattle, "everything that creepeth upon the ground," and the other "beasts of the earth" — as "good" in itself. But when the creation was combined and united, the Lord declared it "very good" (Gen. 1:31), perhaps because God had created a universe of harmony, a balanced ecosystem, as we would call it today.

It seems very significant that on the fifth day, the Lord created the "great whales," fish, other creatures of the sea, and birds; gave them a special blessing; and commanded them to "be fruitful, and multiply, and fill the waters in the seas, and let fowl multiply in the earth" (Gen. 1:22). This verse seems to authorize the maintenance of healthy, abundant, and reproducing populations of these creatures, many species of which have been or are today being wiped out by human activity.

In the first six days of the first creation story, God made the light to divide night and day; the earth and the seas; the grass, herb-yielding seed, and fruit-bearing fruit; the stars, the seasons, the suns and moon; living creatures; and cattle and creeping things. Interestingly, after each of the acts of creation, Genesis 1 says specifically, "And God saw that it was good."

But when man and woman are created (vs. 27), God does *not* say this, although the last verse of Genesis 1 does say, "And God saw everything that he had made, and, behold, it was very good." But why are humans specifically omitted from this blessing? Is it because the animals and nature have an innate goodness, but humankind has the freedom to choose between good and evil?

The Israelites considered natural resources and beauty to be important features of the land, indeed blessings from the Lord. In the Book of Deuteronomy (8:7–9), Moses describes the Promised Land as an ecological paradise, noting its rich and beautiful environment, its "fountains and depths that spring out of the valleys and hills." Moses stresses to the Israelites the sanctity of the land and how the Lord cares for it: "the land, whither ye go to possess it, is a land of hills and valleys. . . . A land which the Lord thy God careth for: the eyes of the Lord thy God are always upon it, from the beginning of the year even unto the end of the year" (Deut. 11:11–12).

The Song of Songs (or "Song of Solomon") also praises nature's glory, the wildlife, the fruit trees, the coming of spring, when "the flowers appear on the earth; the time of the singing of birds is come, and the voice of the turtle (dove) is heard in our land; the fig tree putteth forth her green figs, and the vines with the tender grape give a good smell."

## Human Stewardship Responsibilities

Not only does the Bible stress that nature reflects God's glory and greatness, the scriptures make it clear that humans have been given a special responsibility to protect and care for the natural environment. Yet ironically, this biblical mandate has often been used as a license to despoil and destroy instead of an obligation to protect and preserve.

Probably no passage in the Bible has been so misunderstood and misinterpreted as Genesis 1:26, where God gave humankind "dominion" over nature and animals. This has often been mistakenly interpreted as a synonym for superiority, giving humans the right to treat nature and animals as they see fit. However, the Bible makes it clear that this dominion consists of *stewardship* over the natural world. This duty carries the responsibility not to mistreat the earth and to protect it from abuse, as Genesis 1:28 makes clear when God commands humankind to "replenish the earth, and subdue it." Humans have certainly obeyed the commandment to "subdue" the earth, but the obligation also to "replenish" it is largely ignored. (As the Reverend Andrew Linzey puts it, "The notion of dominion is part of early kingship theology in which humans are understood to be God's moral agent in creation and responsible and accountable to Him.")

Genesis 2:8, 15 reinforces this message of stewardship: "And the Lord God planted a garden eastward in Eden; and there he put the man whom he had formed. . . . And the Lord God took the man and put him into the garden of Eden to dress it and to keep it." The words "to dress it and to keep it" are a clear message of the way the Lord expects humans to treat the natural environment. God did not admonish humans to pollute and destroy the garden, but to cherish and preserve it.

Further evidence of human stewardship obligations is found in the Bible's stressing that humans are only "sojourners," temporary residents of the land the Lord loans to them. In Leviticus 25:23, the Lord proclaims, "The land is mine; for you are strangers and sojourners with me." Similarly, Deuteronomy 10:14 proclaims, "Behold, unto the Lord thy God belongeth the heaven, and the heaven of heavens, the earth, with all that therein is."

King David was aware of this responsibility of stewardship over God's creation and wrote of this in Psalm 8:

> Thou hast made him to have dominion over the
> works of thy hands:
> Thou hast put all things under his feet:
> Sheep and oxen, all of them,
> Yea, and the beasts of the field;
> The fowl of the air, and the fish of the sea;
> Whatsoever passeth through the paths of the seas.

But the Bible makes clear that the world and all living things belong to the Lord. This contention is unequivocally summarized in the Psalm 24, which states that "the earth is the Lord's, and the fullness thereof; the world, and they that dwell therein." And the Lord clearly points out in Psalm 50: "For every beast of the forest is mine; and the cattle upon a thousand hills. I know all the fowls of the mountain; and the wild beasts of the field are mine."

## "The Earth Is Full of Thy Riches"

The theme of God's concern for the creation is eloquently summed up by Psalm 104, which blesses the Lord for the Lord's greatness in providing for all creatures; it notes how dependent we all are on the ecological system that God has established, proclaiming: "O Lord, how manifold are thy works! in wisdom hast thou made them all: the earth is full of thy riches."

This psalm goes on to describe how the Lord delights in his works and "renewest the face of the earth" with his spirit, which is in every living creature. The psalm makes it clear that God is the source of the earth's natural wonders:

> Bless the Lord, O my soul.
> Who stretched out the heavens like a curtain; . . .
> Who makest the clouds thy chariot, . . .
> Who makest winds thy Messengers, . . .
> Who didst establish the earth upon its foundations,
> That it should not be moved for ever and ever;
> thou didst cover it with the deep as with a vesture;
> The waters stood above the mountains.
> At thy rebuke they fled. . . .
> The mountains rose, the valleys sank down —
> Unto the place which thou hadst founded for them;
> thou didst set a bound which they should not pass over,
> That they might not return to cover the earth.
>
> (Psalm 104:1–9)

God's care of the animals and God's wisdom in establishing nature's balance and beauty are extolled in this psalm, which celebrates the wonders of creation, including "the trees of the Lord . . . which he hath planted . . . ":

The trees of the Lord are full of sap; the cedars of Lebanon, which he hath planted;

Where the birds make their nests: as for the stork, the fir trees are her house.

The high hills are a refuge for the wild goats; and the rocks for the conies.

He appointed the moon for seasons: the sun knoweth his going down.

Thou makest darkness, and it is night: wherein all the beasts of the forest do creep forth.

The young lions roar after their prey, and seek their meat from God.

The sun ariseth, they gather themselves together, and lay them down in their dens.

Man goeth forth unto his work and to his labour until the evening.

Psalm 104 goes on to observe how God's creatures are all dependent on God:

> ... the earth is full of thy riches.
> So is this great and wide sea, wherein are things creeping innumerable, both small and great beasts.
> There go the ships: there is that leviathan, whom thou hast made to play therein.
> These wait all upon thee; that thou mayest give them their meat in due season.
>
> (Psalm 104:24–27)

Indeed, the Lord replenishes the earth with the divine spirit, which is in every living creature:

> Thou hidest thy face, they vanish;
> thou withdrawest their breath, they perish,
> And return to their dust.
> Thou sendest forth thy spirit, they are created;
> And thou renewest the face of the earth.
>
> (Psalm 104:29–30)

Similarly, Psalm 33 tells us that God's greatness can be seen in the natural beauty of the world and that "the earth is full of the loving kindness of the Lord":

> By the word of the Lord were the heavens made;
> and all the host of them by the breath of his mouth.
> He gathereth the waters of the sea together as a heap; ...
> Let all the earth fear the Lord;
> Let all the inhabitants of the world stand in awe of him.
> For he spoke, and it was;
> he commanded, and it stood.
>
> (Psalm 33:5–9)

Psalm 33 goes on to say that the Lord closely follows and is concerned with the fate of the living creatures that the Lord has made:

> The Lord looketh from Heaven;
> he beholdeth all the sons of men;
> From the place of his habitation he looketh intently
> Upon all the inhabitants of the earth,
> he that fashioneth the hearts of them all,
> that considereth all their doings.
>
> (Psalm 33:13–15)

And Proverbs 3:19–20 tells us,

> The Lord by wisdom founded the earth;
> By understanding he established the heavens.
> By his knowledge the depths were broken up,
> And the skies drop down the dew.

(This verse of Proverbs seems to answer the [rhetorical] question posed by the Lord to Job [38:28]: "Hath the rain a father? Or who hath begotten the drops of dew?")

## The Grandeur of Creation

The idea of the Lord creating and caring for the natural world and its inhabitants is a recurrent theme found throughout the Bible.

In Nehemiah 9:6, we find this prayer of the Levites, praising the Lord for his care for creation: "Thou, even thou, art Lord alone; thou hast made heaven, the heaven of heavens, with all their host, the earth, and all things that are therein, the seas, and all that is therein, and thou preservest them all."

And Psalm 19 begins with this tribute to nature as an expression of the Lord's power: "The heavens declare the glory of God; and the firmament showeth his handiwork."

A similar message, suggesting an equation between the Almighty and nature, is found in the Psalm 147:4–5, 8–9, 14–18:

> He counteth the number of the stars;
> he giveth them all names.
> Great is our Lord, and mighty in power;
> his understanding is infinite....
> Who covereth the heaven with clouds,
> Who prepareth rain for the earth,
> Who maketh the mountains to spring with grass.
> He giveth to the beast his food,
> And to the young ravens which cry....
> He giveth thee in plenty the fat of wheat.
> He sendeth out his Commandment upon earth;
> his word runneth very swiftly.
> He giveth snow like wool;
> he scattereth the hoar-frost like ashes.
> He casteth forth his ice like crumbs;
> Who can stand before this cold?
> He sendeth forth his word, and melteth them;
> he causeth his wind to blow, and the waters flow.

In Psalm 8, David repeats this theme of the grandeur of creation and humankind's smallness in comparison to it. David writes that we are shamed into insignificance by the greatness of the heavens, by the eternity of the stars:

> O Lord, our Lord,
> How glorious is thy name in all the earth!
> Whose majesty is rehearsed above the heavens....
> When I behold thy heavens, the work of thy fingers,
> The moon and the stars, which thou hast established;
> What is man, that thou art mindful of him?
> And the son of man, that thou thinkest of him?

## Job, the Naturalist

Much of the Book of Job is a celebration of nature's awe-inspiring wonders. Job spent much time in the wilderness, among the animals and the natural world, and thus learned first-hand of the workings of nature.

In 30:29, Job laments that "I am a brother to the dragons [jackals], and a companion to owls."* Job summarizes his sympathetic view of nature: "For you shall be in league with the stones of the field, and the beasts of the field shall be at peace with you" (Job 5:23).

A primary thesis of Job is that humans must live in harmony with nature and seek to learn from its wise and mysterious ways:

> But ask now the beasts, and they shall teach thee; and the fowls of the air, and they shall tell thee; or speak to the earth, and it shall teach thee; and the fishes of the sea shall declare unto thee.
>
> Who knoweth not in all these that the hand of the Lord hath wrought this? In whose hand is the soul of every living thing, and the breath of all mankind.
>
> (Job 12:7–11)

Job wrote of God's love of the land for its own sake, and not just as a servant for human beings, which is demonstrated when the Lord speaks to Job from the whirlwind, telling him how the Lord does "cause it to rain on the earth, where no man is; on the wilderness, wherein there is no man; to satisfy the desolate and waste ground; and to cause the bud of the tender herb to spring forth" (Job 38:26–27).

In Job 35–37, Elihu instructs Job in God's laws of nature as a source of knowledge and wonder, giving Job a lesson in ecology, God's power, and humankind's relative ignorance of the natural world. Elihu advises Job:

---

*In some Bibles, this verse reads, "I am become a brother to jackals, and a companion to ostriches."

Look unto the heavens, and see;
And behold the skies, which are higher than thou...
Behold, God is great, beyond our knowledge...
Yea, can any understand the spreadings of the clouds,
The crashings of his pavilion?...
Great things doeth he, which we cannot comprehend.
For he saith to the snow: "Fall thou on the earth,"
Likewise to the shower of rain.
                                    (Job 35:5; 36:26, 29; 37:5–6)

In chapters 38 and 39, the Lord, speaking from the whirlwind, challenges Job's knowledge, asking him if he understood the complexity, the perfection of creation:

Where was thou when I laid the foundations of the earth?
Declare, if thou hast understanding.
Who determined the measures thereof, if thou knowest?...
Who shut up the sea with doors,
When it broke forth, and issued out of the womb?...
And to cause the bud of the tender herb to spring forth,
Hath the rain a father?
Or who hath begotten the drops of dew?
Who provideth for the raven his prey,
When his young ones cry unto God...
Knowest thou the time when the wild goats of the rock bring forth?
...Doth the hawk soar by thy wisdom,
And stretch her wings toward the south?
Doth the vulture mount up at thy command,
And make her nest on high?
She dwelleth and abideth on the rock,
Upon the crag of the rock, and the stronghold.
From thence she spieth out the prey;
Her eyes behold it far off...
And where the slain are, there is she.

The author of the Book of Job was thus a skilled naturalist who had a remarkable knowledge and understanding of the wild creatures of his day. And his message is clear, especially to anyone who has beheld and been transfixed by a sky full of bright stars on a dark night: "Stand still, and consider the wondrous works of God.... The wondrous works of him who is perfect in knowledge" (Job 37:11, 19). Indeed, the Lord tells Job (38:7) that the creation of the earth evoked great rejoicing, "when the morning stars sang together, and all the sons of God shouted for joy."

Thus does the Book of Job use metaphors from nature and the animal kingdom to describe God's unfathomable power and wisdom and humankind's obligation to respect the natural world:

> Teach us what we shall say unto him;
> For we cannot order our speech by reason of darkness. . . .
> About God is terrible majesty.
> The Almighty, whom we cannot find out, is excellent in power.
>
> (Job 37:19, 22–23)

Job even suggests (30:1) that some animals are better than some people, for there were persons whom he did not deem worthy to put out with his sheep dogs.


### God Provides for the Animals

Throughout Psalms and elsewhere in the Bible, God is portrayed as being always concerned with providing for the needs of animals, which in turn express their gratitude to the Lord. Psalm 147:9 says that the Lord "giveth to the beast his food."

And in Psalm 104:10–14, the Lord

> Sendest forth springs into the valleys. . . .
> They give drink to every beast of the field.
> The wild asses quench their thirst.
> Beside them dwell the fowl of heaven;
> From among the branches they sing. . . .
> The earth is full of the fruit of thy works.
> Who causest the grass to spring up for the cattle.

This same theme is repeated throughout Psalm 145:14–16:

> The Lord is faithful in all his words, and gracious in all his deeds.
> The Lord upholds all who are falling,
> and raises up all who are bowed down.
> The eyes of all look to thee, and thou givest them their food in due season.
> Thou openest thy hand, thou satisfiest the desire of every living thing.

And Psalm 84:3–4 states that not only are sparrows and swallows welcome to nest in the temple of the Lord and raise their young there, but they are "ever praising the Lord."

In the Book of Joel (1:20), the wild animals cry out to the Lord to give them water:

> Yea, the beasts of the field pant unto thee;
> For the water brooks are dried up.

In Psalm 148:7–10, the creatures and creation of nature are called on to join in praising the Lord:

> Praise the Lord from the earth,
> Ye sea-monsters, and all deeps;
> Fire and hail, snow and vapour,
> Stormy wind, fulfilling his work;
> Mountains and all hills,
> Fruitful trees and all cedars;
> Beasts and all cattle,
> Creeping things and winged fowl.

This theme of the creatures praising God also appears in Isaiah 43:20: "The beast of the field shall honor me, the dragons and the owls;* because I give waters in the wilderness, and rivers in the desert, to give drink to my people, my chosen." And the Book of Psalms ends with the exhortation for all the creatures of the earth to praise the Lord, with the last verse of the last psalm (150:6) stating, "Let every thing that hath breath praise the Lord."

## And the Earth Abideth Forever

The Bible makes it clear that there is a harsh punishment for damaging nature and abusing the land, such as the "desolation" described in Leviticus 26:31–35.

In Jeremiah 9:9–11, the Lord condemns the Israelites for causing the destruction and disappearance of nature and wildlife and vows to turn Israel's cities into a wilderness:

> For the mountains will I take up a weeping and wailing, and for the habitations of the wilderness a lamentation, because they are burned up,† so that none can pass through them; neither can men hear the voice of the cattle; both the fowl of the heavens and the beast are fled; they are gone. And I will make Jerusalem heaps, and a den of dragons;‡ and I will make the cities of Judah desolate, without an inhabitant.

When Jeremiah asks why "is the land perished, and laid waste," the Lord answers, "Because they have forsaken my law which I set before them."

In the Book of Habakkuk (2:17), the prophet warns the Israelites that those who have destroyed the forests and animals of Lebanon shall themselves be destroyed:

> For the violence done to Lebanon shall cover thee,
> And the destruction of the beasts, which made them afraid;

---

*Some translations say, "the jackals and the ostriches."
†Or, "desolate."
‡Or, "jackals."

> Because of men's blood, and for the violence done to the Land,
> To the city and to all that dwell therein.

*The Living Bible — Paraphrased* translates this passage as follows:

> You cut down the forests of Lebanon — now you will be cut down! You terrified the wild animals you caught in your traps — now terror will strike you because of all your murdering and violence in cities everywhere.

In a striking parallel to today's pollution problems, Elisha's first miracle in his public ministry is described in 2 Kings 2:19–22, in which the prophet remedies a crisis of water shortages (or pollution) that is causing miscarriages in the land.[1] In this story the men of Jericho tell Elisha that in their city there is no water (or it is polluted), and the ground is barren (or is causing miscarriages). In response, Elisha cast salt in the headspring of the waters and said, "Thus saith the Lord, I have healed these waters; and there shall not be from thence any more death or barren land. [Some Bibles say," . . . any more death or miscarriages."] So the waters were healed unto this day."

And the Bible gives us hope that our world will survive the destruction being wrought by humans, for ultimately nature will prevail: "One generation will passeth away, and another generation cometh; and the earth abideth forever" (Eccles. 1:4).

## The Intelligence of Animals

The Holy Land is at the crossroads of three continents, and its swamps and wetlands have for centuries been vital waystations for flocks of birds migrating between Europe, Africa, and Asia.

The people of the Bible noted with awe and wonder the annual migration of storks, egrets, pelicans, cranes, herons, and other birds; they were inspired by the periodic arrival and departure of these creatures of such beauty and seeming intelligence. The prophet Jeremiah (8:7–8) asks how humans can be arrogant about their intelligence: "How do ye say: 'We are Wise,'" when animals often seem to know their roles better than we:

> Yea, the stork in the heaven
> Knoweth her appointed times;
> And the turtle [dove] and the swallow and the crane
> Observe the time of their coming;
> But my people know not
> The ordinance of the Lord.

Indeed, the implication here is that not only do the animals obey the Lord, but that they do so better than humans.

The Book of Proverbs likewise extolls nature's wisdom and advises us to:

> Go to the ant, thou sluggard
> Consider her ways, and be wise
> Which having no chief,
> Overseer, or ruler
> Provideth her bread in the summer,
> And gathereth her food in the harvest.
> (Proverbs 6:6–8)

Proverbs 30:24–28 goes on to describe how wise some of nature's creatures are:

> There are four things which are little upon the earth,
> But they are exceeding wise!
> The ants are a people not strong,
> Yet they provide their food in the summer;
> the rock-badgers are but a feeble folk,
> Yet make they their houses in the crags;
> The locusts have no king,
> Yet go they forth all of them by bands;
> The spider thou canst take with the hands,
> Yet is she in kings' palaces.

Proverbs also tells those who have fallen into the power of another to "deliver thyself as a gazelle from the hand of the hunter" (Prov. 6:5).

Sometimes the Bible depicts animals as having more sense than humans. In Numbers 22:22–35, the Angel of the Lord rebukes Balaam for beating his faithful ass ("upon which thou hast ridden all thy life"), which tried to save him by turning off the road where the Angel was waiting to attack Balaam. After Balaam had beaten his ass three times, it meekly asks Balaam:

> What have I done unto thee, that thou has smitten me these three times? . . .
> Am I not thine ass, upon which thou hast ridden all thy life long unto this day?
> Was I ever wont to do so unto thee?

After this eloquent plea on behalf of this beast of burden, the Angel rebukes Balaam for smiting his animal that showed more perception than he did, saying "unless she had turned aside from me, surely now I had even slain thee, and saved her alive."

(Interestingly, people familiar with horses, asses, and burros insist that these equines have an uncanny sense of danger [such as the presence of a hidden rattlesnake], and often cannot be made to go in a direction where they feel imperiled.)

Isaiah 1:3 conveys a similar message, that animals are smart enough to know their masters, but humans are not:

> The ox knoweth his owner,
> And the ass his master's crib;
> But Israel doth not know,
> my people doth not consider.

And the bear is favorably portrayed not just as wise but as a devoted, protective parent, willing to go to great lengths to guard its children. In 2 Samuel 17:8, King David's son, Absalom, is warned of the brutal temperament his father has developed, "as a bear robbed of her whelps in the field."

This reference to a mother bear's devotion to her cubs appears over and over again in the Bible. King Solomon suggested that it was better for a man to encounter "a bear robbed of her whelps ... rather than a fool in his folly" (Prov. 17:12). And the prophet Hosea (13:8) writes of God's anger toward idol worshippers, saying that the Lord "will meet them as a bear that is bereaved of her whelps."

### Reverence for Animals in the New Testament: Jesus' Humane Teachings

The New Testament contains many favorable references by Jesus and his disciples to protecting nature and its life forms.

Jesus' appreciation for animals is demonstrated by the repeated analogies and references to animals that he used in his teachings. He often referred to his followers and those who worship the Lord as sheep; and Jesus compared his care for Jerusalem with a hen's concern for her brood. Often in his teachings, Jesus compared himself to such animals as the lamb and the dove, known for their innocence, meekness, and docility.

In Luke 12:6, Jesus stresses that even the lowliest of creatures is loved by God: "Are not five sparrows sold for two pennies? And not one of them is forgotten before God." Matthew 10:29 also reported this statement of Jesus that God cares for all creatures. In teaching of God's wisdom and love for humankind, Jesus said, "Are not two sparrows sold for a farthing? And one of them shall not fall on the ground without your Father."

Among Jesus' many other references to birds that were recorded (and surely others were not) was his statement in the Sermon on the Mount: "Behold the fowls of the air; for they sow not, neither do they reap, nor gather into barns; yet your heavenly Father feedeth them" . . . (Matt. 6:26; Jesus is quoted as having made an almost identical statement about ravens in Luke 12:24). Jesus was, of course, familiar with wildlife and nature, since "he was in the wilderness forty days . . . and he was with the wild beasts" (Mark 1:13).

Throughout the Sermon on the Mount, Jesus uses nature and pastoral imagery to illustrate his points and upholds the creatures of nature as worthy of being emulated. In stressing the lack of importance of material possessions such as fancy clothes, Jesus observes that "God so clothes the grass of the field" and cited wildflowers as possessing more beauty than any human garments ever could:

> Consider the lilies of the field, how they grow; they toil not, neither do they spin.
> And yet I say unto you, that even Solomon in all his glory was not arrayed like one of these.
> 
> (Matthew 6:28–30; Luke 12:27)

In the Sermon on the Mount, Matthew 5:7 quotes Jesus as summarizing the humane ethic: "Blessed are the merciful, for they shall obtain mercy." Luke 6:36 quotes a version slightly different in words but not in meaning: "Be ye therefore merciful, as your Father also is merciful."

Jesus also used the Jewish laws of humane treatment of animals to justify healing a crippled woman on the Sabbath, saying: "Does not each of you on the Sabbath untie his ox or his ass from the manger, and lead it away to water it?" (Luke 13:15)

In Matthew 12:11, Jesus tells his followers. "What man of you, if he has one sheep and it falls into a pit on the Sabbath, will not lay hold of it and lift it out?" Later, in Matthew 23:37, Jesus tells of how often he has wanted to gather his people together, "as a hen gathers her brood under her wings." In this metaphor, repeated in Luke 13:34, Jesus compares his love to that of a creature known to be very protective of its young.

In John 10:11, Jesus says, "I am the good shepherd. The good shepherd lays down his life for the sheep." Here, Jesus makes the point that there is no sacrifice — not even one's life — too great to be made for those under one's care — including animals.

Jesus also notes with pity instances in which donkeys were overloaded and oxen fitted with uncomfortable yokes. He refers in Matthew 11:28–30 to those "who labor and are heavy laden," saying, "I will give you rest. Take my yoke upon you."

And in 1 Timothy 5:18, Paul advises that those who preach and teach should be honored, "for the scripture says, 'You shall not muzzle an ox when it is treading out the grain' [Deut. 25:4], and 'The laborer deserves his wages'" (Matt. 10:10).

In Paul's letter to the Romans (8:18–25), he tells how all creation — even the suffering animals and plants — is patiently waiting for the day when God will resurrect his children:

> For the creation waits with eager longing for the revealing of the Sons of God. . . . The creation itself will be set free from its bondage to decay and obtain the glorious liberty of the children of God. We know that the whole creation has been groaning in travail together until now. (RSV)

And in his letter to the church at Colossae, Paul describes Jesus as "the image of the invisible God, the firstborn of every creature: For by him were all things created, that are in heaven, and that are in earth. . . ." (Col. 1:15–16). Then Paul goes on to refer to the gospel "which was preached to every creature which is under heaven" (vs. 23).

Many Christians see deep significance in the story of Jesus' beginning his life among animals (Luke 2:7). Denied shelter and lodging by the humans of Bethlehem, Jesus' parents, Mary and Joseph, were forced to use a manger for Jesus' birthplace. There Jesus was born, presumably in the company of such animals as donkeys, oxen, cows, sheep, goats, and other creatures. Turned away by humans, the only companionship the holy family could find on the first "Christmas Eve" was that of animals.

And, of course, the Holy Spirit came to Jesus in the form of a dove, just as a dove brought the news to Noah that the Great Flood had ended.

Jesus stressed that he accepted and believed in the teachings of the Old Testament, which contains a strong humane message. Jesus' frequent didactic references to animals and nature confirmed his awareness of this theme, and he often represented animals as being under God's providence. Not only did Jesus never exclude animals from the merciful attitude he advocated that people adopt; he also made it clear that he endorsed Mosaic law, Jewish tradition, and the teachings of the prophets, saying in the Sermon on the Mount (Matt. 5:17) that he had not "come to abolish the law and the prophets . . . but to fulfill them."

The Book of Isaiah, so often cited by Jesus and his disciples, is full of exhortations to show kindness and compassion to animals and to respect nature (see pp. 50–51).

And Jesus' repeatedly stated entreaties to practice love, mercy, and compassion are consistent with, and indeed fundamental to, the humane and preservation ethic. (The claim by some Christians that many of Jesus' humane statements on animals were not included in, or were edited out of, the New Testament, is discussed on p. 181.)

### "The Lord Is My Shepherd"

It has been argued that since humans *seek* mercy from what is *above* them, they have an obligation to *show* mercy to what is *below* them. Indeed, the Bible often draws an analogy between the Lord's care for people and humans' obligations toward animals.

Jesus often quotes the Old Testament to compare his mission toward people to that of a shepherd toward his flock.

Psalm 23:1–4 eloquently sets forth this symbolic relationship between people, sheep, and their respective shepherds:

> The Lord is my Shepherd, I shall not want.
> He maketh me to lie down in green pastures;
> he leadeth me beside the still waters....
> Yea, though I walk through the valley of the shadow of death,
> I will fear no evil,
> For thou art with me;
> thy rod and thy staff they comfort me.

Later, the Psalms reiterates this allegorical relationship:

> For he is our God,
> And we are the people of his pasture, and the flock of his hand.
> (Psalm 95:7)

Isaiah 40:10–11 repeats this thesis in referring to the coming of the savior, describing how humans could expect the kind treatment a shepherd should show to his animals.

> Behold, the Lord God will come with strong hand, and his arm shall rule for him.... He shall feed his flock like a shepherd: he shall gather the lambs with his arm, and carry them in his bosom, and shall gently lead those that are with young.

The prophet Ezekiel continues this analogy; the entire chapter 34 is pastoral in language, seemingly the writings of a shepherd addressed to a sheep-raising people. As verses 15–16 put it,

> I will feed my flock, and I will cause them to lie down, saith the Lord God. I will seek that which was lost, and bring again that which was driven away, and I will bind up that which was broken, and I will strengthen that which was sick.

Ezekiel goes on to write:

> Therefore thus saith the Lord God unto them, . . . I will save my flock, and
> they shall no more be a prey; . . . and I will set up one shepherd over them,
> and he shall feed them. . . . And ye my sheep, the sheep of my pasture, are
> men, and I am your God, saith the Lord God.
>
> (Ezekiel 34:20–31)

Ezekiel's teachings are repeated in much of the writings of Christianity and became an integral part of its basis. Throughout the New Testament, this analogy of sheep and shepherds is used by Jesus and the apostles to spread their new faith.

Matthew 10:1–6 tells us that Jesus sent out his twelve disciples, charging them to go "to the lost sheep of the house of Israel." And in Luke 15:4–7, Jesus compares finding a lost sheep to saving sinners:

> What man of you, having a hundred sheep, if he has lost one of them, does not leave the ninety-nine in the wilderness, and go after the one which is lost, until he finds it? . . . Even so, I tell you, there will be more joy in heaven over one sinner who repents than over ninety-nine righteous persons who need no repentance.

Later, the Christian scriptures compare the savior to the sacrificial lamb. In the Gospel according to John (1:29), Jesus is described by him as "the Lamb of God, who takes away the sin of the world." In John 10:16, Jesus, again using the sheep metaphor, for the first time extends the benefit of his teachings to include not only the Israelites but all humankind: "And I have other sheep, that are not of this fold; I must bring them also, and they will heed my voice. So there shall be one flock, one shepherd."

### Animal Imagery in Revelation

Elsewhere in the New Testament, animals are accorded reverential treatment, especially in the arcane and mysterious book of Revelation.

For example, in chapters 4 and 5, humans and animals participate on an equal basis in ceremonies performed before "the heavenly throne," and at one point (5:5–6), the animals are deemed *more* worthy than humans to open the sacred scroll.

In Revelation 9:4, we read that "it was commanded them that they should not hurt the grass of the earth, neither any green thing, neither any tree; but only those men which have not the seal of God in their foreheads." Revelation 11:18 even states that the Lord "shouldest destroy them which destroy the earth."

In Revelation 15 and 16, some see a symbolic prophecy of the punishment of God's wrath, arguing that it is perhaps being fulfilled today through humankind's destruction of the natural environment.

One of the four animals standing before the Lord's throne gives the seven angels "seven golden vials full of the wrath of God" (15:7), which are then poured upon the earth.

As a result, terrible sores break out upon men; the sea "became as the blood of a dead man, and every living soul died in the sea"; and the rivers also became like blood (Rev. 16:2–4). Does this macabre scene not resemble what we are today doing to our air, water, rivers, and oceans, polluting them, killing off their living creatures, and causing cancer and other diseases among humans?

Some also see a prophecy of destruction through nuclear radiation or war in Revelation 16:8–9, wherein the "angel poured out his vial upon the sun; and power has given unto him to scorch men with fire. And men were scorched with great heat."

Various other verses in Revelation seem to suggest that humans will be punished for destroying their fellow creatures and so much of the earth, and that the animals will have preeminence over people in the New Earth. Revelation 17:17 states, "For God hath put in their hearts to fulfill his will, and to agree, and give their kingdom unto the beast, until the words of God shall be fulfilled."

In 19:17–18, the animals seem to be given revenge for having served as food for humans for so long, and the tables are turned:

> And I saw an angel standing in the sun; and he cried with a loud voice, saying to all the fowls that fly in the midst of heaven, "come gather yourselves together unto the supper of the great God. That ye may eat the flesh of kings, and the flesh of captains, and the flesh of mighty men ... and the flesh of all men, both free and bond, both small and great."

The apocalypse described in Revelation 22:1–2 gives us a vision of a new world, clean and unpolluted, and bringing forth food:

> Then he showed me the river of the water of life, bright as crystal, flowing from the throne of God ... on either side of the river, the tree of life with its twelve kinds of fruit, yielding its fruit each month; and the leaves of the tree were for the healing of the nations.

Whatever the meaning of this symbolism, the clear implication of this book of the Christian gospel is that not just people, but animals and all the creation, will be redeemed into a heavenly state at the appropriate time.

## Do Animals Have Souls?

In addition to the repeatedly expressed thesis that humans and animals receive God's love and will share a similar fate, there are also numerous passages in the Bible that suggest or clearly indicate that animals have souls and presumably will share the hereafter with humans. Genesis 1:30 tells us that within every creature, "every beast of the earth, and every fowl of the air, and everything that creepeth upon the earth...there is a living soul." (The original version of the Bible, and current Jewish Bibles, use this terminology. The King James Version concordance uses the phrase "wherein there is a life" instead of "wherein there is a living soul," but footnotes to this provide the latter phrase as an alternative.)

And Job 12:7-10 says of the world's animal life, "Who knoweth not among all these, that the hand of the Lord hath wrought this? In whose hand is the soul of every living thing." Ecclesiastes 3:18, 20-21 makes the same point:

Concerning the estate of the sons of men...they themselves are beasts.
...All go unto one place; all are of the dust, and all turn to dust again.
Who knoweth the spirit of man that it goeth upward, and the spirit of the beast that goeth downward to the earth?

In addition to the aforementioned verses, there are numerous other passages in the Bible's original Hebrew that refer unmistakably to animals' having souls.

But in most modern versions of the Bible "*nephesh*," the Hebrew word for the "soul," has been mistranslated and its meaning changed. The Hebrew words for "soul" (*nephesh*) and "living soul" (*nephesh chayah*) are mentioned on several occasions in Genesis, and when they refer to humans, they are translated properly. For example, Genesis 2:7 says of Adam: "And the Lord God formed man of the dust of the ground, and breathed into his nostrils the breath of life; and man became a living soul."

But in nine other passages in Genesis, where the identical Hebrew words are used in reference to animals, the word "soul" is *not* used as the translation in many Bibles. Genesis 1:30 has already been alluded to ("And to every beast of the earth, to every fowl of the air, and to everything that creepeth upon the earth, wherein there is life" (or, "a living soul"). Also among these passages is Genesis 1:20, which should read: "And God said, let the waters bring forth abundantly the moving creatures that hath a living soul." But most modern Bibles substitute the word "life" for "living soul," or use "living creatures."

Some Bibles, such as the King James Authorized Version revised and edited by W. C. Sanderson (1953), indicate in a footnote that "soul" or "living soul" are alternative translations for "life" in these passages quoted above.

Other such altered passages include Genesis 1:21 ("And God created great whales and every living soul that moveth"), and Genesis 1:24 ("And God said, let the earth bring forth the living soul after its kind, cattle and creeping things, and beast of the earth after his kind: and it was so.") In both these passages, "creature" is usually substituted for "soul."

There are, however, some passages that retain their original (and accurate) translations. In Numbers 31:28, the Lord tells Moses to divide up among the people the cattle, sheep, asses, and human prisoners captured in battle and to give to the Lord "one soul of five hundred" of both animals and people. (Numbers 16:22 also refers to "the God of the spirits of all flesh.")

And Revelation 16:3 speaks of the "soul" of sea creatures: "And the second angel poured out his vial upon the sea; and it became as the blood of a dead man; and every living soul* died in the sea.

Genesis further suggests that the animals were given life, and thus a soul, in the same way as was Adam in Genesis 2:7, when "God . . . breathed into his nostrils the breath of life; and man became a living soul." Similarly Genesis 7:21–22 tells us of the Great Flood:

> And all flesh died that moved upon the earth, both of fowl, and of cattle, and of beast, and of every creeping thing that creepeth upon the earth, and every man: all in whose nostrils was the breath of life.

This clearly implies that whatever method was used to bestow "the breath of life" to Adam was also utilized with all other creatures.

An extensive and scholarly examination of this question is undertaken by Elijah D. Buckner in his book *The Immortality of Animals* (1903), who concludes:

> . . . The Bible, without the shadow of a doubt, recognizes that animals have living souls the same as man. Most of the quotations given are represented as having been spoken by the Creator Himself, and he certainly knows whether or not He gave to man and lower animals alike a living soul, which of course means an immortal soul. . . . [2]

---

*Since the New Testament was written in Greek, in this passage, the Greek word for soul, *psyche*, is used in the original.

# Chapter 2

# Animal Sacrifices: Condemned by the Prophets

## Animal Sacrifices

The frequent sacrificing of animals in the Old Testament appears to contrast sharply with, and violate, the Bible's admonitions to respect animals and treat them kindly. But, ultimately, the Bible's humane message is reaffirmed by the vehemence with which animal sacrifices are later condemned by the prophets and Hebrew leaders.

Although ritual sacrifices of domestic animals appear frequently in the Old Testament, strict and detailed rules governed these ceremonies to ensure, at least theoretically, that the animal was spared undue suffering. The animal sacrificed was accorded dignity and respect, and great emphasis was placed on bringing about as swift and painless a death as possible.

Such rituals appear to have been originally introduced as a substitute for human sacrifices, especially of children, which were commonly practiced during biblical times by the Hebrews and the heathen tribes of the area. Animal sacrifices eventually came into disfavor and were strongly condemned by the Hebrew prophets. Isaiah (1:11–13) made clear God's distaste for the ritual killing of animals, relating how the Lord told the Israelites to bring him no more sacrifices since they were "an abomination." Later, in Isaiah 66:2–3, the Lord equates the killing of an animal with the murder of a human: "He that killeth an ox is as if he slew a man; he that sacrificeth a lamb as if he cut off a dog's neck."

In Psalm 40:6, David writes, "Sacrifice and offering thou didst not desire." This same message appears throughout the books of Isaiah, 1 Samuel, Psalms, Proverbs, Amos, Micah, Hosea, Jeremiah, and elsewhere. These teachings were repeated by Jesus and are found in Matthew, John, and Hebrews.

## The Brutality of the Era

The Israelites lived in a time when callous and massive brutality *toward people* was the order of the day, to say nothing of the way helpless animals were often treated. In both respects, the Israelites were far advanced for their times and led the way in breaking out of the heathen barbarism of their day.

Yet, the early Israelites were still just emerging into the dawn of civilization from a dark and barbaric past. Their neighbors practiced human sacrifice, with children and virgins being favorite objects; conducted licentious religious rites, sometimes using animals; and waged a continuous war of slaughter and destruction against their own people as well as other tribes.

While the early Israelites set up codes of law and conduct to eliminate and humanize these barbaric customs, they nevertheless continued to indulge in a more enlightened version of some of these practices. For example, the death penalty was abolished for many offenses, but it was maintained for a variety of seemingly trivial infractions of civil and religious law, such as disobedience to parents or homosexuality.[1]

In conquering the Promised Land and adjacent areas, the Israelites (as well as their neighbors) often wiped out entire villages, killing off all the inhabitants — men, women, and children. When prisoners were taken, they were often executed or enslaved.[2]

A system of slavery, or bondage, of their own people also existed among the Israelites themselves (e.g., the selling of one's daughter or oneself to escape poverty), although it was a much more benign form of servitude than that practiced elsewhere.[3]

Thus, placing a value on *human* life, and substituting an animal for a human in offering a sacrifice, was a *major step forward* for these ancient people, however barbaric it may seem to us today. As the great twelfth-century Jewish philosopher Moses Maimonides said of offering up animals, "The sacrifices were a concession to barbarism."[4]

The contrast between the Israelite culture and that of their neighbors can be clearly seen in 2 Kings 3, which describes a battle between the Israelites and the Moabites. Both hoping for good fortune, the Israelites offer an animal sacrifice (vs. 20); and the King of Moab, when the battle turns against him, offers up his own eldest son and burns the prince on a wall (vs. 27).

## Primitive Origins of Sacrifice

The practice of making sacrifices to one or more gods goes back to the very origins of human society, and is, in the words of one scholar, "as old as the human race . . . a virtually universal custom of mankind from time immemorial."[5] This primitive impulse seems to stem from two basic instincts: the desire to show submission, deference, and gratitude to a supreme being, and to obtain forgiveness and reconciliation from a deity.

The early Greeks and Romans, Germans, Celts, Scandinavians, Slavs, and many other nations and cultures indulged in the sacrificial killing of infants, virgins, aged parents, prisoners-of-war, thieves, and slaves. The ancient Semites practiced these rituals as well, and excavations in areas of Palestine have uncovered heathen altars surrounded by cemeteries containing the skeletons of dozens of infants showing signs of having been burned in a fire.[6]

Probably the best-known example of the Israelites' tendencies to offer human sacrifices is found in Genesis 22, where Abraham prepares to offer up his son Isaac as a burnt offering, but ends up sacrificing a ram instead. The biblical scholar Rabbi J. H. Hertz writes that the purposes of this incident, apart from being a "supreme test to Abraham's faith," was "to demonstrate to Abraham and his descendants after him that God abhorred human sacrifice . . . unlike the cruel heathen deities, it was the spiritual surrender alone that God required."[7]

Another well-known instance of human sacrifice occurs in Judges 11, where Jephthah, who was judge over Israel for six years, offered up his only child, his own daughter. Before going into battle against the Ammonites, Jephthah vowed to the Lord that, if he were victorious, he would "offer up for a burnt offering" the first person to come out of his house to greet him (vs. 30–31). When he did return after subduing the Ammonites "with a very great slaughter," his daughter came out to meet him with timbrels and with dances . . . (vs. 33–34). Jephthah sadly explained to her what he had vowed, and she agreed that the promise had to be kept. So, after allowing her two months in the mountains with her friends, she returned to accept her fate. Thereafter, it became a custom for Israelite girls to spend four days each year lamenting the fate of Jephthah's daughter (vs. 36–40).

2 Kings 16:3 tells of the evil king of Judah, Ahaz, who reigned for sixteen years around 742 B.C.E. and sacrificed not only animals but his own child as well: "he . . . made his son to pass through the fire, according to the abominations of the heathen." In the following chapter (17:15–17), the Israelites were continuing their evil ways and "went after the heathen that were round about them . . . and they caused their sons and their daughters to pass through the fire." 2 Chronicles 28:3 also refers to King Ahaz, who "burnt his children in the fire, after the abominations of the heathen." 2 Chronicles 33:6 speaks of King Manasseh, who became king at twelve years of age, reigned for fifty-five years, and "caused his children to pass through the fire in the valley of the son of Hinnom."

Psalm 106:35–38 discusses how the Israelites learned to offer sacrifices from their heathen neighbors, including the practice of sacrificing their children:

> But [they] were mingled among the heathen, and learned their works.... Yea, they sacrificed their sons and their daughters unto devils, and shed innocent blood, even the blood of their sons and of their daughters, whom they sacrificed unto the idols of Canaan: and the land was polluted with blood.

Even King Solomon (1 Kings 11:7, 33) built altars to other gods, including Molech, the god of the Ammonites, where such sacrifices were carried out.

## Condemnation of Child Sacrifice

In sacrificing their children, the Israelites were clearly acting contrary to their own laws. Leviticus 18:21 outlaws the sacrificing of children to the idol Molech: "And thou shalt not let any of thy seed pass through the fire to Molech."

In Deuteronomy 12:30–31, Moses warns the Israelites not to adopt the religious practice of their Canaanite neighbors and specifically forbids the Israelites from adopting their heathen practices, "for even their sons and their daughters they have burnt in the fire to their gods." Deuteronomy 18:10 likewise outlaws child sacrifice, saying that "there shall not be found among you any one that maketh his son or his daughter to pass through the fire."

Isaiah 57:5 condemns those "with idols under every green tree, slaying the children in the valleys under the clifts of the rocks."

Jeremiah 7:31 also discusses, as does Psalm 106:37, the Israelites' sacrificing of their own children. They built an altar at Tophet "to burn their sons and their daughters in the fire," which the Lord not only did not command be done, but did not even think of, Jeremiah writes.

Jeremiah 19:4–5 repeats God's condemnation of the Israelites, who "have filled this place with the blood of innocents; they have built also the high places of Baal, to burn their sons with fire for burnt offerings." And again in 32:35, Jeremiah prophesies that the Israelites will be subjected to "the sword... famine... and pestilence" because they did "cause their sons and their daughters to pass through the fire unto Molech; which I commanded them not, neither came it into my mind, that they should do this abomination."

In Ezekiel 16:20–21, the Lord condemns the Israelites for making graven images:

> Moreover, thou hast taken thy sons and thy daughters, whom thou hast borne unto me, and these thou hast sacrificed unto them to be devoured. Is this of thy whoredoms a small matter, that thou has slain my children, and delivered them to cause them to pass through the fire for them?

Again in Ezekiel 20:26, the Lord condemns the Israelites for "polluting" themselves with the very gifts the Lord gave them by burning their firstborn children as offerings to other gods.

The prophet Micah (6:6–8) condemns both the human and animal sacrifices that were practiced. In their place, he offers a comprehensive substitute ethic for leading a good life and obeying God's laws:

> Wherewith shall I come before the Lord and bow myself before the high God? Shall I come before him with burnt offerings, with calves of a year old? Will the Lord be pleased with thousands of rams, or with ten thousands of rivers of oil? Shall I give my first born for my transgression, the fruit of my body for the sin of my soul? He hath shewed thee, O man, what is good; and what doth the Lord require of thee; but to do justly, and to love mercy, and to walk humbly with thy God.

## The First Humane Slaughter Laws

When the Israelites did begin to substitute animals for humans in their sacrifices, they demonstrated a remarkable degree of compassion for the creatures to be slaughtered, considering the brutal customs of the times.

In contrast to the callous customs and laws governing the killing of humans and animals by the other people of that era, the Israelites adopted strict rules to ensure that the sacrificed animals were slaughtered as humanely as possible (although such terms must of course be considered in a relative context).

In setting forth the laws governing the sacrificing and consuming of these animals, a great emphasis was placed on avoiding unnecessary pain and suffering and ensuring as swift a death as possible for the animal. This sharply contrasts with the prevailing practices of that day, where tribes would hack the limbs from live animals and drink their blood in order to try to gain the strength of the creature.

Apart from health considerations, Moses' laws were designed as much to eliminate or prevent the practice of these cruel customs as to sanction sacrifices and meat-eating. This emphasis on kindness to animals was apparent in the fact that on the Hebrews' march from Egypt to the Promised Land it was considered the most serious crime with the most severe penalties, apart from murder, to kill an animal outside the gates of the temple.[8]

Another relatively humane aspect of the sacrificial system was the requirement spelled out in Exodus 22:29 and Leviticus 22:27–28 that a newborn animal remain with its mother for the first week of its life before being sacrificed, and that the mother and young may not be killed on the same day. As the renowned Jewish philosopher and biblical scholar Moses Maimonides explained this latter prohibition, it is intended to prevent the young from being slain in the sight of the mother (see p. 195).[9]

(Some of these humane laws in effect thousands of years ago compare favorably with modern-day "factory farming" practices, where animals are often kept in extremely cruel circumstances. Veal calves, for example, are normally taken from their mothers at birth, denied mother's milk and other nutrition, and deliberately undernourished to produce an anemic condition that gives the veal its tenderness and light appearance.)

The Israelites also believed that the sacrificed animal, when burnt, ascended to heaven, thus mitigating any feelings of remorse the offerer may have toward these gentle animals. The Hebrew word for burnt offering is *olah*, which signifies "that which ascends."[10]

### The Prophets Condemn Sacrifices: Isaiah

As the Hebrew tribes began moving forward into the light of civilization, having abandoned the still widespread custom of child sacrifice, animal sacrifices also began to come under strong attack. The later Old Testament prophets were vehement in condemning animal sacrifices, and through these prophets, the Lord ordered that such practices be ended, calling them "an abomination."

When the great judge and spiritual leader Samuel denounces King Saul (1 Sam. 15:22) for failing to obey the Lord's command, Samuel says to him: "Hath the Lord as great delight in burnt offerings and sacrifices, as in obeying the voice of the Lord? Behold, to obey is better than sacrifices, and to hearken than the fat of rams."

The prophet Isaiah (1:11–13) makes clear God's distaste for the ritual killing of animals:

> To what purpose is the multitude of your sacrifice to me?
> saith the Lord;
> I am full of the burnt offerings of rams,
> And the fat of fed beasts,
> And I delight not in the blood
> of bullocks, or of lambs, or of he-goats....
> Bring no more vain oblations;
> It is an offering of abomination unto me.

Like Micah (6:6–8), Isaiah (1:15–17) goes on to offer more sensible and humane ways to serve the Lord and atone for one's sins (including perhaps the sin of senseless killing of and cruelty toward animals):

> Your hands are full of blood. . . .
> Cease to do evil;
> Learn to do well;
> Seek justice, relieve the oppressed
> Defend the fatherless, plead for the widow.

Again in chapter 59:3 and 65:1–3, Isaiah repeats this message.

The final chapter of Isaiah (66:3) also condemns animal sacrifices in stark and unmistakable terms:

> He that killeth an ox is as if he slew a man;
> He that sacrificeth a lamb, as if he broke a dog's neck.

## Psalms: Offer the Sacrifice of Thanksgiving

In Psalm 40:6, David praises the "wonderful works" of the Lord, and writes that "sacrifice and offering thou didst not desire; mine ears hast thou opened: burnt offering and sin offering thou has not required."

This message is reiterated by the psalmist Asaph, in Psalm 50:8–15, where the Lord emphasizes that the Lord neither wants nor needs animal sacrifices, but rather desires from the people true thanks and fulfilled promises:

> I will not reprove thee for thy sacrifices;
> And thy burnt-offerings are continually before me.
> I will take no bullock out of thy house,
> Nor he-goats out of thy folds,
> For every beast of the forest is mine,
> And the cattle upon a thousand hills.
> I know all the fowls of the mountains;
> And the wild beasts of the field are mine.
> If I were hungry, I would not tell thee;
> For the world is mine, and the fullness thereof.
> Do I eat the flesh of bulls,
> Or drink the blood of goats?
> Offer unto God the sacrifice of thanksgiving. . . . [11]

Psalm 50 (vs. 23) ends with the Lord's again making it clear that the only sacrifice the Lord wants is one of thanksgiving:

> Whoso offereth the sacrifice of thanksgiving honoreth Me;
> And to him that ordereth his way aright
> Will I show the salvation of God.

## "I Desire Mercy, and Not Sacrifice"

In the book of the prophet Amos (5:21–22), the Lord also strongly condemns animal sacrifices:

> I hate, I despise your feasts,
> And I will take no delight in your solemn assemblies.
> Yea, though ye offer me burnt-offerings and your meal-offerings
> I will not accept them.
> Neither will I regard the peace offerings of your fat beasts.

Instead, the Lord again offers a better alternative (vs. 24):

> But let justice well up as waters,
> And righteousness as a mighty stream.

Proverbs 21:3 conveys this same message, that "to do righteousness and justice is more acceptable to the Lord than sacrifice." And Proverbs 15:8 states that "the sacrifice of the wicked is an abomination to the Lord; but the prayer of the upright is his delight."

The prophet Hosea (6:6) also states unequivocally that God desires mercy and knowledge, not sacrifices: "For I desire mercy, not sacrifice, And the knowledge of God rather than burnt offerings." In 8:13, Hosea suggests a possible motive for carrying out sacrifices as an excuse to eat meat (see p. 54): "They sacrifice flesh for the sacrifices of mine offerings, and eat it; but the Lord accepteth them not."

These teachings — especially those of Hosea — are repeated in the New Testament, sometimes word for word. The fact that Jesus on at least two occasions quoted Hosea shows how strongly he felt about stressing this. In Matthew 9:13, Jesus says, "Go and learn what this means, 'I desire mercy, and not sacrifice.'" In Matthew 12:7, Jesus says, "And if you had known what this means, 'I desire mercy, and not sacrifice,' you would not have condemned the guiltless."

## Jeremiah: "Your Burnt Offerings Are Not Acceptable"

Throughout his writings, Jeremiah attacked the truthfulness and integrity of the priests and prophets of his day, the people who legitimized and conducted the sacrifices. In 5:31, he says: "An appalling and horrible thing is come to pass in the land: The prophets prophesy in the service of falsehood, and the priests bear rule at their beck; and my people love to have it so." In 6:13, Jeremiah writes: "For from the least of them even unto the greatest of them, everyone is greedy for gain; and from the prophet even unto the priest, everyone dealeth falsely." This is repeated almost word for word in Jeremiah 8:10.

The Book of Jeremiah contains repeated and extensive warnings to the Israelites to abandon the practice of animal sacrifice and their other heathen ways. In Jeremiah 6:20, the Lord admonishes the Israelites that "your burnt-offerings are not acceptable, nor your sacrifice sweet to me."

Throughout, the prophet Jeremiah strongly condemns sacrifices and writes that such practices would lead to the land being given back to the animals. In Jeremiah 7:21–22, the Lord scornfully rejects sacrifices, saying sarcastically, "Put your burnt offerings unto your sacrifices, and eat flesh. For I spake not unto your fathers, nor commanded them in the day that I brought them out of the land of Egypt, concerning burnt offerings or sacrifices."

This is clear reference to the fact that when the Lord gave to Israel the laws of Sinai, including the Ten Commandments (Exod. 19 and 20), no mention was made of sacrifices.

## The New Testament Condemns Sacrifices

These teachings are reflected throughout the New Testament. The disciple Paul wrote that Jesus "entered once for all into the Holy Place, taking not the blood of goats and calves but his own blood, thus securing an eternal redemption" (Heb. 9:12). In Hebrews 10, Paul repeats and reiterates the uselessness of animal sacrifices, "For it is impossible that the blood of bulls and goats should take away sin." And Paul relates how Jesus said to God, when he came into the world: "Sacrifices and offerings thou has not desired, but a body hast thou prepared for me; on burnt offerings and sin offerings thou has taken no pleasure" (vs. 5–6).

In explaining and analyzing Jesus' action, Paul stresses (vs. 8–9) that Jesus "abolishes the first [sacrifices and offerings] in order to establish the second ['to do thy will']." Again, Paul repeats his point in vs. 11: "And every priest standeth daily ministering and offering oftentimes the same sacrifices, which can never take away sins."

And the fact is often overlooked that when Jesus drove the money changers out of the Temple (John 2:13–16), he also threw out those who were offering for sale animals to be sacrificed, "those that sold oxen and sheep and doves." The purpose of the money changers, of course, was to enable those offering sacrifices to purchase animals for immolation.

Biblical scholars have largely ignored the significance of Jesus' cleansing the Temple of "those who sold pigeons" and, implicitly, other animals being sold for sacrifice (Mark 11:15–19; Matt. 21:12–17; Luke 19:45–48; John 2:13–16). When considered with the passage in Mark (12:28–34; also Matt. 22:34–40 and Luke 10:25–28) concerning the uselessness of sacrifices, Jesus' opposition to animal sacrifices is clear.

## The Economic Motivation for Sacrifices

Despite the condemnation of so many of their leaders, the Jews continued the tradition of animal sacrifices until the Roman occupation of Jerusalem and the destruction of the Temple in 70 C.E.. The Romans and some other peoples continued it even longer.

There are many theories as to why this custom was so widespread and persisted through the ages, even among such a humane people as the Jews; but the financial and other benefits are obvious. According to one of the oldest treatises advocating vegetarianism, *De Abstinentia*, written by Porphyry (232?–304?), the Greek scholar and philosopher who lectured in Rome, animal sacrifices were often used as an excuse for eating meat. The deity would be offered a tiny or inedible portion of the carcass, with the remainder being consumed by the offerer or the priest. This view was also held by an early father of the Christian church, Clement of Alexandria (150?–220), who stated in his work *Stromata* (Miscellanies), "But I believe sacrifices were invented by men to be a pretext for eating flesh."[12]

Confirmation of these accounts can be found throughout the Bible. 1 Samuel 2:13–16 tells how the priests were so anxious to consume the sacrifices that they often could not wait for it to be cooked, but ate it raw, sometimes "taking it by force."

In fact, the Israelite political-economic system, of which sacrifices were an integral part, was clearly, if not outright corrupt, highly favorable to the priestly caste (the Levites and the "sons of Aaron": Numbers 18:1–17). By law, it required periodic tributes not just of sacrificial animals but also of food and other goods (and always the most choice of what was available) be rendered unto the priests (who could not own property). This was often done under the pretext of tithing or giving up a portion of one's wealth to the Lord.

The requirement that the priests be given the meat of sacrificed animals for food is, in fact, spelled out in the Mosaic law, e.g., Leviticus 6:26, 7:30–36, and Numbers 18:8–19. Deuteronomy 18:1–3 requires that the priests from the tribe of Levi may not own or inherit any property but "shall eat the offerings of the Lord made by fire," and that the priests shall be given the prime cuts from sacrificed ox and sheep.

Reverend V. A. Holmes-Gore speculates that the sacrifice merchants may have had to pay a significant percentage or rental fee to the top Temple officials and concludes:

> It is clear that the whole sacrificial system was a source of ill-gotten gain to the permanent officials and especially the high-priestly family. It is therefore clear that the priests would strongly oppose any humanitarian attempts to stop their appalling traffic in the lives of the creatures.[13]

The biblical scholar Alfred Edersheim gives an account of life in these days that strongly confirms the theory that economic motives helped perpetuate the sacrificial system. In his book *The Temple: Its Ministry and Services as They Were at the Time of Jesus Christ* (1881), he states that sacrifices "had been foreign elements imported into it [Judaism] — tolerated, indeed, by Moses, but against which the prophets earnestly protested and incessantly labored." He goes on to describe the large number of people that this system required be employed to maintain it, including over five hundred priests on some feast days.[14]

But employment was not the only benefit that accrued from the sacrificial system. As Edersheim points out, food, hides, and of course money were other fringe benefits enjoyed by the offerers and especially the priests.

An example of the magnitude of some of the sacrifices that took place is found in 1 Kings 8:63–65, where King Solomon is said to have sacrificed as a peace-offering 22,000 oxen and 120,000 sheep in order to "dedicate the house of the Lord." Later that day, more sacrifices were made, a great feast was held, and the celebration lasted "seven days and seven days, even fourteen days."

Moreover, this economic system provided a basis for cooperation and collaboration between *some* of the Jewish priests and their Roman overlords. According to Edersheim,

> The Emperor Augustus had a daily burnt-offering brought for him of two lambs and a bullock; and ever afterward this sacrifice was regarded as indicating that the Jewish nation recognized the Roman emperor as their ruler. Hence, at the commencement of the Jewish war, Eleazar carried its rejection, and this became . . . the open mark of the rebellion.[15]

All this is not to say that this system was a totally corrupt and evil one. These same laws required that donations be given to the poor, e.g., "the stranger, the fatherless, and the widow, that they may eat within the gates, and be filled" (Deut. 26:12). Moreover, having no property,

the priests had to depend on these offerings from the people to sustain themselves. But what is not arguable is that such an arrangement
provided great encouragement for the ruling class to perpetuate the sacrificial system as a means of procuring food, especially choice cuts of
meat.

The idea that slaughtering animals is pleasing to, and will appease,
God and/or the higher powers has persisted in modern days among
some sects. Animals are commonly killed and mutilated in voodoo rituals and in Moslem religious ceremonies. For example on January 23,
1980, when Iran's ruling holy man, Ayatollah Khomeini, was admitted
to the hospital because of a heart condition, between two and three thousand sheep and cows were reported sacrificed in the streets and outside
mosques in prayer rites for him in the holy city of Qom.[16]

Moreover, animal sacrifices frequently take place throughout the
United States, usually by Satanists, voodoo believers, and practitioners
of Santeria, a secretive Afro-Cuban cult that is a blend of Catholicism
and voodoo, and is widely practiced in Cuba, in Brazil, throughout the
Caribbean, and in several large cities in the United States.[17]

# Chapter 3 _____

# The Early Christian Saints: Compassion and Love for Animals

The Christian church got off to a good start in its relationship to animals. The saints of the first thousand years or so are traditionally depicted as having close and friendly relationships with various wild and domestic creatures, even wolves and lions. The most famous of these legends concerns St. Francis of Assisi, the patron saint of animals.

There are hundreds, even thousands, of such stories of other saints; and, as the Irish historian W. E. H. Lecky (1838–1903) wrote in his monumental work, *History of European Morals from Augustus to Charlemagne* (1869):

> It was very natural that the hermit, living in the lonely deserts of the East, or in the vast forests of Europe, should come into an intimate connection with the animal world, and it was no less natural that the popular imagination, when depicting the hermit life, should make this connection the center of many picturesque and sometimes touching legends.[1]

"These legends," Lecky said, "are worthy of special notice in moral history as representing the first, and at the same time one of the most striking, efforts ever made in Christendom to inculcate a feeling of kindness and pity towards the brute creation."[2]

According to Reverend Andrew Linzey, author of *Christianity and the Rights of Animals,*

> St. Francis is not alone in his concern for "brother and sister" creatures — as he called them. The lives of more than two-thirds of canonized saints — east and west — demonstrate a practical concern for, and befriending of, animals, which was often in sharp contrast to the conventional view of their contemporaries.[3]

Whatever the basis in fact for these stories — and many are obviously exaggerated or apocryphal — they do demonstrate the attitude toward animals commonly held by the church's most revered figures of that era.

## The Early Saints

Some of the best-known and most-loved saints of the Christian church had close relationships with animals.

St. Jerome (340?–420), who published the Vulgate, the Latin version of the Bible, is traditionally depicted as living with his pet donkey or lamb. A lion he is said to have befriended by pulling a thorn out of its paw appointed itself his bodyguard,[4] supposedly shepherding the donkey out to pasture each morning and home again each night.[5]

The cell of St. Theon was regularly visited by goats, wild asses, and buffaloes. And then there is the legend of St. Gent, who is said to have captured a wolf that had killed one of two cows with which he was plowing, harnessed the wolf, and had it plowing with the other cow.[6]

St. John Chrysostom (345?–407), one of the fathers of the Greek Church and the patriarch of Constantinople, spent ten years in the desert leading a life of study and asceticism. He wrote:

> The Saints are exceedingly loving and gentle to mankind, and even to brute beasts. . . . Surely we ought to show them great kindness and gentleness for many reasons, but, above all, because they are of the same origin as ourselves.[7]

Thus, St. Chrysostom had the foresight to perceive the evolutionary brotherhood of humans and animals some fifteen hundred years before Darwin scientifically established this fact!

St. Basil (330?–379?), known as Basil the Great, the bishop of Caesarea and founder of monastic institutions, reportedly had the following prayer in his liturgy:

> The Earth is the Lord's and the fullness thereof. O God, enlarge within us the sense of fellowship with all living things, our brothers the animals to whom thou has given the earth as their home in common with us. We remember with shame that in the past we have exercised the high dominion of man with ruthless cruelty, so that the voice of the earth, which should have gone up to thee in song, has been a groan of travail. May we realize that they live, not for us alone, but for themselves and for thee, and that they have the sweetness of life.[8]

Even the founder of Western monasticism and the Benedictine order, St. Benedict (480?–543?), befriended the wildlife at his monastery at Monte Cassino. His biographer, Abbot Tosti, wrote in 1896:

> Men like St. Benedict, always intent on the love of the Creator, could not withhold their love from the things He had created. Hence, they felt themselves bound by bonds of fraternal love with everything in God's universe.... [9] [T]he irrational animals, by divine ordination, often gave their services to these holy men, who, in the desert, far from human society, committed their lives into the hands of God alone. Wherefore, though defenseless and solitary, they never died from the violence of wild beasts.[10]

It is said that a group of monks at Vicovaro became unhappy with their superior Benedict's rules, and one attempted to kill him by poisoning a loaf of bread. But when St. Benedict, through divine intervention, became aware of this, he called upon his pet raven, which he fed at mealtimes, to carry off the loaf and hide it where it would not be found.[11]

Ravens, known for their great intelligence, also figure prominently in the lives of other saints. St. Meinrad, the hermit, befriended a pair of ravens, which witnessed his murder and helped discover the killers. After thieves looking for valuables in his cave murdered Meinrad, the birds followed them into the village and made such a commotion around them, flapping and carrying on, that an investigation was undertaken. The murderers were punished, and a shrine was established there that to this day remains a place of pilgrimage.[12]

Ravens are said to still be cherished in many Benedictine monasteries;[13] and flocks of ravens used to assemble at the tomb of St. Apollinar of Ravenna on his festival day.

When the English monk St. Cuthbert (635?–687) admonished some ravens for taking the thatch of his shelter to make their nests, they understood him, showed humility, and obeyed.[14] Cuthbert had relations with other creatures as well. When he called the birds, they came; and once, like St. Kieranus, he revived a dead bird by praying for it.[15] On another occasion Cuthbert called upon an eagle for assistance; it caught and brought to him a large fish, which he and his companion shared with the bird half and half.

The English theologian, scholar, and historian St. Bede (673–735), also known as the Venerable Bede, recorded the following incident involving St. Cuthbert:

> At dawn, he came out of the sea and falling on his knees continued his prayer. Whilst he was doing this, two animals called sea-otters* came out

---

*In modern times, sea otters are known to occur only along the North Pacific coast of the continental United States and Alaska, but seals do exist off Britain.

of the sea and lying before him on the sand, warmed his feet with their breath and wiped them with their hair. After receiving his blessing, they returned to their native element.[16]

St. Giles, in the seventh century, was reportedly crippled while defending his pet deer. According to legend, St. Giles was an Athenian who made a hermitage in a French forest near the mouth of the Rhone river, surviving on herbs and his pet hind's milk. When the king of the Visigoths, Flavius Wamba, was out hunting, he chased the pet to the hermitage and became so impressed by Giles's holiness that he built him a monastery.[17] Giles became the patron saint of beggars, cripples, and blacksmiths. He is one of the most popular of the medieval saints, and in Britain alone some 160 churches are dedicated to him.[18]

### "Saints and Beasts" in European History

Some of the best-known tales of "saints and beasts" have been compiled and recounted by Lecky in his *History of European Morals*. Wild animals supposedly accompanied St. Theon on his walks, and he, in turn, gave them water to drink from his well. St. Kieranus wept, prayed over, and healed a mortally wounded bird that had been attacked by a hawk. When St. Aengussius cut his hand while chopping wood, birds gathered around him and loudly bemoaned his accident.[19] St. Erasmus was the protector of oxen, which would kneel down at his shrine, and St. Antony was the protector of pigs.[20]

Lions as well as birds figure prominently in these saintly legends and are associated with Jerome, John the Silent, Simeon, Gerasimus, and many other saints. Lions are said to have buried both St. Paul the hermit and St. Mary of Egypt. When a weak and elderly monk named St. Zosimas was traveling to Caesarea with an ass carrying his possessions, a lion killed and ate the ass. However, when Zosimas ordered the lion to carry his load to the city gates, it did so.[21]

Similarly, St. Helenus summoned a wild ass from its herd to carry his possessions through the wilderness.[22] Both he and St. Pachomius (the fourth-century Christian monk of Egypt who founded the first monastic institution, on an island in the Nile) traversed the Nile River on the back of a crocodile. And St. Scuthinus crossed the Irish Channel on a "sea monster."[23]

Deer are also the subject of many of these apocryphal tales, with stags accompanying the saints on their journeys, carrying their loads, and plowing their fields. The hunted stag very commonly figured in these legends and was often protected by saintly hermits, who sometimes converted the hunter to Christianity. On St. Regulus's festival day, wild stags would assemble at his tomb. And in the midst of a deer hunt, both the hounds and the stag halted to kneel down and pray together at the remains of St. Fingar.[24]

Stags are also held responsible for the conversions of St. Hubert, the eighth-century patron saint of hunters, and of St. Eustachius, the second-century Roman martyr and one of fourteen saints called "helpers in need" for those sick, in danger, or in need. Hubert is said to have been converted while hunting a stag, which turned toward him with a luminous crucifix on its head and spoke to him in a human voice. He later became bishop of Maestricht and Liege. Legend also has it that Eustachius, a Roman general, was similarly converted by the image of Jesus between a stag's antlers.[25]

After St. Macarius of Alexandria restored the sight of a young blind hyena brought to his door by its mother, she, in gratitude, brought him some wool. When Macarius admonished the hyena for stealing and killing a sheep, the hyena hung its head in shame, and, still bowing, swore not to rob again. There are similar tales of a lion's having its blind cub's sight restored by the prayer of a saint, and then bringing him an animal skin. And a wolf showed great remorse for taking a loaf of bread from the hermit, who usually shared his supper with the creature.[26]

St. Colman, the seventh-century Irish monk and bishop of Lindisfarne, is supposed to have had three companions — a rooster, a mouse, and a fly, all of whom cooperated to help Colman keep his devotional schedule. The rooster crowed to announce the hour of prayer; the mouse bit his ear until the sleepy saint aroused; and the fly would alight on the line of the book Colman was studying to keep his place in case his mind wandered or he had to leave the room.[27]

St. Anthony of Padua (1195–1231), the Franciscan monk who preached throughout Italy and France and was canonized in 1232 by Pope Gregory IX,[28] is credited with attracting a group of fish that came to hear him preach.[29]

### Befriending Swans, Horses, and Wolves

Stories handed down through the ages depict many other saints as animal lovers. In the sixth century, St. Columba (521–97) and twelve disciples left Ireland and settled on the island of Iona, off the west coast of Scotland, and founded a mission there. The island is known as the cradle of British Christianity, since it is from Iona that Christianity is said to have spread to the British Isles. While on Iona, Columba once sent a monk to take care of a swan that had arrived there exhausted, until it had recovered.

Columba had a favorite horse, which indicated the imminence of the saint's death through its lamentations. When the Irish saint returned home to bid farewell to his community, his old gray horse, which used to draw his laundry cart and had now been put out to pasture, ambled across the field to him and nuzzled him affectionately, as if to say adieu. Columba, saddened and moved by the experience, said to his old friend who had accompanied him: "Our creator has revealed to this poor creature what He did not reveal to thee, rational man as thou art."[30]

The image of the kind and compassionate wolf, made most famous in the legend of Romulus and Remus being suckled and raised by a mother wolf, also found its way into the story of the sixth-century Irish bishop St. Ailbe. Soon after he was born to a slave girl, her master ordered her to take the child into the wilderness and leave him. There, he was found by a wolf, which took care of him until a hunter came across the child and returned him to civilization. Many years later, after he had become the bishop of Emily, a wolf being chased by hunters took refuge in his home, put its head on his lap, and asked for his help, to which Ailbe replied:

> I will protect thee, old mother. When I was little and young and feeble, thou didst nourish and cherish and protect me, and now that thou are old and gray and weak, shall I not render the same love and care to thee? None shall injure thee. Come every day with thy little ones to my table, and thou and thine shall share my crusts.[31]

### God's Animals

A charming collection of these legends of saints and animals has been compiled by the Reverend Ambrose Agius in his book *God's Animals*. One of the earliest of the Christian saints, John the Apostle, amused himself during the last years of life with a pet partridge. When two of his dedicated disciples seemed surprised and embarrassed to encounter him fondling his pet bird, believing John to be totally engrossed in his mysticism and apocalyptic visions, the saint responded with his now-famous reply, "The bow which is always bent loses its spring."[32]

There was also the fourth-century saint Blasius (or St. Blaise), the Christian bishop of Sebaste, Armenia, who is the patron saint of wool combers, supposedly having been martyred by having his flesh ripped with wool combers' irons and being beheaded. The saint is said to have established an animal hospital in the wilderness that helped the wildlife, which in turn protected and cared for him.[33]

One of the great animal-loving saints of Ireland was St. Patrick (389?–461?). It is Patrick who was entrusted by Pope Celestine I with "converting the Irish race" and who established churches and the Catholic faith throughout northern Ireland. He is also credited with introducing Latin as the language of the church and with founding the monastery at Armagh,[34] where he is said to have saved a mother deer and her baby. When St. Patrick and his companions flushed the doe and her fawn, he refused to let them be harmed and carried the fawn to a safe location.[35]

Commenting on this incident, Richard Power writes in *The Ark* that it was this courageous, compassionate act that served to impress, and convert, these pagan hunters: "By saving the fawn they were about to kill, St. Patrick made the Christian religion meaningful to the hardened Ulster warriors. Before that act of compassion, his preaching had failed to convince them."[36]

Another Irish saint, Kevin of Glendalough, declined an angel's offer to level some hills to be used as the foundation for his monastery, saying, "I have no wish that the wild creatures on these mountains should be sad because of me." As the story goes, while in the Wicklow mountains (some thirty miles from Dublin) St. Kevin was visited one day by an angel, who had apparently been observing him for some time. The angel offered to make the saint's life a little more comfortable, saying:

> I would sweep away these hills
> and crags and rocks and wooded dells,
> where little grows and no one dwells;
> I'll give you pastures lush and green
> for kine to graze, a winding stream,
> and gentle fields to grow your grain
> in place of this uncouth domain.

But Kevin, shaking his head, declined the offer, saying:

> I pray you humbly, let them stand,
> the rugged hills, the broken land;
> for I do love like any child
> the hunted creature of the wild;
> and every bird that climbs the sky
> is free to wander just as I
> or dwell in peace beside the lake,
> to make them homeless for my sake
> would grieve me sorely night and day.[37]

In recounting this tale of his patron saint, the Reverend Kevin Daley observes that "St. Kevin's respect for the animals grew from his closeness to God in prayer, and his love communicated itself to the animals so that the most fierce became tame at his feet."[38]

## English Saints

There are numerous English saints who loved animals, including those of the Saxon invasion of the fifth century. St. Werburgh of Chester made a deal with some geese that had been damaging church property that no action would be taken against them if they left and caused no more trouble. But when one of her attendants unwittingly killed one of the geese, they returned, honking and protesting loudly, until St. Werburgh brought the fowl back to life.[39]

In France, the Marquise of Rambures has also collected various tales of the saints and animals in her book *L'Eglise et la pitié envers les animaux* (The church and kindness toward animals, 1908). It recounts a tale told by Father Matthew Kelly, of Maynooth Seminary, Ireland, that St. Kevin was able to tame the wildlife around him: "For him, as for other Saints, part of the lost empire of Paradise was restored as the wild beasts of the mountain and the forest became tame in his presence and drank water out of his hand."[40]

The early English mystic St. Guthlac could reportedly call the birds in to feed from his hand; he explained his powers as follows: "Hast thou never learned in Holy Writ that he who led his life after God's will, the wild beasts and the wild birds have become more intimate with him?"[41]

St. Gudival of Ghent once brought back to life a sheep that had been killed "because he saw in it Christ led like a sheep to the slaughter."[42]

St. Anselm of Canterbury (1033–1109), who was appointed archbishop of Canterbury in 1093 and canonized in 1494, "was moved to feelings of compassion for animals, and he wept for them when he saw them caught in the hunter's net."[43]

## Saints in Rome, South America, and Britain

Alban Butler, in *Lives of the Saints*, also recounts numerous saintly legends, such as that of St. Eleutherius who served as pope (or bishop of Rome) from 174 to 189: "They took him up into a mountain; but the beasts of the forest gathered round him like lambs. . . . He was exposed in the amphitheater, but a lion and a lioness let loose upon him only licked his hand and his feet."[44] This tale is, of course, reminiscent of that of the first-century C.E. Roman slave Androcles, who was supposedly thrown into the arena with a lion, which spared him because he had removed a thorn from its foot years earlier when he was hiding out in Africa.

In the Americas, St. Rose of Lima worked out a deal with the mosquitos, whereby they would praise the Lord with the music of their whirring wings and their flying and she would be left unmolested to say her prayers. Her fellow citizen Martin de Porres, who has been canonized, extended his love to include even rats and mice:

> Brother Martin's charity embraced the lower animals and even vermin, excusing the depredations of rats and mice on the plea that the poor little things were insufficiently fed, and he maintained some sort of a Cats' and Dogs' Home in his sister's house. Note also that St. Martin's love for animals was an extension of and not a substitute for his love for his fellow man. For Martin extended his care of the sick to those of the city and was instrumental in establishing the orphanage and a foundling-hospital with other charitable institutions attached.[45]

One of the best known of the English saints is Hugh of Lincoln (1135?–1200), who was called to England from France by King Henry II and became his adviser. Hugh served as bishop of Lincoln and was canonized in 1220.[46] According to *Lives of the Saints*,

> St. Hugh in his little garden was a special attraction to birds and squirrels, of whom he was very fond and over whom he had considerable power. . . . His chaplain and biographer assures us that as Bishop of Lincoln he had as pet a swan at Stow, one of his manors, which would feed from his hand, follow him about, and keep guard over his bed, so that it was impossible for anyone to approach the bishop without being attacked by it.[47]

Hugh was also known for his devotion to the sick and the poor, especially children, and he often visited the leper-house to care for the lepers. He was especially courageous in defending the Jews when they were being attacked and persecuted.

Another English saint, Godric of Finchale, typified many of these gentle figures: "Shy creatures, such as stags, horses, and birds, were not afraid of him, nor did he fear wolves or snakes. All wild animals were his friends, disporting themselves in his company and fleeing to him in danger."[48] And St. Richard of Wyche (Droitwich) was moved by the sight of food animals being taken to slaughter:

> When he saw poultry or young animals being conveyed to his kitchen (he never ate meat himself), he would say half-sadly, half-humorously, "Poor innocent little creatures: if you were reasoning beings and could speak, you would curse us. For we are the cause of your death, and what have you done to deserve it?"[49]

### St. Francis of Assisi

During the medieval period, the church's attitude was not a favorable one for the animals. Yet, at the same time, it produced one of the greatest advocates for animals in history — St. Francis of Assisi (1182–1226). Born as Giovanni Francesco Bernardone, Francis consecrated himself to a life of poverty and religious teaching, lived his latter years as a hermit, and was canonized in 1228 by Pope Gregory IX.

St. Francis, founder of the Franciscan order, taught kindness to animals and even preached to them, with the birds reportedly rejoicing by chirping and flapping their wings in spiritual ecstasy.[50] He would even remove worms from the roads to prevent them from being crushed and brought wine and honey to the bees in winter to keep them from starving.[51]

Some of these tales are doubtlessly exaggerated or apocryphal, but they do demonstrate Francis's well-known concern for animals. As Dr. Michael W. Fox observes in his book *Saint Francis of Assisi, Animals, and Nature*, there are accounts that "have been clearly distorted by inaccuracies of translation from earlier documents," which were compiled from his followers' oral testimonies that were themselves sometimes magnified. However, says Fox,

> What is remarkable, if not disturbing, is that his followers and later chroniclers found his actions and feelings toward nonhuman creation so extraordinary. St. Francis once liberated two lambs, tied up across the shoulders of a farmer, who were bleating pitifully on their way to market where they would be slaughtered. St. Francis removed worms from a busy road and put them at the roadside so that they might not be crushed under the feet of passersby. He would become ecstatic over the sight of a field full of flowers or a grove of trees filled with birdsong. Such actions reveal much about St. Francis and about those who regarded such behavior as extraordinary; others neither felt nor acted in these ways.[52]

There are countless stories of St. Francis and his animal friends. The famous wolf of Gubbio, Italy, after having been admonished by him, put its paw in St. Francis's hand to formalize its promise not to kill any more sheep. The agreement was even witnessed by a notary. Thereafter, the wolf was free to roam the city at will, and it went from house to house and was fed by the people in return for its pledge not to harm them or their flocks.[53]

Birds especially loved the saint. The loud and noisy swallows would keep quiet when he preached; and a falcon would awaken him when it was time for him to say his prayers. Even the grasshoppers helped out, with one of the cooperative insects chirping melodiously to assist Francis in singing his praises to God.[54]

Francis returned the animals' love, and he once expressed his fondest wish as being happiness for the songbirds and farm animals:

If I ever have the opportunity to talk with the emperor, I'll beg him, for the love of God and me, to enact a special law: no one is to capture or kill our sisters the larks or do them any harm. Furthermore, all mayors and lords of castles and towns are required each year on Christmas Day to order their subjects to scatter wheat and other grain on the roads outside the walls so that our sisters the larks and other birds might have something to eat on so festive a day. And on Christmas Eve, out of reverence for the Son of God, whom on that night the Virgin Mary placed in a manger between the ox and the ass, anyone having an ox or an ass is to feed it a generous portion of choice fodder. And, on Christmas Day, the rich are to give the poor the finest food in abundance.[55]

St. Bonaventure (1221–74), the Italian scholastic philosopher, wrote of his fellow friar St. Francis:

He considered all created beings as coming from the paternal heart of God, this community of origin made him feel a real fraternity with them all. He said: "They have the same source as we had. Not to hurt our humble brethren was our first duty to them; but to stop there, a complete mis-apprehension of the intentions of Providence. We have a higher mission. God wishes that we should succor them whenever they require it."[56]

St. Bonaventure noted that St. Francis was especially attracted by the meek innocence of his animal friends: "Filled with an overflowing love, he called all creatures, however small, his brothers, sisters, because he knew they all had the same origin as himself. But he loved with a very special love those who expressed the meekness of Christ."[57]

In his biography of Francis, Thomas of Celano (1200?–1255?), the Italian Franciscan monk who was a follower of Francis, wrote:

When he found an abundance of flowers he preached to them and invited them to praise the Lord as though they were endowed with reason. In the same way he exhorted with the sincerest purity cornfields and vineyards, stones and forests and all the beautiful things of the fields, fountains of water and the green things of the gardens, earth and fire, air and wind, to love God and serve Him willingly. Finally he called all creatures *brother*.[58]

## The Continuing Influence of St. Francis

The influence of St. Francis can still be found in present-day Roman Catholic liturgy. The *Rituale Romanum* contains services for blessing animals and stables, and the benediction for sick animals includes the plea, "Be thou to them, O Lord, the defender of their life and the re-storer of their health."[59] On Christmas eve, in the second nocturne before the midnight Mass, the response is: "O great mystery, and wondrous sacrament, that animals should see the Lord born and lying in a manger."[60]

Cardinal Mercier of Belgium instructed that a sermon on St. Francis and his teachings be given each year, as did Cardinal Rafael Santos, archbishop of Manila, who is 1963 ordained the following:

> We are happy to dedicate a special day this year in order to remind our people of the great value of animals in our daily life and to give them whatever care and personal concern they deserve from us.
>
> But above all we should remember that animals are not only created by Almighty God to serve man's needs, but also to reflect God's goodness and wisdom.

Cardinal Santos also wrote in his pastoral letter of October 1963 that "whatever treatment we give to lesser creatures is a reflection on the state of our soul in relation to their Creator."[61]

Cardinal Arthur Hinsley (1865–1943), the former archbishop of Westminster, has written that "the spirit of St. Francis is the Catholic spirit." Canon Aloysius Roche wrote in *The Ark*: "The Church, by setting the seal of her approval on his life, surely implies that his behavior to the lower animals is part and parcel of the Franciscan message to the world."[62]

Pope Pius XII made St. Francis the Patron of Catholic Action, praising him on February 25, 1939, in *La Vie Intellectuelle*, "because he has presented the spectacle of kindness towards all and goodness, and pushed to establish friendship not only with human beings but with all Creation, and that not only with his lips, but with his heart."[63] Pope Pius also asked the citizens of Rome to celebrate the annual feast of St. Francis by providing a meal for whatever animals they could help.[64]

## Other Medieval Saints

The later medieval period produced other humane saints in addition to St. Francis. A thirteenth-century saint, James of Venice, is said to have often bought and released the birds sold in Italy for little Italian boys to play with. St. James, it is reported, "pitied the little birds of the Lord.... His tender charity recoiled from all cruelty, even to the most diminutive of animals."[65]

There was also St. Bridget (1303?–1373), the nun who is patroness of Sweden and the founder of the Brigittine order. She wrote in her *Revelations*, "Let a man fear, above all, me, his God, and so much the gentler will he become towards my creatures and animals, on whom, on account of me, their Creator, he ought to have compassion." She raised pigs, and a wild boar is said to have left its home in the forest to give itself over to her.[66]

Molua MacOcha, the Irish saint, was famous for his love of animals. It is said that when he died, a small bird was observed mourning his death, and saying that "all living creatures bewail him, for never has he killed any animal, little or big."[67]

Many other saints, too numerous to mention here, were animal lovers; and the multitude of anecdotes about their affection for animals makes it clear that the attitude of many of the church's most revered leaders for hundreds of years was one of compassion and respect for the creatures of the earth.

Even in farming and raising livestock, the monastic traditions frequently established high standards for humane treatment of animals. As Ruth Burtt wrote in *The Ark*,

> The records of the monasteries often show a marked consideration for their working beasts on the part of monastic landlords and this is notably so in the large estates owned by the great abbeys.
>
> Thus, 13th-century rules, laid down by the Abbey of St. Peters, Gloucester, expressly state that the servants of their manors are to take care of the oxen, making sure that the mangers in each stall contain a night's food for each team, and they are to plough without injuring or distressing the beasts.[68]

In his *History of European Morals*, Lecky touched on this same theme:

> The religious man becomes gentle, moderate, and humane in the tribute of work he expects from his animals. He follows up their aptitudes. He sees in them the companions of his labours, and he takes good care not to cut them off from his affection and compassion.
>
> Wherever evangelical piety flourished, it spreads orderliness over country districts. . . .
>
> It is only necessary to go over the farms of the Trappists or the Carthusians in order to see the fatherly supervision of the work and the happy results.[69]

# The Middle Ages and the Renaissance: The Church Sanctions Cruelty to Animals

The Middle Ages are perhaps best remembered for the ritualistic cruelty and suffering inflicted on so many groups of helpless victims, including "witches" and cats, wolves and "werewolves," and other innocents unfortunate enough to be seen by the church and society as agents of the devil.

Pitilessly persecuted mainly because of fear and superstition, people and animals suffered side-by-side, sometimes literally, as when hundreds of thousands of "witches" were burned at the stake, along with their cats. It was an age of terrible, senseless cruelty and suffering, often aided and abetted by the church and carried out in the name of religion.

The Middle Ages are roughly defined as the period of European history from the fifth to the fifteenth centuries, separating antiquity from the Renaissance. Beginning with the Dark Ages, it was a period of great social upheaval and of terrible suffering for many.

### The Church Promotes Hysteria

The tenor of medieval times was characterized by what can best be described as hysteria. The hysteria was of epidemic proportions, resulting in widespread terror, intimidation, accusation and counteraccusation, and the hanging and burning alive of hundreds of thousands of people thought to be witches, sorcerers, heretics, and werewolves. Not surprisingly, cats, wolves, and other creatures also fell victim to these irrational fears that prevailed throughout much of European society.

In Medieval Europe, the church dominated the life of the people. Its power in the formation and transmission of ideas was particularly immense and pervasive, and not just because it ran the institutions of higher learning.

The church also subsidized and thereby controlled to a great extent what could be published. Books were tailored to fit current ideology, thereby perpetuating for centuries whatever myths were compatible with the church's needs. Thus, whatever the church decided should be the attitude toward animals became not only the reigning theology but also the intellectual and philosophical fashion of the day.

Some of the worst damage was done by church-sponsored literature of a seemingly authoritative nature, the pseudo-scientific theories advanced by Greco-Roman medical authorities around the beginning of the Christian era that were used for hundreds of years to justify and inspire cruelty to animals.

The foremost medical authority of that day was a second-century Greek Christian named Galen, whose works were considered unquestionable for centuries in the medical practice of Greece, Rome, and the Arab world.[1]

Galen relied on many worthless folk remedies involving the use of animal saliva or parts, such as powdered wolf's liver, gonads, entrails, and other organs. To Galen and other physicians who followed him through the Middle Ages, animals were of interest only as a source of medicine and as experimental models. Because Galen was a Christian, his writings were supported and disseminated by the church, giving his erroneous treatments and teachings a disproportionate influence until the sixteenth century, when logic and reason began to reassert itself in the practice of medicine.[2]

The type of book on animals enjoying the widest popular appeal was the *Physiologus* ("the naturalist" in Greek), which began to turn up around the first century C.E. Beginning as collections of animal fables, legends, and folklore, they soon became instruments of the church's propaganda machine, and by the second and third centuries, they had adopted a didactic and moralizing tone. Various animals were described and commented on, and a biblical quote was included for each entry, along with an account of the moral lesson to be learned from it. By the twelfth century, the *Physiologus* had been expanded into the bestiary, a similar book of myths and moral lessons about animals also notable for the lack of concern for any scientific objectivity or accuracy.[3]

Thus, misinformation about animals and their behavior, first invented and passed on hundreds of years B.C.E., were perpetuated for over a thousand years through the power and influence of the church. As author Barry Lopez writes in *Of Wolves and Men,*

> The Church, because it largely controlled both the publication of books
> and the institutions of learning, profoundly affected the progress of natu-

ral history by subjecting it to theological constraint, by making it conform to preconceived ideas. What the Church supported, survived. What it regarded as in error — and a secular interest in animals smacked of paganism — did not.[4]

It is ironic that the relatively advanced civilizations of Greece and Rome produced so many brilliant advocates for animals, such as Aesop, Aristotle, Plutarch, Cicero, Pythagoras, Celsus, and others, while at the same time producing such brutality. But the most profound legacy of these states was the scientific data they formulated that was passed on from generation to generation, justifying the abuse of other living creatures.

## St. Thomas's Disastrous Doctrine

One influential Christian who had a profound and damaging impact on animal welfare was the thirteenth-century saint and philosopher Thomas Aquinas (1225?–1274). Thomas advocated and helped refine doctrines that have been used for centuries, even up to the present day, to justify the infliction of suffering on animals.

Thomas was a believer in the Roman Catholic Church's prevailing doctrine that animals have no afterlife, despite the clear references in the Bible to animals' having souls,[5] which he twice admitted.[6] He even taught that they have no inherent rights. Yet he still advocated that people treat animals kindly, though this aspect of the Thomistic philosophy is often ignored.

In *Summa contra Gentiles*, II, 112, Thomas wrote:

> If in Holy Scripture there are found some injunctions forbidding the infliction of some cruelty toward brute animals . . . this is either for removing a man's mind from exercising cruelty upon brutes, should go on hence to human beings; or because the injury inflicted on animals turns to a temporal loss for some man, either the person who inflicts the injury or some other.[7]

In *Summa Theologica*, Thomas reiterated this view: "God's purpose in recommending kind treatment of the brute creation is to dispose men to pity and tenderness towards one another."[8]

Quoting St. Augustine (354–430), the early Christian church father and philosopher who championed orthodoxy and wrote *De Civitate Dei (The City of God)*, St. Thomas wrote of animals in *Summa Theologica* that "by a most just ordinance of the Creator, both their life and their death are subject to our use":

Dumb animals and plants are devoid of the life of reason whereby to set themselves in motion; they are moved, as it were by another, by a kind of natural impulse, a sign of which is that they are naturally enslaved and accommodated to the uses of others. . . . He that kills another's ox sins, not through killing the ox, but through injuring another man in his property. Wherefore this is not a species of the sin of murder but of the sin of theft or property.[9]

Thomas did admit that animals could be the subject of love, but only in the most limited sense:

Now irrational creatures can have no fellowship in human life which is regulated by reason. Hence friendship with irrational creatures is impossible, except metaphorically speaking. . . . Nevertheless, we can love irrational creatures out of charity, if we regard them as the good things that we desire for others, insofar, to wit, as we wish for their preservation, to God's honor and man's use; thus does God love them out of charity.[10]

Yet, even Thomas recognized and admitted that God cares for creatures and that humans should do likewise and not frustrate God's purpose in creating them. Father Jean Gautier quotes Thomas as expressing these views in his work *De moribus divinis: de cura Dei de creaturis:*

It is God's custom to care for all His creatures, both the greatest and the least. We should likewise care for creatures, whatsoever they are, in the sense that we use them in conformity with the divine purpose, in order that they may not bear witness against us in the Day of judgment.[11]

Unfortunately, this and other favorable statements on animals made by Thomas are usually overlooked, and his negative views are emphasized.

The great harm that Thomism had caused to animal welfare was made inevitable long after Thomas's death when he was built up by the church as one of its great theologians and his philosophy accepted *in toto*. This was done without excluding his personal (and some have said, quite heretical) statements on animals, which were inconsistent with the traditions and teachings of the church up until his time.

Thomas was canonized by Pope John XXII in 1323, proclaimed a doctor of the church in 1567 by Pope Pius V, and declared patron of Catholic schools in 1880, at which time Pope Leo XIII made his doctrinal writings on theology the official doctrine of the church.[12] Thus, by not correcting or excluding Thomas's philosophy on animals, these popes implicitly endorsed and perpetuated what many Catholics consider to be a fallacy, a theological error, that has over the centuries been used to justify untold cruelty to God's creatures.

Unfortunately for the animals, this Thomistic philosophy exerted a profound influence on the interpretation of Roman Catholic dogma, overshadowing and replacing the humane ethic of the Bible. It came to be used to justify cruelty and indifference to animals that would probably have shocked its progenitor.

## The Renaissance: The Burning of Witches and Cats

The Renaissance is heralded as the period that brought humanity out of the Dark Ages, inspiring an upsurge of artistic and literary activity. But the Renaissance also brought with it a renewal and intensification of people's darker impulses, manifested by an eruption of superstition, witch-burning, and the torture and killing of anyone thought to be "heretical" in his or her views or actions. It seems strange that the Renaissance, which brought such a flood of enlightenment to the Dark Ages, would deepen the gloom for animals. Yet, in many ways, this is just what happened.

With the advent of the Renaissance in the fourteenth century — the period marking the transition between the medieval and the modern world — the lot of animals deteriorated. As is so often the case, the justifications for persecuting animals — often religious ones — were also used to rationalize cruelty to humans, so many of whom suffered along with the animals.

In 1484, Pope Innocent VIII (1432–92) formally sanctioned, on behalf of the church, that "sorcerers" and "witches" had the power of evil. He also ordered that pet cats be included when witches were burned at the stake. According to Gerald Carson, "as late as the seventeenth century, it was risky for an old woman to have a cat as a pet." During the next two hundred years, it is estimated that several hundred thousand people — perhaps over a million — were tortured and burned at the stake for practicing witchcraft. The number of cats that also perished is not known, but both felines and women were terribly persecuted, and for similar reasons.[13]

The belief that Satan could and did assume the form of animals was widespread during the Middle Ages. Black cats were the subject of particular suspicion, frequently becoming a symbol of witchcraft. Many cats were summarily put to death and people often refused to own them.

The ceremonial burning of cats was a tradition on certain religious holidays, especially in France. These customs are described in detail by the eminent Scottish anthropologist Sir James George Frazer (1854–1941) in his classic work on cults, myths, magic, and religion, *The Golden Bough*. In Alsace, cats were burned in the Easter bonfire; in the Ardennes, on the first Sunday in Lent; and in the Vosges, on Shrove Tuesday. In the festive midsummer fires, cats were roasted over the bonfire at Gap, in the High Alps; and at Metz, a dozen cats were placed in wicker-cages, and "were burned alive in them, to the amusement of the people."[14]

The Europeans paid dearly for their persecution of cats. The elimination of these predators of rodents brought about a proliferation of flea-carrying rats, which helped cause and spread the bubonic plague. The "Black Death" decimated Europe in the late 1300s, killing off nearly half the population between 1347 and the end of that century.[15]

Other animals were often burned alive in order to break the power of witchcraft. Since German and Welsh witches were thought to assume the form of foxes and snakes, these creatures were also thrown into the midsummer fires, as were chickens (white cocks) in Russia.[16]

Indeed, in the ten centuries preceding the present one, there are accounts of the trials, torture, and execution (often by hanging) of hundreds of animals, mainly by ecclesiastical courts acting under the assumption that animals can be used by the devil to do his work.[17]

But even amid such unfavorable conditions, a few compassionate religious leaders still exhibited compassion toward animals. For example, some came to argue that since animals had no hope of an afterlife, they deserved to be treated that much better while here on earth, since this was the only life they would know. Robert Bellarmine (1542–1621), the Italian prelate, cardinal, and archbishop who was beatified in 1924, was said to leave the fleas in his beard undisturbed, allowing them to bite him, because "we shall have heaven to reward us for our sufferings, but these poor creatures have nothing but the enjoyment of this present life."[18]

## The Persecution of Wolves and Werewolves

There is no better example of how religion can impel and justify cruelty to innocent animals than the persecution of wolves and "werewolves" that took place in the Middle Ages and the Renaissance. The attempt to wipe out the wolf in medieval Europe coincided with, and was accelerated by, the campaign to extirpate werewolves and other perceived enemies of Christian civilization.

An excellent account of the persecution of wolves and "werewolves" can be found in Barry Lopez's book, *Of Wolves and Men*, which describes in detail how the church, especially the Inquisition, used the fear generated by such accusations for its own purposes. [19] Stories of wolves killing livestock were embellished and passed on, soon becoming tales of wolves — or people dressed in wolf skins — killing and devouring children.

It was widely believed that some people could transform themselves at will into a wolf, and that these "werewolves" roamed the countryside committing murders and mutilations, deforming infants, and generally acting as the agents of the devil. They were supposedly most active and dangerous during the twelve-day period between Christmas and Epiphany. The prodigious English poet Geoffrey Chaucer (1340?–1400) wrote in the "Parson's Tale" of "the devil's wolves that strangle the sheep of Jesus Christ."[20]

Ironically, the extirpation of wolves not only failed to provide protection to humans, but often increased losses to farmers by allowing crop-eating (and plague-carrying) rodents to proliferate.

The church adeptly took advantage and profited from the fear and hatred of wolves, skillfully channeling such prejudice to fit its own purposes. This was particularly so in the case of the Inquisition, the tribunal set up by the Roman Catholic Church in the thirteenth century to find and eradicate heresy. This body, Barry Lopez states, "did more to sustain the belief in the legend of the werewolf by fanatical persecution than any other agent or institution."[21]

By exploiting this myth, the church was able to create and sustain a feeling of fear and hysteria on the part of the populace that real devils were living among them. These heretics, in the form of sorcerers, witches, and other such dangerous and powerful entities, were hauled before kangaroo courts and denounced, tortured, and executed by the thousands. This campaign of terror and intimidation allowed the church to consolidate its power and control over the people by extirpating those elements that might generate unrest and opposition.

These tenets were laid out by two Dominicans in the 1487 publication *Malleus Maleficarum* (Hammer of Witches), which in great and tedious detail "proved" the existence of werewolves and the fact that they were in league with the devil and so had to be suppressed. To kill a werewolf was to do the work of the Lord. Thus, through a seemingly scholastic and intellectual methodology, superstition and folklore became the official theological doctrine as well as the prevailing mood of the times. And the horrors of the Inquisition were given a philosophical and moral justification.[22]

The Bible was frequently invoked in support of these claims, including Leviticus 26:22 ("I will also send wild beasts among you, which shall rob you of your children, and destroy your cattle, and make you few in number") and Deuteronomy 32:24 ("I will also send the teeth of beasts upon them").

But the church had more than just evidence, logic, and reason on its side; it also had the ultimate proof: confessions from the werewolves themselves! These were normally extracted either under torture and threats, or from the demented and feebleminded. On January 18, 1573, Giles Garnier, a hermit who lived in a cave outside Lyon, France, was burned alive after confessing to making a pact with the devil and having killed half a dozen children. Another self-admitted werewolf was Jean Grenier, a fourteen-year-old French lad who in September 1603 not only confessed for himself but also implicated his father and another man. His death sentence was commuted and he was sent to live in a Franciscan monastery where, in Lopez's words, "he spent the next eight years running around on all fours, completely demented, physically deformed, and pathologically attached to wolf lore."[23]

This mindless and intense hatred for the wolf, spread and embellished by the church, continued to influence and at times dominate the thinking of Europeans for generations to come, especially in cases where grotesque and heinous crimes were committed.[24]

Not only did this persecution of wolves continue for hundreds of years, but the Europeans who settled the New World brought along their religiously oriented antiwolf prejudices, which was to help doom not only America's wolves but their brothers and sisters, the Indians, as well (see p. 99).

### Progress during the Renaissance: Leonardo, Montaigne, and Luther

While the Renaissance — with its rebirth of learning, study, and appreciation for art — saw a deterioration in the status of animals, it also brought about a more compassionate and enlightened attitude on the part of *some* of the period's greatest figures, such as Leonardo and Montaigne.

Leonardo da Vinci (1452–1519), perhaps the most celebrated figure of that era, excelled as a painter, sculptor, engineer, scientist, and architect. Many of his most beloved paintings are religious in nature, such as his Madonnas with the Christ child, his Virgins, the *Annunciation*, and, of course, *The Last Supper* mural in the monastery of Santa Maria della Grazie in Milan.

One of Leonardo's biographers, E. MacCurdy, in *The Mind of Leonardo da Vinci*, mentions many examples of his kindness to animals.[25] Like the Greek philosopher and mathematician Pythagoras, Leonardo would buy caged birds sold in the streets in order to give them their freedom. He recognized humankind's inherent cruelty, "always warring against his own species, persecuting, harassing, and devastating all things that are on the earth or beneath it in the waters." In condemning the practice of drowning bees to get their honey, Leonardo wrote, "Oh, justice of God! Why dost thou not wake and behold thy creatures thus ill-used?"

Two other prominent humanitarians of that period were close friends: Michel de Montaigne, the essayist, and Pierre Charron, the theologian. Montaigne (1533–92), a Roman Catholic who served as mayor of Bordeaux for two terms, not only defended animals, but was a champion of religious tolerance long before this became fashionable. Like so many others, Montaigne perceived the corrosive effect of cruelty on one's character. He wrote in his *Essays* that those who took pleasure from "spectacles of the slaughter of animals . . . proceeded to those of the slaughter of men."[26]

Charron (1541–1603), a Roman Catholic theologian, moralist, philosopher, and canon of the church, was renowned as a pulpit orator, and was preacher-in-ordinary to Queen Margaret of Navarre. His influence on society and within the church lent considerable weight and respectability to his support for the humane movement.

Another of the key figures of this era also had kind feelings toward animals: Martin Luther (1483–1546), the German priest and religious reformer who led the Protestant Reformation in Germany.

It is not known to what extent, if any, Luther's love for animals led to his break with the Catholic Church, but the church's attitude could have been enough to appall and alienate any humanitarian. In his commentary on Deuteronomy 22:6, which forbids the harming of the mother bird if her eggs or chicks are gathered up, Luther wrote, "What else does this law teach but that by the kind treatment of animals they are to learn gentleness and kindness. Otherwise it would seem to be a stupid ordinance not only to regulate a matter so unimportant, but also to promise happiness and a long life to those whot keep it."[27]

And English historian W. E. H. Lecky relates how "Luther grew sad and thoughtful at a hare hunt, for it seemed to him to represent the pursuit of souls by the devil."[28]

Author Dix Harwood, in *Love for Animals*, mentions a story of a grieving little girl being comforted by Luther, who assured her that her pet dog that had died would surely go to heaven. Luther is said to have told her that in the "new heavens and new earth . . . all creatures will not only be harmless, but lovely and joyful. . . . Why, then, should there not be little dogs in the new earth, whose skin might be as fair as gold, and their hair as bright as precious stones?"[29]

### Descartes: Animals as Machines

Unfortunately, a kind attitude toward animals was rare among the major figures of this period. And by the end of the Renaissance, human philosophical attitudes toward animals reached a nadir, as exemplified by one of the most influential writers of the day, René Descartes (1596–1650).

The French scientist and philosopher Descartes and his followers, the Cartesians, held that animals had neither language nor intelligence, and therefore were merely a sort of machine, or automaton.

Descartes's central thesis was *"Cogito ergo sum"*: "I think, therefore I am." He inferred from this assumption that animals could not think, thus could not feel and had no feelings. As one of Descartes's followers put it, "Animals eat without pleasure; they cry without pain; grow without knowing it, they fear nothing; they know nothing."[30]

In a November 23, 1646, letter to the Marquess of Newcastle, Descartes dismissed the wonders of animal behavior as mechanical in nature, like a clock:

> I cannot share the opinion of Montaigne and others who attribute understanding or thought to animals....
> I know that animals do many things better than we do, but this does not surprise me. It can even be used to prove they act naturally and mechanically, like a clock which tells the time better than our judgment does. Doubtless when the swallows came in spring, they operate like clocks. The actions of honeybees are of the same nature.... They act only by instinct and without thinking.[31]

In his *Discourse on Method*, Descartes urged his readers to dissect a beef heart and note the valves and ventricles that made it a thermal machine. This was used to justify any conceivable abuse of animals, including the dissecting of unanesthetized dogs and other creatures for medical experimentation. An example of the excesses this led to is demonstrated by the incident in which the French metaphysician and philosopher Nicolas de Malebranche (1638–1715) attributed the howls of his dog he had just kicked to "the creaking of the gearing and the turnspit."[32]

### Voltaire and Other Rebuttals to Descartes

But Descartes's views were not universally held, and several leading contemporaries rejected his theories on animal behavior. One of these was his contemporary Jean de la Fontaine (1621–95), the noted author of numerous books of fables on animals who not only believed that animals had souls, but that they could think and act rationally.

Another who disagreed with Descartes was the French critic, philosopher, and encyclopedist Pierre Bayle (1647–1706), the acknowledged founder of eighteenth-century rationalism who championed freedom of thought and religion. Born a Protestant, he converted to Catholicism, but later returned to his former church. His famous article entitled "Rorarius" expressed the view that Descartes's beliefs were in error and that animals could indeed have souls that, like those of humans, were eternal.

One of the best known and most vehement critics of Descartes was the famous French writer and satirist Voltaire (1694–1778). In a stinging rebuttal to Descartes, Voltaire, who had been educated by Jesuits, stated in the sections on animals in his *Philosophical Dictionary:* "What a pitiful, what a sorry thing to have said that animals were machines bereft of understanding and feeling, which perform their operations always in the same way, which learn nothing."

Voltaire wrote that it was ridiculous to assume that humans feel distress and pleasure and have memory and understanding, but not to bring that same judgment to bear on a dog which has lost its master,

> Which has sought him on every road with sorrowful cries, which enters the house agitated, uneasy, which goes down the stairs, up the stairs, and from room to room, which at last finds in his study the master it loves, and which shows him its joy by cries of delight, by its leaps and by its caresses.

Voltaire bitterly condemned not only the conclusions but the methodology of the Cartesians:

> Barbarians seize this dog, which in friendship surpasses man so prodigiously; they nail it on a table, and they dissect it alive in order to show the mesentric veins. You discover in it all the same organs of feeling that are in yourself. Answer me, machinist, has nature arranged all the means of feeling in this animal, so that it may not feel? Has it nerves in order to be impassable? Do not suppose this impertinent contradiction in nature.

Few people today would admit to being Cartesians. But lest we be too quick to condemn this callous philosophy of three hundred years ago, we should be aware that similar tendencies are still present in, and indeed dominate, several sectors of our society that are involved in the exploitation of animals. As the highly esteemed naturalist, essayist, and critic Joseph Wood Krutch (1893–1970) said of the Cartesians in his book *The World of Animals,*

> the tendency to move in that direction is always present. In its mildest form, it is the tendency to regard animals as so nearly machines that any attempt to consider their mental or emotional life is dismissed as mere sentimentality or anthropomorphism. In its technical aspect, it is the father of behaviorism, the attempt to reduce all animal behavior to instinct and the conditional reflex.[33]

When one hears or reads the defenses of animal exploitation put out by the medical research lobby, the fur industry, and other groups involved in profiting from animal suffering, one cannot help but be struck by how many Cartesians are still among us.

## The Church, the Popes, and Bullfighting

During the Renaissance, the Catholic nations of Europe often exhibited some of the most callous treatment of animals. But even there, remarkable progress was made on some problems.

Perhaps the most prominent issue was bullfighting, a "sport" as notable for its flagrant cruelty as for its popularity with the masses. An examination of the attempts to condemn this sadistic spectacle reveals the limitations on the church's power to restrict cruel blood sports when they enjoy such strong public support.

Pope St. Pius V strongly and courageously condemned bullfighting, and harsh punishment was called for in the 1567 papal bull *De Salute Gregis*, which was formally sustained in the code of canon law of 1917. The pope characterized bullfighting as "contrary to Christian duty and charity, ... those bloody and disgraceful spectacles of devils and not of human beings." He forbade attendance at bullfights under penalty of excommunication and specifically banned all clergy from such events.[34]

However, the papal bull created such a storm of protest that Pius's successor, Gregory XIII (1502–85), tempered the severity of the bull in 1575 by removing the threat of excommunication. But the next pope, Sixtus V (1521–90) reinstated this penalty in 1583. Again, extreme pressure was brought to bear on the church to relent. The king of Spain, the bigoted Philip II (1527–98), who helped develop the Inquisition, even argued that such an amusement was necessary in order to train and prepare the knights for war.[35]

In 1595, Pope Clement VIII (1536–1605) removed most of the former prohibitions and punishments, banning only friars and monks from attending bullfights.

Yet, despite these enormous pressures brought to bear at such a sensitive time for the church, it never renounced its original opposition to bullfighting (see pp. 122–124). But neither has it taken sufficient action to end these "bloody and disgraceful spectacles."

*Chapter 5* _____

# Changing
# the "Animal Hell
# of Merry England"

The English are universally thought of as a dignified and reserved people, notable for their many groups and individuals devoted to animal welfare. Yet, for centuries, England was the scene of some of the most brutal public entertainments involving the torture of animals, usually undertaken with the enthusiastic approval and often participation of the church.

Even up until relatively recent times, English schools were extremely dangerous places for animals. E. S. Turner, in *All Heaven in a Rage*, writes that "in general, any dog, cat, or bird venturing near a public school could expect to be maimed or killed.... [At] Eton College, abuse of animals was almost part of the curriculum."[1]

While the brutal English animal-torturing spectacles continued well into the nineteenth century, they had long before become controversial; and by the eighteenth century, they had lost much of their fashionable appeal. Indeed, the discrediting of these public contests did not happen overnight, but were the result of a growing animal welfare movement led by some — a very few — of England's most prominent spiritual leaders.

The ultimate result was more compassionate treatment of animals — and humans. And often the same people were leading the fight on behalf of both groups. Many of those who fought slavery and child labor in the nineteenth century were also active in the animal protection movement.

### The Massive Popularity of Animal Torture

For hundreds of years, Shrove Tuesday, the end of the season of merry-making just before Lent, was an occasion for the populace to engage in the "sport" of cock-throwing. This delightful pastime consisted of pelting a rooster with sticks and clubs until it was dead. If its legs were broken before it was killed, it was mounted on splints and the game continued. Roosters were not absolutely essential to the game, and sometimes cats were used instead. The English statesman and author Sir Thomas More (1478–1535) was reportedly famous for his skill at this "sport." It was finally suppressed by the London magistrates in 1769.[2]

Historian W. E. H. Lecky, in his *History of European Morals*, cites three possible origins for the hatred of roosters and the popularity of cock-throwing, one of which was as punishment for being connected with St. Peter's denial of Jesus: "... this night, before the cock crow, thou shalt deny me thrice" (Matt. 26:34).[3]

When not being tortured and killed by humans, roosters were often used to maim and slay each other. In twelfth-century England, cock-fighting became a popular recreation for youngsters, and in some areas "church bells were rung in honor of the survivor."[4]

Bull-baiting was another popular English "sport"; it originated in the early thirteenth century, and became a favorite of the English and Irish peoples from that time onward. The game consisted of tying a bull to a stake, allowing it eight or so yards of rope, and then loosing a trained bulldog on it.

The English were especially proud of their bulldogs, and one widely circulated story of that time concerned a bull-baiter who was trying to sell some pups for five guineas each. In order to demonstrate their superior genetic heritage, he took their aging mother and had her cling tightly to a bull while he methodically cut her feet off one by one.[5]

The appeal these animal displays held for the populace of Queen Elizabeth I (1533–1603) is difficult to exaggerate or describe. Thomas Cartwright (1535?–1603), the English Puritan clergyman who campaigned against the Church of England and was imprisoned for "nonconformity," complained in his 1572 "Admonition to Parliament against the Use of the Common Prayer": "If there be a bear or a bull to be baited in the afternoon, or a jackanapes [ape or monkey] to ride on horseback, the minister hurries the service over in a shameful manner, in order to be present at the show."[6]

But gradually such animal spectacles began to fall into disfavor, especially among the "better" classes; and they came under increasingly strong attack from influential publications and writers such as the diarists Samuel Pepys (1633–1703) and John Evelyn (1620–1706).[7]

According to Lecky, the rowdiness surrounding these spectacles eventually led to their being discredited and abolished. During the latter half of the eighteenth century, he wrote in his *History of European Morals*, "There was constant controversy on the subject ... and several forgotten clergymen published sermons upon it, and the frequent riots resulting from the fact that the bear-gardens had become the resort of the worst classes assisted the movement."[8] Finally, by 1769, cock-throwing had been largely ended by the London magistrates, but bull-baiting continued well into the 1800s.

## Ending the Bloody Spectacles

Changing what Charles Niven calls the "Animal Hell of Merry England" was no easy task, for "the Englishman's insatiable appetite for atrocious cruelty" served a distinct purpose: "Such cruelty helped brutalize the youth of the country when Britain's greatness depended on waging European wars, fighting Spaniards on the open seas, and subduing natives armed with primitive weapons in colonial territories." [9]

While the pervasive popularity of such cruelty to animals shocks us today, one must also realize that many humans during these times were not treated much better. Gerald Carson, in *Men, Beasts, and Gods*, observes that this cruel treatment of animals was hardly remarkable from a society that tolerated slavery and torture, and in which popular recreation included attending public hangings (for such crimes as picking pockets) and observing the mentally ill inmates at Bedlam.[10]

Gerald Carson offers another example of the natural extension of cruelty from animals to humans: "When dwarfs were objects of fashionable amusement, a French duchess had a locksmith make a pair of iron collars, one for the neck of her dwarf girl, the other for Her Grace's monkey."[11]

And when the most barbaric of the animal spectacles at last ceased, it was not because of any serious opposition from the church. As Lecky was observed, when these "ancient combats of wild beasts" finally "disappeared from Christendom," it was due to changing mores and fashions rather than censure from moralists and religious leaders:

> It is possible that the softening power of Christian teaching may have had some indirect influence in abolishing them; but a candid judgment will confess that it has been very little. During the periods, and in the countries, in which theological influence was supreme, they were unchallenged. They disappeared at last, because a luxurious and industrial civilization involved a refinement of manners.

As these brutal animal contests lost the approval of the upper classes, the possibility of legislating against them became feasible.

## The First Wildlife Protection Laws

In contrast to the treatment of domestic animals, wildlife in Europe has traditionally enjoyed a somewhat protected status — but not because of any humane considerations. Rather, wildlife was conserved for the pleasure of the ruling classes, who wanted to ensure an ample supply of victims for *their* blood sports.

As with many social activities of the feudal system, some blood sports were reserved almost exclusively for the aristocracy and thus retained their upper-class appeal. The most popular of these sports were hawking, hunting, and coursing, the last in which a rabbit was pursued and torn apart by hounds.

At the same time, dogs and wildlife were protected from the peasantry, not out of concern for the animals, but to make sure there would always be enough available for the amusement of the upper classes. Peasants were forbidden to own hunting dogs or weapons, but hunger and poverty led to illegal trapping and poaching, despite severely harsh penalties. A serf who killed a deer had his eyes gouged out; his right hand was cut off for resisting a game warden, and death was the penalty for the second offense. Such laws had the added utility of helping to deny weapons to the peasants and maintaining class distinctions.[12]

Ironically, the first steel-jaw, leg-hold traps (called gin traps in England) were used by gamekeepers to catch poachers hunting deer in the royal forests.[13]

As we shall see, recent decades have brought about tremendous improvement in the laws and public attitudes dealing with the protection of wild and domestic animals. Though many horrors remain, we can look back with disbelief on what was considered normal only a hundred years ago. But it is indisputable that organized religion, having helped promote and justify massive slaughter of and cruelty to animals, played a negligible role in ending the most flagrant of these abuses.

## The Seventeenth Century: A Real Beginning

By the time the seventeenth century had begun, widespread revulsion with public displays of cruelty to animals had prompted the beginning of what would become a real humane movement in England. Toward the beginning, a few courageous and enlightened individuals stand out as having spoken up in defense of animals, as Edward Fairholme and Wellesley Pain point out in their history of the R.S.P.C.A.[14]

One of the most interesting and contradictory of the English theologians was Sir Thomas More (1478–1535), who served as an archbishop and a Carthusian monk. He defended King Henry VIII against the reform measures of Martin Luther and supported radical reform of the clergy and a more rational theology. But, as lord chancellor, he was quite harsh on heretics and opposed liberalizing the laws against heresy. He was beatified by Pope Leo XIII and canonized in 1935.[15]

Sir Thomas More's attitudes on animals were equally contradictory and extreme, though he was one of the earliest British religious leaders to publicly advocate kindness to animals. He was said to have been famous for his skill at cock-throwing, but he is best known for his book *Utopia*, which contains many liberal and humane ideas considered revolutionary for the times. Published in 1516, it outlines his thoughts on the ideal society, including religious toleration, educating women as well as men, and common ownership of land. He urged an end to hunting, calling it "a thing unworthy to be used of free men." And he condemned cruelty to animals, saying that it would lead to cruelty to humans. In his description of the perfect society, butchers had the lowest status, because of their responsibility for the killing and suffering of animals.[16]

Despite his contradictory attitude toward animals, Sir Thomas's writings were quite important in influencing public attitudes; and they helped set the stage for the first real progress to be made in English society in the next two centuries.

When the Quaker movement was founded in the mid-seventeenth century by George Fox (1624–91), English humanitarians gained an important ally in their twenty-two-year-long struggle to enact animal protection legislation.

This new and enlightened attitude that was emerging was greatly strengthened by the "father of English natural history," John Ray (or Wray) (1627?–1705). Ray made the first systematic description and classification of animal and vegetable species and wrote numerous botanical, zoological, and theological works. In 1691, Ray published a classic book, *The Wisdom of God Manifest in the Works of His Creation*, which was widely studied at the time and acclaimed for the next century. His main thesis was the sanctity and value of the natural world.[17]

An advocate of a meatless diet, Ray made two main points in his book. The first was that the Lord can best be found and understood through studying and appreciating the works of "His Creation":

> Let us then consider the works of God and observe the operation of His hands. Let us take notice of and admire His infinite goodness and wisdom in the formation of them. No creature in the sublunary world is capable of doing this except man, and yet we have been deficient therein.[18]

Ray's other fundamental proposition was that animals were put on earth for their own sake and not just for that of humans: "If a good man be merciful to his beast, then surely a good God takes pleasure that all His creatures enjoy themselves that have life and sense and are capable of enjoying."[19]

## Religion and Animals in the Eighteenth Century

By the eighteenth century, an effective social reform movement had sprung up and begun to grow and gain strength. Growing demands were heard for drastic social reforms, including the abolition of slavery and the prevention of cruelty to children — and animals. The source of much of this ferment was the evangelical movement led by John Wesley (1703–91), the founder of Methodism, and his brother Charles (1707–88).

John Wesley, saying "I look upon all the world as my parish," traveled some 250,000 miles on horseback,[20] evangelizing and calling for fair treatment for the lower classes and for animals. In so doing, he strongly invoked the wrath of the ruling classes for being a threat to social order and stability. In one sermon he preached, Wesley alluded to animals having souls, saying "Something better remains after death for these poor creatures also." He taught that animals "shall receive an ample amends for all their present sufferings."[21]

Wesley was a vegetarian who based his dietary habits on the ideal state as exemplified by Isaiah in his vision of the millennium, wherein "on the new earth, no creature will kill, or hurt, or give pain to any other."[22]

Wesley taught that animals would be part of the "great deliverance," including "all that are capable of pleasure or pain, of happiness or misery." Thus, it was the obligation of humans to "be tender of even meaner creatures, to show mercy to these also," for animals and humans, "the whole animated creation," were all part of "the golden chain of God's creatures," and "were the offspring of one common father."[23]

Another important English theologian and contemporary of Wesley, who often disagreed with him on other matters but shared his humane views, was Bishop Joseph Butler (1692–1752). Raised in a Presbyterian family, he joined the Church of England, successively becoming a rector, bishop, and dean of St. Paul's.[24] In *The Analogy of Religion* (1736), Bishop Butler became one of the first clergymen to teach the immortality of animal souls: "Neither can we find anything in the whole analogy of Nature to afford even the slightest presumption that animals ever lose their living powers, much less that they lose them by death."[25]

Butler, as bishop of Durham, wrote that it was "invidious" to assume that for animals there existed an insuperable difficulty, that they should be immortal, and by consequence capable of everlasting happiness." He also hypothesized that "in the natural immortality of brutes," animals could "become rational and moral agents."[26]

Another of the early English clergy to include love of animals in his theology was the Reverend John Hildrop, who felt that it was natural and logical to treat animals with love and respect. He reasoned that, since animals were created for God's glory, the Deity would hardly want to be wasteful and see them destroyed. In his book *Free Thoughts on the Brute Creation* (1754), Reverend Hildrop pursued these arguments, contending that humans should do what they can to reduce the enormous suffering of the animals on the earth, for which the creatures would surely be recompensed with immortality.[27]

But change did not come about overnight, and preaching from the pulpit on behalf of animals still held its dangers. Reverend James Granger, a vicar of the Church of England from Sheplake, Oxfordshire, went to prison for twice preaching against cruelty to animals.

His first "offense" was committed on October 18, 1772, when he delivered a sermon taking his text from Proverbs 12:10, "A righteous man regardeth the life of his beast." Dedicating the sermon to a neighbor he had often seen whipping his horses, Reverend Granger admonished him to mend his ways:

> For God's sake and thy own, have some compassion upon these poor beasts....I give thee fair warning, that a worse punishment waits for thee in the next; and that damnation will certainly come, according to thy call....I advise thee to fall upon thy knees, and ask God forgiveness for the cruelty....[28]

When the sermon was later published under the title "An Apology for the Brute Creation, or Abuse of Animals Censured," he described how his congregation received these courageous words: "The foregoing discourse gave almost universal disgust to two considerable congregations. The mention of dogs and horses was censured as a prostitution of the dignity of the pulpit, and considered as proof of the author's insanity."[29]

Aware that cruelty to animals often leads to a similar attitude toward people, Reverend Granger wrote in a foreword to his sermon: "This discourse is not only intended for such as have the care of horses, and other useful Beasts; but also for children, and those that are concerned in forming their Hearts."[30]

After twice preaching the sermon and having been admonished by his bishop, Reverend Granger was sent to jail for having the temerity and bad taste to be a few decades — or centuries — before his time.

One of the most effective Englishmen of that day working on behalf of the oppressed — both human and animal — was the famous English jurist and economist Jeremy Bentham (1748–1832). Bentham gained his fame expounding utilitarianism ("the greatest happiness of the greatest number"); but he also fought tirelessly against slavery and for legal protection for animals. He is best remembered among humanitarians for his statement on animals, "The question is not, Can they *reason*? nor Can they *talk*? but Can they *suffer*?"[31]

## The Great English Poets of the Eighteenth Century

This new emerging humane attitude in England was reflected by those most prominently involved in the arts. One of these was the great English poet Alexander Pope, whose epigram *Essay on Man* (1733) is among the most famous and widely read poems ever written. In it he expanded John Donne's thesis that "no man is an island, entire of itself" to the concept that all living creatures, including humans, are involved with, and dependent on, each other:

> Has God, thou fool! work'd solely for thy good,
> Thy joy, thy pastime, thy attire, thy food? . . .
> Is it for thee the lark ascends and sings?
> Joy tunes his voice, joy elevates his wings. . . .
> While Man exclaims, "See all things for my use!"
> "See man for mine!" replies a pamper'd goose:
> And just as short of reason he must fall,
> Who thinks all made for one, not one for all.

Pope was also a proponent of the meatless diet and expressed his horror at the cruelty visited upon food animals, such as the whipping to death of pigs with knotted ropes to tenderize the meat.

By the end of the eighteenth century, some of England's most famous writers and poets were espousing the humane cause. Samuel Taylor Coleridge (1772–1834), who preached in Unitarian chapels and was a Scholar at Jesus College in Cambridge, wrote in his classic work *The Ancient Mariner* (1798):

> He prayeth best, who loveth best,
> all things, both great and small;
> For the dear God who loveth us,
> He made and loveth all.

Robert Burns (1759–96), the Scottish national poet, bitterly lambasted hunters in his poem "To the Wounded Hare."

Percy Bysshe Shelley (1792–1822) advocated kindness to animals, and practiced it by abstaining from eating meat. In "A Vindication of Natural Diet," he wrote that one who follows a natural, vegetarian diet will find abhorrent such amusements as sport hunting, which stem from corrupting and poisoning one's body.

And poet William Cowper (1731–1800), who composed sixty-seven hymns, wrote, "I would not enter on my list of friends, though grace'd with polish'd manner and fine sense, the man who needlessly sets foot upon a worm."

Other English poets who, in later years, supported the humane movement include Robert Browning and Alfred Lord Tennyson, as well as the painter and satirist William Hogarth.

Charles Niven points out that these expressions of indignation and humane concern for animals were few and far between and that "the cruelty during that period was simply appalling." Still, this "literary effort during the years 1740 to 1800 was slowly softening up the resistance of the general public to change."[32] And these courageous figures set the stage for the early nineteenth-century battles that began in Parliament to enact legal protection for animals.

## The Eighteenth Century Ends with Progress

By the late eighteenth century, people's attitudes toward animals had begun to improve, due in part to the writings of some influential men of the church, such as the British novelist and vicar Laurence Sterne (1713–68). He once caught a fly that had been bothering him at dinner and released it out the window, saying "Go...fly should I hurt thee? This world surely is wide enough to hold both thee and me."[33]

In 1776, what may have been the first book devoted to *teaching* kindness to animals was published: *A Dissertation on the Duty of Mercy and Sin of Cruelty to Brute Animals*, by Dr. Humphrey Primatt. Dr. Primatt believed that "if all the barbarous customs and practices still subsisting amongst us were decreed to be as illegal as they are sinful, we should not hear of so many shocking murders and acts of inhumanity as we now do."[34]

In 1786, the curate of Middleton, the Reverend Richard Dean, published *An Essay on the Future Life of Brute Creatures*, urging his readers to treat animals kindly, and not to "treat them as sticks, or stones, or things that cannot feel.... Surely ... sensibility in brutes entitles them to a milder treatment than they usually meet from hard and unthinking wretches."[35]

On October 4, 1790, a watershed event occurred when a man was prosecuted for ripping the tongue out of a horse with one hand while beating it over the head — for ten minutes — with the other. At this time, there were no laws protecting animals, so the man was acquitted.

Three years later, two Manchester butchers were fined twenty shillings apiece for cutting the feet off live sheep and then driving them through the streets. Had the sheep been their own property, no actions likely could have been brought.[36]

## The Fight in Parliament for Legislation

The need for some type of legislation to provide at least minimal protection to animals had long been apparent. This was especially so, since the English system was admired around the world and became the basis for the legal system of jurisprudence in America and other countries as well.

During this period, the mistreatment of an animal could be prosecuted only if it could be proven that the act harmed or lowered the value of *someone else's* property. For example, one could not beat and cripple another's horse, thus damaging the person financially. But one could torture one's own horse to one's heart's content.[37]

The first effort to have Parliament enact legislation to protect animals came in April 1800, when Sir William Pulteney introduced a bill to outlaw bull-baiting. This attempt failed, as did one two years later. One argument often made against the legislation was that "it would be wrong to deprive the lower orders of their amusements."[38] In 1809, Lord Thomas Erskine (1750–1823), Lord High Chancellor of England, drafted legislation for "Preventing Wanton and Malicious Cruelty to Animals."

The unusual preamble to the bill, Erskine admitted, employed "language calculated to make the deepest impression on the human mind," and commenced with a spiritual appeal:

> Whereas it has pleased Almighty God to subdue to the dominion, use, and comfort of man the strength and faculties of many useful animals and to provide others for his food; and whereas the abuse of that dominion by cruel and oppressive treatment of such animals is not only highly unjust and immoral, but most pernicious in its example, having an evident tendency to harden the heart against the natural feelings of humanity....[39]

On May 15, 1809, Lord Erskine introduced his bill in the House of the Lords, where — quite surprisingly — it passed. However, it was defeated in the House of Commons by a vote of 37 to 27. Although Erskine's bill did not pass, it was nevertheless a great beginning and an important step forward in the eventual enactment of such legislation.[40]

In 1822, at last, humane legislation was successfully enacted in England. The person largely responsible for this measure was the tough and witty Irish M.P., Richard Martin (1755?–1834), called "Humanity Martin" by his good friend King George IV (1762–1830).

In 1821, Martin introduced his bill to prohibit the abuse of horses and other animals. Commonly known as "Humanity Martin's Cattle Bill," it was greeted with such uproarious laughter — especially when the suggestion was made and defended that asses should be included — that the reporter from *The Times of London* could not hear what was being said. Nevertheless, the bill passed the House of Commons. Unfortunately, it never got out of the House of Lords.[41] But Martin was not a person easily intimidated or discouraged. Once, as a member of the Irish House of Commons (before the union with Britain), he is reported to have faced down a mob of several thousand with only a small pocket pistol, and in so doing won their cheers.

Martin persisted in his efforts, saying that "every preacher in London has spoken in support of the bill." And the following year, on July 22, 1822, Martin's Act at last became the law of the land — the first such law to be passed by any nation. (In 1641, the American colony of Massachusetts adopted a law forbidding cruelty to domestic animals, the first such law passed by a Western governmental body. See p. 97.)

This 1822 law, known formally as "An Act to Prevent the Cruel and Improper Treatment of Cattle," empowered magistrates to punish anyone engaging in cruelty to horses, cattle, and sheep, with a fine of from ten shillings up to five pounds, or imprisonment for not more than three months in jail. Since the passage of "Martin's Act," as the law was called, numerous other laws and amendments have broadened protection to animals in England.[42]

Sadly, Martin never received proper credit or reward for his great accomplishment. Because of his financial problems, he lost his inheritance — the huge estate in Western Ireland known as Connemara. And when he died in his eightieth year in January 1834, his obituary notice in the *Times* referred to him as "the late eccentric M.P. for Galway." Fairholme and Pain point out that "Martin was always on the side of the oppressed, whether they were human or animal. But these efforts went largely unappreciated, even his work to enact such social reforms as having the death penalty abolished for forgers, and to secure the right of counsel for the accused."

Charles Dickens (1812–70), the great novelist whose books about the poverty and mistreatment of the poor inspired many social reforms, wrote of Martin: "It was a pity he could not exchange a little of his excessive tenderness for animals for some common sense and consideration for human beings!"

Martin is mentioned parenthetically in a footnote in the English historian W. E. H. Lecky's voluminous work, *History of European Morals* (1869), and is described as follows: "an eccentric Irish member [of Parliament], who was generally ridiculed during his life, and has been almost forgotten since his death; but to whose untiring exertions the legislative protection of animals is due."[43]

In retrospect, the remarkable things is not that it took animal protectionists so long to have humane legislation enacted (from 1800 to 1822), but that it was passed at all. William Wilberforce (1759–1833), the great antislavery crusader, first advocated an end to the slave trade in 1787 and did not meet with success until 1807 — twenty years later. It is thus

hardly amazing that legislation to protect animals — also strongly supported by Wilberforce — took two years longer to succeed than the fight
to emancipate humans.

Ironically, the year after Martin's death, in 1835, a bill sailed through
Parliament with surprising ease, giving some real protection to domestic animals. Sponsored by Joseph Pease, the act passed the House of
Commons with almost no opposition and the House of Lords without
discussion and received the Royal Assent on September 9. It provided
for a fine of between five and forty shillings for cruelty to any domestic
animal, and it outlawed the using of a place for cock-fighting and for
baiting animals such as bulls, bears, and dogs.[44] Had he lived to see
this victory, Humanity Martin's pride would surely have been exceeded
only by his amazement.


## The Nineteenth Century: Cruelties Continue

The dawning of the nineteenth century brought with it a strong mo-
mentum toward greater compassion for animals and hope for further
progress. But there was still a multitude of problems to be dealt with.

By 1835 the bear- and bull-baiting gardens of England had been abolished and closed, but other barbarisms continued unabated. Cat skinners
continued to whip off a cat's fur to sell, often leaving the unfortunate
animal still alive in the street. Many people in London actually made a
living by stealing cats, skinning them alive, and then selling the pelt.

Other widespread cruelties included whipping pigs to tenderize the
flesh, shopkeepers using caged squirrels on rotating treadmills to attract business, and various performing animals taught unnatural tricks
through torture and deprivation.

In 1882, Reverend James King wrote of this period: "The most reckless, savage punishment, and the most disgusting disregard to the bodily
sufferings of animals, were exhibited unconcealed in the highways and
streets daily.... The protests of humane people were silenced by ridicule
which came from the platform, the pulpit, and the senate."[45]


## Helping Animals — and People

Many of the most important leaders of the animal protection movement were also active in efforts to help oppressed humans of that day,
such as antislavery and child labor campaigns. John Colam, secretary of
the Royal Society for the Prevention of Cruelty to Animals (R.S.P.C.A.),
helped found the National Society for the Prevention of Cruelty to
Children.

The founder and first secretary of the R.S.P.C.A. — the oldest animal protection organization in existence — was an Anglican priest, the Reverend Arthur Broome. He devoted his full time to helping animals, and, as a result of the public's apathy, was imprisoned for his and the society's debts — a singular distinction for a clergyman of the Church of England!

It was originally founded as a Christian society "based on Christian principles," one of whose main activities was sponsoring sermons of humane education in London churches. Three clergymen are among its initial supporters. The small group of people who met in 1824, at the famous Old Slaughter's Coffee-House in St. Martin's Lane, to form the R.S.P.C.A. included William Wilberforce, the English philanthropist and leader in the fight to abolish slavery in the British Empire.[46]

As the Reverend Lorne Lemoine has written, "In many places animal welfare organizations have amalgamated with parallel movements for the protection of children. For the same kind of mentality which would sanction the maltreatment of an animal might well countenance the abuse of a child."[47]

The main impact religion appears to have had during this period in ameliorating cruelty to animals came when the Puritans ordered a halt to bear-baiting. They attacked it along with other amusements, and there is disagreement about their motives in doing so. The English writer and statesman Thomas Macaulay (1800–1859) has written that "bear-baiting, then a favourite diversion of high and low, was the abomination of the austere sectaries. The Puritans hated it, not because it gave pain to the bear, but because it gave pleasure to the spectators."[48]

But American historian Samuel Eliot Morrison disputes Macaulay, saying he "could seldom resist the temptation to make a wise-crack!" Morrison points out that the Puritans who settled in the Massachusetts Bay Colony enacted in 1641 a law forbidding cruelty to domestic animals and allowing cattle drivers to rest their cows in unenclosed fields without trespass.[49]

Another clergyman active in late nineteenth-century England was an eloquent and prolific writer on the subject of animals, the Reverend John George Wood (1827–89). He was not only a popular lecturer in the field of natural history, but wrote numerous books as well, including *My Feathered Friends* (1856), *Man and Beast — Here and Hereafter* (1874), and several other works. Wood, in the latter publication, expressed the view that most people were unkind to animals because they were unaware that the creatures had souls and would enjoy eternal life.[50]

## Darwin's Scientific Heresies

Nineteenth-century England produced one of history's greatest scientists, a man whose theories continue to have a profound impact on several areas of science and the humanities. This renowned figure — Charles Robert Darwin (1809–82) — was also a strong advocate of kind treatment for animals, and his theory of evolution helped establish a scientific basis for the kinship between human beings and animals.

Indeed, Darwin's work corroborated scientifically the religious belief, articulated by St. John Chrysostom, that animals "are of the same origin as ourselves." Not surprisingly, Darwin's books, *On the Origin of Species by Means of Natural Selection* (1859) and *The Descent of Man* (1871), hypothesizing the evolution of humans from anthropoid apes, set off a storm of controversy, especially in religious quarters.

Darwin's theory of evolution by natural selection was first published in 1858 by the Linnaean Society of London, in a joint paper co-authored by the English naturalist Alfred Russel Wallace (1823–1913).

Although Darwin's theories were construed by many as an attack on revealed religion, he contended that the concept of a planned and orderly creation was more complimentary to the deity than the idea of a haphazard one. Darwin's teachings helped support scientifically the biblical view of humans and animals being part of an integrated biological community and living together in a cooperative and mutually beneficial arrangement.

Darwin was himself a strong defender of animals and helped promote England's 1876 Cruelty to Animals Act, which regulated experiments on animals. He once stated that "sympathy with the lower animals is one of the noblest virtues with which man is endowed."[51]

Darwin had a keen insight into animal intelligence and behavior. Because of his distinguished scientific reputation, his revelations on the remarkable similarities between humans and animals in such areas as intelligence, emotions, and social structures could not be derisively dismissed as sentimental anthropomorphism.

Darwin concluded that humans and animals had more similarities than differences:

the difference in mind between man and the higher animals, great as it is, certainly is one of degree and not of kind. We have seen that the senses and intuitions, the various emotions and faculties, such as love, memory attention, curiosity, imitation, reason, etc., of which man boasts, may be found in an incipient, or even sometimes in a well-developed condition, in the lower animals.[52]

Thus did the most renowned scientist of the day lay the scientific foundation for changing the prevailing view of animals, from machines to fellow creatures much like ourselves. It was a heresy as great, and perhaps greater, than his theory of evolution.

*Chapter 6* _____

# The Settling of America: Religious Reverence, and Hatred, for Animals

I care not for a man's religion whose dog or cat are not the better for it.
— Abraham Lincoln[1]

In the New World, European settlers found a nature paradise, full of wildlife and wilderness that both entranced and terrified these early pioneers. The Puritan ethic of the early settlers had a paradoxical impact on nature and animals in America. In 1641, the Massachusetts Bay Colony had the distinction of passing the first American law prohibiting cruelty to animals. But at the same time, wilderness, wolves, and other wildlife were seen as evils to be tamed or destroyed, as were the native Americans, the Indians.

But, as in Europe, attitudes began to change gradually for the better; and some of America's greatest statesmen, such as Benjamin Franklin and Thomas Paine, advocated kindness to animals. By the end of the Civil War, the American humane movement began to grow and increase in strength, and several prominent American clergymen were active and influential in securing much of the progress that was made.

## The World's First Anticruelty to Animals Law

As colonies of European settlers began to spring up throughout the New World, novel political and social concepts, such as liberty and democracy, were also established. Another less well-known but equally revolutionary idea also came into being: legal protection for animals for their own sake.

Among those advocating such a viewpoint were the Puritans who established the Massachusetts Bay Colony in 1630. In 1641, only eleven years after having settled in the colony, the Puritans drafted and adopted

97

the first recorded law in America to protect animals. According to Emily Stewart Leavitt, author of *Animals and Their Legal Rights*, "America has the distinction of being the first country to acknowledge the rights of animals by enacting statutory legislation to protect them from cruel treatment."[2]

The process began in 1638, when the General Court of Massachusetts asked Reverend Nathaniel Ward, a "learned lawyer," to compile a legal code for the colony. Ward (1578?–1652) was an Anglican clergyman who was dismissed for nonconformity. He was driven out of England for heresy by Bishop William Laud (1573–1645), the archbishop of Canterbury, who tried to extirpate Calvinism in England and Presbyterianism in Scotland. (Laud was later committed to the Tower of London and, in 1645, beheaded.) Ward settled in Agawam (now Ipswich), Massachusetts, in 1633, where he became a pastor and compiled his work, "The Body of Liberties." The Puritans voted to have it printed, and it was formally adopted by the court in December 1641.[3]

This legal code contained one hundred "liberties" that the Puritans stated should "be respectively impartiallie and inviolably enjoyed and observed throughout our Jurisdiction for ever." The table of contents lists as Liberty 92, "Cruelty to animals forbidden"; it reads as follows:

OFF THE BRUITE CREATURE

92. No man shall exercise any Tirranny or Crueltie towards any bruite Creature which are usuallie kept for man's use.

93. If any man shall have occasion to leade or drive Cattel from place to place that is far of, so that they be weary, or hungry, or fall sick, or lambe [lame]. It shall be lawful to rest or refresh them, for a competent time, in any open place that is not Corne, meadow, or inclosed for some peculiar use.[4]

The Puritans noted emphatically that these "liberties" had the effect of laws.

Massachusetts was thus the first Western governmental body to incorporate mercy for animals into law, doing so almost two centuries before England.[5] Amazingly, it was to be another two centuries before one of the American states passed a general anticruelty law with the strength and scope of the Massachusetts statute.

## Destroying America's Wilderness

While the Puritan ethic helped to stimulate the passage of America's first law to protect animals from cruelty, it had a decidedly negative impact on most wild animals and their wilderness habitat. The colonists brought with them from Europe the engrained hatred for wolves instilled during the Dark Ages and thence cultivated and exploited by the ecclesiastical and civil authorities. These elusive and mysterious creatures of the twilight and the dark, whose eerie and mournful howls pierced the forest and could frighten the bravest of men, became the subject of countless bloodchilling legends. While in Europe the wolf was considered the dog of the devil, here there was no need to invent werewolves and other imaginary savages, for the wilderness abounded with those other creatures of fear and hatred, the Indians. These brothers of the wilderness came to symbolize for the settlers the perils and malevolence of this unknown world. As in Europe, organized religion fed these fears, and Protestant preachers condemned the savagery of these twin pagan forces of the forests.

Before long, the colonists began to deal with what they saw as forces of evil. As Barry Lopez discusses in his book *Of Wolves and Men*, walls were built around towns to keep out wolves and Indians, and a war of extermination against them began to be waged. Since they seemed so similar, the same weaponry was utilized against both groups. They were commonly shot on sight and were given less legal protection than game animals. (A Massachusetts statute of 1638 governing the discharge of firearms within the city provided that "whoever shall shoot off a gun on any unnecessary occasion, or at any game except an Indian or wolf, shall forfeit five shillings for every shot.")

Poisoning was another method of extermination, using baited meat for the wolves and smallpox-infected blankets for the Indians. Wolf pups were dug out of their lairs and killed or burned in the den. Indian children were kidnapped and sent to missionary schools to be indoctrinated with Christianity and made "civilized."[6] Wolf bounties were also instituted, beginning in 1630 in Massachusetts, with Virginia following suit two years later, followed by the other colonies.

Among the early American religious figures who helped lead the onslaught against the wilderness was the congregational clergyman Cotton Mather (1663–1728). He not only supported the trial and execution of numerous "witches" that took place in 1692–93, but also inveighed against the presence of the wilderness as something of an insult to the Lord. He and other Puritan ministers preached the theme that untamed nature represented a challenge to the devout colonists to prove their faithfulness by obliterating this "howling wilderness" and changing it to a "fruitful field."[7]

In the colonists' religiously inspired war against nature, there was never any doubt as to what the outcome would be. In 1756, before taking office as the second president of the United States, John Adams wrote of how much improved the country had become, with the destruction of wilderness, wildlife, and the Indians. As he put it, when the colonists first arrived: "The whole continent was one continued dismal wilderness, the haunt of wolves and bears and more savage men. Now the forests are removed, the land covered with fields of corn, orchards bending with fruit and the magnificent habitations of rational and civilized people."[8]

## The Indians' Respect for Nature — and the Whites' Destruction of It

The New World was a great experiment in democracy. And in the more democratic traditions of the early American settlers, wildlife was thought of as belonging to *everyone*, and not just to the nobility. As a result, the largely unrestricted taking of wildlife soon became the rule, governed mainly by the Roman tradition of wild animals belonging to whoever killed or captured them. From the 1600s to the early 1800s, the exploitation of wildlife was carried out virtually without limits of any kind.[9]

The whites' callous and destructive attitude toward wildlife and nature contrasted sharply with the reverential, or at least respectful, way many of the American Indian tribes treated what they considered kindred creatures and sacred land. The Native Americans were shocked by the wanton slaughter of wildlife undertaken by the European intruders, and many correctly perceived that the disappearance of wild animals like the buffalo would someday seal their doom as well.

The attitude toward nature held by many Native Americans is exemplified by the now-popularized saying attributed to them, "We do not inherit the Earth from our parents. We borrow it from our children." And it is said that the six nations of the Iroquois Confederacy and the Sioux Indians based their decision-making process on considering the effects an action or decision would have on the next seven generations.[10]

So strong was the conservation ethic and appreciation for wildlife held by many Indian communities that it would be considered remarkable even by today's standards. This reverence for nature formed the basis for much of their religious culture. Some Indians believed, for example, that "the capital of life existing in the universe is constant, and every share taken from the animal kingdom must be compensated by a shortening of the life of man."[11]

According to conservation writer Mike Frome,

> To the Cherokee Indians, environment was the controlling force in their lives. So strong was this conviction that their religious beliefs were based on it.... Every animal, stone, and tree were believed to have their own spirits and particular reasons for being. Ceremonials were devoted to fulfillment of man's rather small role in the grand design of the universe.[12]

Some animals enjoyed a special, revered status among certain tribes. In the mythology of many Indians, the coyote was especially admired. To the Crow Indians of the Northwest, it was considered the creator of the earth and all living things, according to wildlife author Hope Ryden. The Navajos of the Southwest called it "God's dog," and the Aztecs of Mexico also deified the coyote.[13]

Some Indian tribes of the northwestern United States held the killer whale in sacred reverence. They believed that humans who spear-hunted for food in the sea became killer whales in their next life. Once, when a young brave killed one and brought it back, the elders of the tribe went to the shore and prayed for forgiveness.[14]

Even when hunting, the North American Indians had a profound sense of conservation concerning the animals they killed and seemed to appreciate the need to exercise prudence and humility in taking them. To many Indians, the game belonged not to them but to a Great Spirit, an Owner of the Animals, who gave the hunters animals and allowed them to be taken under certain conditions. But if these stipulations were not fulfilled or the hunters were not worthy, the animals would be kept away from them, especially if the hunter did not treat the animals with respect.[15]

"Hunting is holy, game animals are holy. And the life of a hunting people is regarded as a sacred way of living because it grows out of this powerful, fundamental covenant," writes author Barry Lopez.[16]

As Reverend James E. Carroll has written, the Indians, when hunting, felt a spiritual obligation to the Creator:

We would do well to emulate the ideal of the Indian's attitude toward animals. When the Indian hunter stalked his game, he did so with skill and mercy. He offered a prayer to his god or gods that his aim would be true. If his arrow or spear didn't hit a vital spot, he considered it a solemn responsibility to end the animals' suffering as quickly as possible. To kill for sport *only* was unthinkable to the American Indian. The animals had been given him by God for his sustenance, and he would not presume to abuse such a gift.[17]

Not all Indians hunted in such a careful and conscientious manner. The methods used by some Indian tribes to hunt buffalo were to sneak up within arrow range in the hide of an antelope or wolf, or to hide in ambush in rocks or brush. But other tribes, especially those on the prairies located near cliffs, utilized more wasteful (if safer) ways of killing buffalo. They would drive the buffalo along rock ridges they had constructed leading to precipices, and thence over the cliffs. So many buffalo could be taken in this manner that often only the tenderest cuts of meat were kept, sometimes just the tongues. But even with such often wasteful killing methods, the Indians hardly put a dent in the buffalo population.[18]

And the Indians could be quite unsentimental when it came to domestic animals. The dog was a staple of the diet for some Indian tribes; its hair was used for weaving; and it was employed as a beast-of-burden before the Spaniards introduced the horse into America, pulling sleds and carrying food and firewood. They were not considered pets in the way we use the term, and dogs that got into food supplies or caused other such problems did not last very long.[19]

### "This Earth Is Sacred"

The Indians were shocked and dismayed by the Europeans' destruction of nature and tried to preserve the sanctity of the land and the animals even as the whites were attempting to take the country for themselves. Some of the statements attributed to the Indian leaders of that day are eloquent and moving in their pleas for the whites not to destroy the spiritual quality of the land.

In his widely quoted letter to President Franklin Pierce (1804–69), Chief Sealth of the Duwamish tribe in the state of Washington (after whom the city of Seattle is named) pleaded with the white conquerors to preserve and cherish the land they were about to take from him:

> How can you buy or sell the sky — the warmth of the land? The idea is strange to us. Yet we do not own the freshness of the air or the sparkle of the water. How can you buy them from us? Every part of this earth is sacred to my people. Every shining pine needle, every sandy shore, every mist in the dark woods, every clearing and humming insect is holy in the memory and experience of my people.
>
> If I decide to accept your offer to buy our land, I will make one condition. The white man must treat the beasts of this land as his brothers. I am a savage and do not understand any other way.
>
> I have seen a thousand rotting buffaloes on the prairies left by the white man who shot them from a passing train. What is man without the beasts? If all the beasts were gone, men would die from great loneliness of spirit, for whatever happens to the beast also happens to man. All things are connected. Whatever befalls the earth, befalls the sons of the earth.
>
> One thing we know — our God is the same. This earth is precious to Him. Even the white man cannot be exempt from this common destiny.[20]

Chief Standing Bear has described how his people, the Lakota Sioux, also had a profound respect for wildlife:

> Life was a glorious thing, for great contentment came with the feeling of friendship and kinship with the living things about you. The white man seems to look upon all animal life as enemies, while we look upon them

as friends and benefactors. They were one with the Great Mystery. And so were we.[21]

He has described how his people saw nature as "Mother Earth" on which they depended for their sustenance:

The Lakota was a true naturalist — a lover of nature. He loved the earth and all things of the earth. . . . Kinship with all creatures of the earth, sky, and water, was a real and active principle. . . . Wherever the Lakota went, he was with Mother Earth. No matter where he roamed by day or slept by night, he was safe with her. This thought comforted and sustained the Lakota and he was eternally filled with gratitude.[22]

A similar land ethic was expressed by the Lenape Indians from the Wissahickon Valley in Pennsylvania, in their reply to the founder of the colony of Pennsylvania, William Penn (1644–1718), who preached and wrote as a member of the Society of Friends (Quakers):

You ask us to believe in the Great Creator and Ruler of the Heaven and Earth, and yet you do not believe or trust Him, for you have taken the Land unto yourself which we and our friends occupied in common. You scheme night and day how you may preserve it so that none can take it from you. Yes, you even scheme beyond your own life and parcel it out between your children. . . . We believe in God the Creator and Ruler of Heaven and Earth. He maintains the Sun; he maintained our fathers for so many, many moons. He maintains us, and we . . . are sure that he will also protect our children. . . . And so long as we have this faith we trust in Him, and never bequeath a foot of ground.[23]

Still today, the Indian's respect for the environment and reverence for "Mother earth" often conflict with the whites' disregard for nature and their desire to tame it.

Nakoma Volkman, of the Native American Center of Southeast Minnesota, in Rochester, writes: "The earth is my floor and it is sacred — the sky is my cathedral, my altar [is] all about. I must cry when Mother Earth is hurt. If nature is damaged or destroyed forever, I cannot live — life cannot be sustained."[24]

The destruction and desecration in recent decades of natural areas important and sacred to the Indians are too numerous to be included here, but it is clear that their forebodings about how the white man would treat the land were well-founded. And in ruining so much of the Native Americans' spiritual heritage, we have also destroyed much of our own.

In so doing, we are endangering our very survival, as pointed out by Chief Oren Lyons, clan chief of the Onondaga, New York, branch of

the Iroquois, and director of Native American studies, State University
of New York at Buffalo:

> Indigenous people have a long-term moral perspective on the earth and its
> life. We have no complex answers, but only the simple principle of respect
> for all life, for the trees, the rivers, the fish, the animals.
>
> The world is very complex today, but values still remain simple,
> the principles of life remain simple. If we break those rules of life and
> procreation, we break the cycle of life and life will disappear.
>
> The Earth will not disappear, but people will. We're not going to de-
> stroy the world. The world has its own time cycle. But we are still only a
> biological experiment.[25]

In *Daybreak*, a Native American publication, Oren Lyons describes
how the wisdom of his ancestors, and other native peoples, applies to
the present situation:

> The spiritual philosophies and politics of indigenous peoples around the
> earth are just now beginning to be heard and understood. The visions
> of our grandfathers, great leaders of North, Central, and South American
> Indians, are now being quoted because what they predicted would happen,
> has happened, and is happening.
>
> As Chief Sealth (Seattle) said to a mid-nineteenth century president
> of the United States, "This we know. The earth does not belong to man;
> man belongs to the earth.... To harm the earth is to heap contempt upon
> its creator. Continue to contaminate your bed, and you will one night
> suffocate in your own waste."[26]

## Early American Defenders of Animals

While most mainstream religious denominations in early America ignored or were hostile to humane and conservation precepts, a few groups
placed great emphasis on them.

One was the United Society of Believers in Christ's Second Appearance, known as the Shakers, which based its reverence for the
environment on religious principles. Their order once settled colonies
in seven states, and built a village — Shakertown, at Pleasant Hill,
Kentucky — that was intended to be God's kingdom on earth. Their
remarkably advanced social and ecological concepts encompassed not
just equality of the sexes and races, but also humanitarianism toward
animals, including forbidding the wearing of spurs and kicking of
animals.[27]

Posted in the barns of many Shakers was an admonition that summed
up their attitude:

> A man of kindness, to his beast is kind.
> Brutal actions show a brutal mind.
> Remember, HE who made the brute,
> Who gave thee speech and reason, formed him mute;
> He can't complain; but God's omniscient eye
> Beholds thy cruelty. He hears his cry.
> He was destined thy servant and thy drudge,
> But know this: His Creator Is Thy Judge.[28]

The founder of the sect, Ann Lee (1736–84), often made references to kindness of animals; and more extensive teachings relating to this were introduced in the mid-nineteenth century and have become part of the church's doctrine.

Born in Manchester, England, Lee joined the Shaking Quakers, or Shakers; and in 1774, she immigrated to America, where she and her followers set up the first Shaker colony in the United States at Watervliet, New York. Ann Lee is reported to have taught that a person who mistreated animals could not be a Christian and to have advocated "justice and kindness to all the brute creation."[29]

In 1845, official sets of orders and rules were compiled and codified and were read at meetings; Section VII consisted of "The Order Concerning Beasts, Etc." These rules went so far as to regulate the keeping of dogs, cats, and other creatures as pets, and further stated that:

No beasts belonging to the people of God may be left to suffer with hunger, thirst or cold, in consequence of neglect, on the part of those who have the care of them. But all should be kept in their proper places, and properly attended to according to their needs.

No beasts or any living thing may be wantonly pained, injured, or tortured. And no living thing may be chastened or corrected in a passion.[30]

*The Divine Book of Holy and Eternal Wisdom*, published by the Shakers in 1849, describes a revelation from "the Holy Angel" setting forth a number of laws, two of which forbid abuse of animals and state that humans are answerable to God for their treatment of other creatures.[31]

As is so often the case, those who practiced kindness to animals did so for people as well. The Shakers opened their homes to orphans and unwanted children and during the Civil War cared for wounded and hungry soldiers from both sides.[32] The Shakers once numbered six thousand, but the sect has now dwindled to less than a dozen people, living in New Gloucester, Maine, and Canterbury, New Hampshire.[33]

The now-defunct Bible Christian Church, a nineteenth-century movement, existed in the United States for a little over a century, teaching vegetarianism and love for animals. The church was organized in England in 1800; one of its early converts (in 1809) was William Metcalfe (1788–1862), who immigrated to Philadelphia in 1817 with forty-one followers to establish a church community in America.[34]

Metcalfe was an ardent vegetarian and cited numerous biblical references to support his belief that humans were intended to follow a meatless diet for both health and humane reasons (see pp. 179–180).

The Society of Friends (Quakers) also took a kindly view toward animals (see p. 140). The ardent abolitionist John Greenleaf Whittier (1807–92), known as "the Quaker poet," summed up the belief of many Quakers when he wrote, "The sooner we recognize the fact that the mercy of the Almighty extends to every creature endowed with life, the better it will be for us as men and Christians."

And John Woolman (1720–72), a Quaker preacher and abolitionist, traveled throughout the southern and the northern colonies attacking slavery and inveighing against cruelty to animals. In his famous *Journal* (published posthumously in 1744 and often reprinted), he wrote of the remorse he felt after tossing stones at, and killing, a robin. This event shocked him into committing himself to "exercise goodness towards every living creature."[35]

The Mormon pioneers, who settled in Utah and other areas of the West, were also guided by an ethic of respect for the land and the animals, and the early leaders of the faith strongly emphasized such precepts (see pp. 142–145).

Other early American defenders of animals included the American Revolutionary leader Thomas Paine (1737–1809). The son of a Quaker corsetmaker in England, Paine published the famous pamphlet *Common Sense* (January 10, 1776) urging the declaration of independence. He strongly felt that kindness to animals was a moral obligation and wrote: "The moral duty of man consists of imitating the moral goodness and beneficence of God manifested in the creation toward all his creation. Everything of persecution and revenge between man and man, and everything of cruelty to animals is a violation of moral duty." Paine is also credited by some with authorship of a poem entitled "Cruelty to Animals Expressed," which stated the view that, in the end, cruelty brings torment to the perpetrator.[36]

Even the American statesman Benjamin Franklin (1706–90) wrote in his autobiography how his love for animals helped impel him partially to adopt a vegetarian diet. Seeing some codfish being caught, he once wrote that he considered "the taking of every fish as a kind of unprovoked murder, since none of them had, or ever could do us any injury that might justify the slaughter."[37]

## Nineteenth-Century Humanitarians

In the nineteenth century, several of America's great early poets expressed a religious and humane ethic in their works. Henry Wadsworth Longfellow (1807–82) devoted several of his poems to a religiously oriented theme of kindness to animals. In "The Birds of Killingworth," there are overtones of divine retribution for the decision of a town to kill off its bird population to save the grain the birds eat. Longfellow described the pleasure and music the birds bring, making clear that he considered them God's creatures, with the sparrows chirping "as if they still were proud of their race" was mentioned in the Bible, and the ravens crying out, "Give us, O Lord, this day our daily bread!"

At the town meeting, the only person who speaks in defense of the birds is the town teacher, the preceptor. He praises "The birds, who make sweet music for us all/in our dark hours, as David did for Saul. . . . Whose habitations in the tree tops even/are half-way houses on the roof to heaven!"

He also asks how the children can be taught compassion amid such brutality toward other creatures:

> How can I teach your children gentleness,
> And mercy to the weak, and reverence
> For Life, which, in its weakness or excess,
> Is still a gleam of God's omnipotence.

After the birds are killed off, the town is infested with insects, just as the preceptor had predicted. Finally realizing the error of their ways, the townspeople bring in birds "from all the country round" to repopulate the woods and fields. Thus did Longfellow make his point, that kindness to animals and a respect for the balance of nature are not only moral virtues, but are in people's own selfish interest.[38] In others of his poems, such as "The Emperor's Bird's Nest," Longfellow expressed similar themes.[39]

Other leading nineteenth-century figures from the arts and humanities also contributed to influencing public opinion on behalf of animals. The antislavery activist Harriet Beecher Stowe (1811–96), whose book *Uncle Tom's Cabin, or Life Among the Lowly* (1852), helped solidify feeling in the North against slavery, had a compassionate feeling toward animals and believed them to be a gift from the Almighty. As she once wrote: "We should remember in our dealings with animals that they are a sacred trust to us from the Heavenly Father. They are dumb and cannot speak for themselves."[40]

Her brother, abolitionist clergyman Henry Ward Beecher (1813–87), who crusaded against slavery and for women's suffrage and for his last forty years was pastor of the Plymouth Congregational Church in Brooklyn, New York, expressed similar sentiments toward animals:

> For fidelity, devotion, love, many a two-legged animal is below the dog and the horse. Happy it would be for thousands of people if they could stand at last before the judgment seat of Christ and say: "I have loved as truly and I have lived as decently as my dog" — and yet we call them only brutes.[41]

## John Muir's Sacred Wilderness

Other religion-oriented Americans fought against the terrible destruction of wildlife and wilderness that was taking place. One of the best known of these was the Scottish naturalist, geologist, and author John Muir (1838–1914), who founded the Sierra Club in 1892 and explored the American wilderness from Indianapolis through California and Alaska. He focused his studies on the Yosemite Valley and was instrumental in persuading Congress to establish Yellowstone National Park in 1889, as well as in influencing President Theodore Roosevelt to set aside 148 million acres of forest reserves.

Muir campaigned tirelessly for saving the wilderness, authoring numerous articles and books on the subject and invoking a spiritually based ethic for nature preservation.[42]

He strongly opposed sport hunting, and during his years of wilderness travels, he never carried a gun, once saying, "Making some bird or beast go lame the rest of its life is a sore thing on one's conscience, at least nothing to boast of, and has no religion in it."[43]

In one battle over the flooding of a beautiful valley to construct a power dam, Muir wrote of his opponents, "The Temple destroyers, devotees of ravaging commercialism, seem to have a perfect contempt for nature, and instead of lifting their eyes to the God of the Mountains, lift them to the Almighty Dollar."[44]

Once in Florida, admiring a palm tree, Muir observed that "they tell us that plants are not like man immortal, but are perishable — soul-less. I think this is something that we know exactly nothing about."[45] And after a dangerous encounter with an alligator, he noted:

> Doubtless these creatures are happy, and fill the place assigned to them by the great Creator of us all. Fierce and cruel they appear to us, but beautiful in the eyes of God. . . . How narrow we selfish, conceited creatures are in our sympathies. How blind to the rights of all the rest of creation.[46]

Muir once even "communed with" and enthralled "a congregation of birds, squirrels, and chipmunks," which he claimed watched attentively as he sang and whistled a series of Scottish airs.[47] On another occasion, while in the mountains of Yosemite, Muir wrote that nature's beauty mirrors the Deity's:

> All of God's universe is glass to the soul of light. Infinitude mirrors reflecting all receiving all. The Stars whirl and eddy and boil in the currents of the ocean called space.... Trees in camplight and grasses and weeds impressive beyond thought so palpably Godful in form and in wind motion.... The pines spiring around me higher higher to the Star-flowered sky are plainly full of God.... Oh the infinite abundance and universality of Beauty. Beauty is God. What shall we say of God that we may not say of Beauty.[48]

(Almost a century later, Muir's writings helped inspire Richard Cartwright Austin, who for twenty-five years was a Presbyterian minister in "the ravaged coalfields of Appalachia," where he worked in the early 1970s, to secure federal legislation to control strip mining. Austin set out to explore the trails of Yosemite and ended up writing several books on his ministry in "environmental theology," including a Christian perspective on Muir entitled *Baptized into Wilderness*. Austin writes that "The Protection of nature must be rooted in love and delight — in religious experience.... Wilderness is sacramental; it can help us meet God.")[49]

## Humane Legislation in the United States

Although cruelty to animals was in some cases punishable under Common Law, it was not until about two hundred years after Massachusetts passed its landmark ordinance that the first general anticruelty statute in one of the states of the United States was enacted. In 1828, the New York state legislature passed a law giving protection to certain domestic animals, such as horses, oxen, cattle, and sheep.[50]

The next state to pass such legislation was the initiator of such a law *two centuries earlier:* Massachusetts, in 1835, followed by Connecticut and Wisconsin in 1838. By 1898, all of the states and territories had enacted such laws except Alaska, Arizona (which did so in 1913), and the Virgin Islands (which acted in 1921).[51]

The humane and animal protection movement did not really get organized in America until after the US Civil War. After visiting the R.S.P.C.A. in London (then in its forty-first year) in 1865, Henry Bergh (1813?–1888) determined to form a similar organization in the United States.

The following year, the New York legislature charted the American Society for the Prevention of Cruelty to Animals (A.S.P.C.A.) in New York City, giving it the power to investigate cruelty cases and arrest individuals. Bergh was appointed president of this first humane society in the Western Hemisphere. Soon, similar groups were formed in Boston and other American cities to care for stray, injured, and mistreated dogs, cats, horses, and other animals in the nation's urban centers.[52]

Bergh also succeeded in having New York pass an improved anti-cruelty statute in 1866, which included a section prohibiting the abandonment of disabled horses and mules. The following year, he drafted and had passed an even more comprehensive animal protection law, which has served as the basis for similar laws that now exist in forty-one states and the District of Columbia.[53]

For the sake of those who delight in asking how such a humanitarian could devote his time to helping animals when so many *people* were suffering, it should be noted that Bergh, around 1874, helped found the New York Society for the Prevention of Cruelty to Children — the first organization in the United States dedicated to helping children and protecting them from abuse.[54]

Toward the end of the nineteenth century, a clergyman, Reverend Thomas Timmins of Portsmouth, England, helped organize what appears to be the first mass effort in America to *teach* kindness to animals. Reverend Timmins traveled to America to work and consult with George T. Angell (1823–1909). Angell founded the Massachusetts S.P.C.A. in 1868 and published in Boston what has been credited with being the first periodical in the world devoted to animal welfare, the magazine *Our Dumb Animals*.[55]

On June 2 of that year, the first edition of some two hundred thousand copies was distributed free by the police to almost every household in Boston. Soon, police in other cities began to do the same, and towns were reached through the postmaster. The magazine is still being published in Boston by the American Humane Education Society, which Angell also founded and is now part of the Massachusetts S.P.C.A.[56]

Timmins and Angell succeeded in organizing American students into "Bands of Mercy," based on the English movement, and by 1912 there were over three million elementary school students enrolled in the over eighty-five thousand chapters. The members wore badges and pledged as their motto, "I will try to be kind to all living creatures, and try to protect them from cruel usage." This movement eventually attained worldwide proportions before declining after World War II.[57]

Angell considered as one of his most important accomplishments the arrangements he worked out in 1883 with the National Education Association (N.E.A.), to form "American Teachers Bands of Mercy" within the N.E.A., which numbered some three hundred groups at one time.[58] Today, a century later, no such organization exists within the schools, perhaps helping to explain the apparent moral decline of our young people and our society.

# Contemporary Western Religion: Its Successes and Its Failures

# The Catholic Church: From Hostility, to Indifference, to Concern

In the nineteenth and twentieth centuries, the Catholic Church's attitude toward animals and nature has varied from hostility, to indifference, to the initial glimmerings of concern. During this period, and up to the present time, church leaders can be found representing any and all of these positions.

However, in recent years, amazing progress has been made in moving the church toward if not yet into the ranks of those advocating protection of animals and the environment. It has been a long and difficult journey, and there is still a long way to go; but the distance that has been traveled is enormous.

### Sanctioning Cruelty and Abuse

The church's largely negative attitude toward animals during the Renaissance persisted into modern times. The Irish historian W. E. H. Lecky wrote in 1869 that "on the whole, Catholicism has done very little to inculcate humanity to animals" and pointed out that the Catholic countries of Europe were "those in which inhumanity to animals is most wanton and most unrebuked."[1]

In the 1850s, Pope Pius IX is reported to have refused to allow the opening in Rome of a society for the protection of animals on the grounds that it was a theological error to believe that humans had any obligations toward other creatures.[2]

Anna Kingsford (1846–88), the English antivivisectionist and vegetarian, wrote in her book *The Credo of Christendom* of the need for Christianity to teach kindness to animals:

Who can doubt it who visits Rome — the city of the Pontiff — where now I am, and witness the black-hearted cruelty of the "Christians" to the ani-

mals which toil and slave for them?... They will tell you "Christians have
no duties to the beasts that perish." Their Pope has told them so. So that
everywhere in Catholic Christendom the poor, patient, dumb creatures
endure every species of torment without a single word being uttered on
their behalf by the teachers of religion.[3]

Sometimes the representatives of the church have gone to extraordinary lengths to justify acts of cruelty to animals, while attempting to
maintain the principle that one should not engage in such acts as an
end unto itself. The result of this moral and philosophical hair-splitting
has been to condone almost any mistreatment of animals for which the
slightest justification can be conjured.

An early version of the *Catholic Dictionary*, thirteenth edition (1884),
under the heading "Animals, Lower," states:

> As the lower animals have no duties... so they have no rights.... The
> brutes are made for man, who has the same right over them which he has
> over plants or stones.... It must also be lawful to put them to death or to
> inflict pain on them, for any good or reasonable end, such as the promotion
> of man's knowledge, health, or even for the purposes of recreation.... But
> a limitation must be introduced here. It is never lawful for a man to take
> pleasure directly in the pain given to brutes, because in doing so, man
> degrades and brutalizes his own nature.[4]

Another publication extremely damaging to animal welfare was the
often-cited 1888 or 1901 book by Jesuit Father Joseph Rickaby, *Moral
Philosophy*, in which he wrote:

> Brute beasts, not having understanding and therefore not being persons,
> cannot have any rights.... We have no duties to them — not of justice —
> not of religion.... We have then no duties of charity, nor duties of any
> kind, to the lower animals, as neither to sticks and stones.... It is wanton
> cruelty to vex and annoy a brute beast *for sport*.... But there is no shadow
> of evil resting on the practice of causing pain to brutes *in sport*, where the
> pain is not the sport itself, but an incidental concomitant of it.[5]

Father Basil Wrighton, of the Catholic Rectory in Reading, England,
and a leader of the Catholic Study Circle for Animal Welfare, has attributed much of the blame for the cruelty to animals that has prevailed
over the years to the sanction provided by this work and similar ones by
writers speaking in the church's name, but which "are not infallible pro-
nouncements of the Church.... Their authority is no greater than that
of the writers themselves."[6]

## Defending the Animals

At the same time that the church was so stubbornly endorsing mistreatment of animals, a few nineteenth-century Catholic leaders were
actively promoting the opposite view. Roman Catholic Cardinal John
Henry Newman (1801–90), the renowned English theologian and former Anglican leader of the Oxford movement, wrote in *The Grammar of
Assent* (1870) that "cruelty to animals is as if a man did not love God."
He also wrote of "cruelty shown to poor brutes":

> They have done us no harm. . . . They have no power whatever of resis-
> tance. It is the cowardice and tyranny of which they are the victims that
> make their sufferings so especially touching. There is something so very
> dreadful, so Satanic, in tormenting those who have never harmed us, and
> cannot defend themselves, who are utterly in our power.[7]

Another prominent cardinal of that time, Henry Edward Manning
(1808–92), archbishop of Westminster, spoke out against cruelty to animals, especially painful medical experiments. In a letter dated July 13,
1891, he wrote: "We owe ourselves the duty not to be brutal or cruel;
and we owe to God the duty of treating all His creatures according to
His own perfections of love and mercy."[8]

The great English poet and Jesuit Gerard Manley Hopkins (1844–
89) found in nature "God's grandeur," expressing his reverence in a
poem of that title. He wrote lovingly of God's creation, saying that "the
world is charged with the grandeur of God." And despite the damage
done by humans, "nature is never spent; there lives the dearest fresh-
ness deep down things." In "Inversnoid," he eloquently pleaded for the
preservation of wildness and wilderness:

> What would the world be, once bereft
> Of wet and of wildness? Let them be left,
> O let them be left, wildness and wet;
> Long live the weeds and the wilderness yet.[9]

## Twentieth-Century Voices of Compassion

By the mid-twentieth century, a strong movement was underway within
the church to bring compassion for animals to the forefront of its concern.
A strong condemnation of cruelty to animals appeared in the March
10, 1966, edition of the official Vatican weekly newspaper *L'Osservatore
della Domenica* under the name of its editor, the well-known theologian
Msgr. Ferdinando Lambruschini:

Man's conduct with regard to animals should be regulated by right reason, which prohibits the infliction of purposeless pain and suffering on them.

To ill-treat them, and make them suffer without reason, is an act of deplorable cruelty to be condemned from a Christian point of view. To make them suffer for one's own pleasure is an exhibition of sadism which every moralist must denounce.[10]

In France the Reverend Jean Gautier, a doctor in canon law, a director of the Grand Seminary in Paris (St. Sulpice), and a noted authority on Roman Catholic philosophy, wrote in his book *Un prêtre et son chien* (A priest and his dog): "For cruelty to defenseless beings we shall one day have to answer before him who trieth the heart and the reins. Not with impunity is the weakness of animals abused."[11]

In his 1957 book, *The Status of Animals in the Christian Religion*, C. W. Hume noted that the catechism that children use for first Communion and for confirmation in France included the answer, "it is not permissible for me to cause suffering to animals without good reason, to hurt them unnecessarily is an act of cruelty."[12]

## The Movement in England

The animal welfare movement within the church has been especially strong in Britain.

British Jesuit Father John Bligh has said, "A man is not likely to be much of a Christian if he is not kind to animals."[13] Cardinal Francis Bourne (1861–1934), who also was archbishop of Westminster, has been quoted as telling the children in Westminster Cathedral in April 1931: "There is even in kindness to animals a special merit in remembering that this kindness is obligatory upon us because God made the animals, and is therefore their creator, and, in a measure, His Fatherhood extends to them."[14]

In Britain and Ireland, one of the most active and effective groups working to protect animals has been the Catholic Study Circle for Animal Welfare (CSCAW). Organized in London between 1929 and 1934, its first official meeting was held on July 9, 1935, and later that year its still-active publication, *The Ark*, was launched.[15]

From the beginning, the CSCAW has received official recognition from the ecclesiastical authorities, including successive archbishops of Westminster, who have served as presidents of the Circle. The Circle and its officers and members received the personal blessing of Pope Pius XII in 1958, and from Pope Paul VI in 1967. Similar organizations have also been formed in Australia, Canada, and France.[16]

An editorial in the December 1961 edition of *The Ark* stressed that the group would attempt to secure reaffirmation of the "principles of humane treatment of animals enunciated by various Popes, but woefully ignored by contemporary clerics or swept aside as irrelevant to a priest's normal responsibility." It also urged "the reintroduction of at least two questions into the catechism taught to all children all over the world":

1. Is cruelty to animals a sin? Yes, a very cowardly and disgraceful sin (Bishop Bellford).

2. Why is cruelty to animals a sin? Because it performs an act that deviates from the order and purpose of the Creator (Cardinal Zigliara).[17]

The Reverend Kevin Daley, as chairman of the CSCAW in London, has written that "the work of animal welfare" is an "essential part of the work of a Christian."[18]

One of the founders of the Circle was Don Ambrose Agius (b. 1890), Mark of Ealing Abby and author of the classic work, *God's Animals*. As a chaplain during World War I, he was wounded on the Western front; and while serving as a parish priest in Liverpool during World War II, his church was destroyed by bombs. A prolific writer, he has authored numerous articles, booklets, and papers on human moral obligations toward animals.[19]

In 1966, the Very Reverend Agius set forth a methodical legal and historical basis for his arguments. He wrote of the two basic rights animals have: "*ratione Creatoris*," meaning animals cannot be maltreated without infringing on the rights of their Creator; and "*ratione ordinis creatae*," disturbing God's natural order. Asserting that "cruelty is sinful," he noted that when the Holy Office — which is authoritative to Catholics — was asked, "Have animals rights of any kind as against their masters or owners?" the reply was affirmative, as it was for two other questions: "Does the Holy Office hold it to be sinful to torture dumb animals? Does the Holy Office hold such sins to be degrading to the soul and disposition to the tormentor?" Therefore, he wrote, "We may insist that anyone who has dealings with animals is bound by certain moral obligations, binding under sin, to treat them according to the purpose of the Creator."[20]

In his 1970 book *God's Animals*, Reverend Agius summarizes "what it all adds up to" and eloquently states what he sees as the teachings and duties of the Christian church, and its believers, toward animals:

It is a moral obligation for every Christian to fight cruelty to animals because the consequences of cruelty are destructive of the Christian order....

The Bible, which is the handbook of God's attributes and of the principles of His action, tells us that cruelty to animals is wicked and that it is
opposed to God's will and intention. . . .
    The duty of all Christians [is] to emulate God's attributes, especially
that of mercy, in regard to animals.
    To be kind to animals, is to imitate the loving kindness of God.[21]

In his foreword to Reverend Agius's book, Cardinal John Heenan,
archbishop of Westminster, wrote in 1970,

Animals . . . have very positive rights because they are God's creatures. If
we have to speak with absolute accuracy, we must say that God has the
right to have all his creatures treated with respect. . . . Only the perverted
are guilty of deliberate cruelty to animals or, indeed, to children.[22]

This is not to say that all modern-day British Catholic leaders have
answered the call of St. Francis. Some clergymen are quite open about
their love for killing God's creatures. In September 1968, a British Roman
Catholic bishop, the most Reverend David Cashman, bishop of Arundel
and Brighton, admitted that he was "mad about" shooting birds and
mammals with a shotgun, saying that "it's the nearest thing to heaven,
in human terms, that I know."[23]
    Another widely publicized incident occurred in the summer of 1979,
in the central English village of Brant Broughton, when a "chirpy" sparrow got trapped in the rafters of the St. Helen's Parish Church and broke
into song during a guitar recital being recorded for a radio broadcast.
The church rector, Reverend Robin Clark, then asked the congregation
to leave, summoned a marksman with an air gun, and had the offend-
ing sparrow shot. The killing of the sparrow was big news throughout
England, the United States, and all over the world, with the front page
of the London *Daily Telegraph* declaring, "Rev. Robin orders death of
a sparrow."[24] Editorials and public opinion strongly condemned the
act, and many were reminded of how the Bible says that sparrows are
welcome to live in the House of the Lord (Ps. 84:2–5).

### The Struggle in America

In America, Catholics working for animals and the environment have
faced an uphill fight, confronting an often hostile hierarchy and an indifferent public. A widely publicized instance of the church's antagonistic
attitude toward humane work took place in the mid-1960s, when Mother
Cecilia Mary, a courageous seventy-six-year-old nun, was threatened
with dismissal as a sister in the church. Her "sins" had been defying
orders from the Vatican to close her shelter for stray animals, run by

her and five elderly nuns, and return to her duties helping people. After forty years as mother superior at a priory, Mother Cecilia had retired in 1963 and used her inheritance to start a shelter for hundreds of lost and homeless animals.

But Mother Cecilia was as tough as she was compassionate. Saying that "charity is higher than any obedience," she defied the order and wrote to Pope Paul, saying, "May I remind Your Holiness that many years ago we were all travellers in the Ark together." She was later exonerated by the pope and continued to operate her shelter for hundreds of dogs, cats, horses, goats, and other unfortunate creatures who needed her help.[25]

Among the earliest organized efforts to work for animal protection in the United States was the National Catholic Society for Animal Welfare (NCSAW, now called the International Society for Animal Rights [ISAR]). Despite years of effort, it was never able to attract more than a handful of leading clergymen to its cause. As its president, Helen Jones, wrote in 1966: "The Church should be a leader in the movement for the protection of animals, but it is not even in the procession. . . . The attitude of the Church today toward the suffering of animals is for the most part one of utmost indifference."[26] However, the group did succeed in using its limited resources to promote a religiously based appeal for animal protection before it was dissolved in the 1980s and became ISAR.

A Roman Catholic priest, Msgr. LeRoy E. McWilliams of North Arlington, New Jersey, as president of NCSAW testified in October 1962 in favor of legislation to minimize the suffering of laboratory animals, telling the congressional representatives:

> The first book of the Bible tells us that God created the animals and the birds, so they have the same father as we do. God's fatherhood extends to our "lesser brethren." All animals belong to God; He alone is their absolute owner. In our relations with them, we must emulate the divine attributes, the highest of which is mercy. God, their father and creator, loves them tenderly. He lends them to us and adjures us to use them as He Himself would do.

Msgr. McWilliams also sent a letter to all seventeen thousand Catholic pastors in the United States appealing for them to understand "what Christianity imposes on humans as their clear obligation to animals."[27]

In 1970, Reverend J. Barrie Shepherd, chaplain and assistant professor of religion at Connecticut College, wrote in the *Catholic World* that humans were obliged to respect and care for nature because "God rejoices in the earth's goodness," and humankind's salvation and that of the natural environment are intertwined.

Reverend Shepherd disputes the Christian tenet, left over from medieval days, that their world is a "barren land" to be endured in order to achieve "the heavenly bliss of the world to come":

> The world is *not* an inferior realm of material things from which man must rise into the realms of pure spirit. This world in its heavens and its earth, its oceans and its seas, its mountains and its hills, its flora and its fauna, is good, is *very* good. The verdict is repeated seven times in Genesis One. And God rejoices in its goodness.[28]

Since the 1950s, *Voice of the Voiceless*, a magazine founded and edited by the late C. Richard Calore in Los Angeles, has spoken out on behalf of animals, publishing articles, stories, poems, and quotations, mainly by clergy, emphasizing kindness to animals. But Calore often pointed out the difficulty in getting anyone in the church interested or involved in such work (see pp. 131–132).[29]

Some of the devout found they could best serve the Lord by taking direct action against those destroying God's creation. The Sisters of Loretto in central Appalachia filed a lawsuit against the Blue Diamond Coal Company (owned by prominent Catholics) aimed at correcting the company's damaging safety and environmental policies. As *Washington Post* columnist Colman McCarthy, a prominent Catholic writer and environmentalist, wrote in 1979, the nuns were simply carrying out "a few of the church's teachings": "How can you love God, they wonder, by despoiling the land?... the sisters are doing little more than applying the generalities outlined in a recent pastoral letter from Appalachia's bishops on the victimization of coal miners and abuses to the land."[30]

Today, Catholics are among the most active leaders of environmental and animal protection groups, and some have founded organizations to carry on such work. For example, Virginia Bourquardez founded and heads the International Network for Religion and Animals (INRA), in Silver Spring, Maryland;[31] and Dr. Donald Conroy, a Catholic priest, runs the North American Conference on Religion and Ecology (NACRE), in Washington, D.C.[32]

And as we shall see in chapter 9, these and other Catholics have been in the forefront of the revolution of the 1980s in the church's growing involvement in environmental theology.

## Continuing to Defend Cruelty

Although the church has come a long way in recent decades toward recognizing the worth of the nonhuman creation, elements of the church still sanction abusive practices.

In a 1988 Christmas sermon, the archbishop of Udine, Italy, is reported to have stated, "It is not a sin to beat a dog or leave it to starve to death."[33] And each March on the eastern shore of Canada off Newfoundland, "sealing" ships and hunters receive a blessing from the local priests before moving out to the ice floes offshore to club to death tens of thousands of baby harp seals.

In 1979, the respected Jesuit magazine *America* published an editorial entitled "Canadian Seals and Tourism," defending the annual Canadian-Norwegian seal hunt in which some 180,000 baby seals were clubbed to death and skinned in front of their nursing mothers. (The annual quotas have since been reduced substantially.) While parroting the Canadian government's propaganda about the slaughter being humane and scientifically justified, it strongly attacked as "irresponsible" the campaign being waged by conservationists like the Humane Society of the United States, the International Fund for Animal Welfare, the Sea Shepherd Conservation Society, and the Fund for Animals "to force Canada to stop the seal hunt." The editorial even defended the humaneness of the hunt, although it admitted that "killing Canadian seals by smashing their skulls and cutting open their chests is not a pretty sight."

Canadian clergy have even defended and acted as spokespersons for the fur industry. In 1986, Most Reverend Peter Sutton, chairman of the Roman Catholic Bishops of the North, and the Right Reverend Jack Sperry, Anglican bishop of the Arctic, attacked the conservationists' anti-fur campaign, blaming them for harming aboriginal peoples who hunt seals and other fur-bearing animals.[34]

Other Catholics remain puzzled by such attitudes on the part of their co-religionists. As Colman McCarthy has pointed out,

> A long raised but rarely answered question is this: If it was God's plan for Christ to be born among animals, why have most Christian theologians denied the value and rights of animals? Why no theology of the peaceable kingdom? ... Animals in the stable at Bethlehem were a vision of the peaceable kingdom. Among theology's mysteries, this ought to be the easiest to fathom.[35]

### Church Rituals and Traditions Honoring Animals

The Roman Catholic liturgy contains numerous prayers and benedictions for animals. The *Benedictio Equorum et Animalium* (blessing of horses and other animals) entreats, "May these animals receive, O Lord, thy benediction, and by it be preserved in body, and be delivered from all evil, through the intercession of the blessed Anthony."

There is also the *Benedictio Pecorum et Jumentorum* (blessing of cattle and horses), and the *Benedictio Stabuli Equorum, Boum, et aliorum Armentorum*, the blessing of a stable for horses, oxen, and other creatures, the latter of which states:

> Lord God Almighty, who didst well that thy only-begotten Son, Our Redeemer, should be born in a stable, and lie in a manger between the animals: bless, we pray thee, this stable...that for horses, cattle, and other living creatures it may be made a wholesome place and safe from all aggression.

There are various other blessings for animals contained in the church's liturgy, some expressing appreciation for their help in worship services. Bees are blessed for making not just honey but also the wax used in religious ceremonies; silk worms, for providing the material used in the vestments worn at Mass; and horses, for participating in the processions of the Blessed Sacrament in Germany. There are additional public blessings of pets and of farm and domestic animals, such as the feast of St. Anthony in Rome.[36]

In Spain, Italy, and France, on the holiday of St. Anthony, the patron saint of lower animals, mules, donkeys, horses, and sheep are sprinkled with water, blessed, and sanctified. In some areas, pictures of the saint are hung in the stables to protect the animals.[37]

## The Church and Bullfighting

For hundreds of years, the church has expressed an attitude of strong disapproval of bullfighting, as discussed earlier in this book (see p. 81). Yet, the church has never taken sufficient action to outlaw these cruel spectacles, which continue to be tremendously popular in Spain, Mexico, and some other Catholic countries.

Indeed, religious symbolism remains an integral part of the ceremony accompanying the killing of the bulls. Before tormenting and torturing the bulls to death, matadors piously pray, and sometimes offer their capes to drape statues in the church.[38] In Seville, the bullfighters have their own Madonna and church. As writer Cleveland Amory, president of the Fund for Animals, has pointed out,

> Not only are the bullfights held on feast days, but no small part of the nomenclature of bullfighting comes from religion. The fight begins with the band playing the Spanish quick step march named for the patron saint of all bullfighting, La Virgen de la Macarena. One of the stylized "passes" of the cape is called "the veronica pass" after St. Veronica, who wiped tear drops of agony from the face of our Lord.[39]

In addition to the church's earlier attacks on these spectacles, bull-fighting has been strongly condemned by Cardinal Pietro Gasparri (1852–1934), the secretary of state of the Vatican and expert canonist who was largely responsible for formulating the revisions in the code of canon law. On October 23, 1920, he wrote:

> In spite of the spirit of humanity engendered in the New Testament, man's barbarity is expressing itself again in the bullfight. There is no doubt that the Church utterly condemns now, as she has always done, as did his Holiness St. Pius V, these bloody and shameful exhibitions.[40]

On September 21 of the following year, he reiterated his opposition to bullfighting: "For a long time the Holy See has condemned them. The Bull of Pius V is well known. I desire with all my heart that the Pope's directions should be observed."[41]

In a proclamation to the French and Spanish bishops expressing the views of the Holy See, Cardinal Gasparri pointed out the harm that watching bullfights can cause to impressionable youngsters:

> Once again the bishops of France and Spain are enjoined to do their utmost to dissuade their flocks from going to bull-fights, especially from taking children to see them; the cruelty of those spectacles sows in their young minds morbid seed which certainly bears bad fruit. The Holy See earnestly calls for a more intense campaign against the bullfight.[42]

In 1956, when the Spanish bullfighting industry offered to give Pope Pius XII (1876–1958) an expensive and luxuriously bejewelled bull-fighter's cape, along with a million *pesetas*, protests poured in from around the world, including one in Latin from the Catholic Study Circle for Animal Welfare. As a result, the gifts of the Cape d'Honneur and the money were never accepted. According to the Reverend Ambrose Agius, instead of receiving the proposed delegation of bull breeders, managers of bull rings, bullfighters, and other industry representatives, the pope met with the leaders of the Barcelona Federation for the Protection of Animals and Plants.[43]

Pope Pius's refusal to be associated with bullfighting was consistent with the precedent established by one of his predecessors, Pope St. Pius V, who, in 1567, issued a papal decree condemning it and forbidding Catholics to attend under pain of excommunication (see p. 81). Later, the church softened the penalties for, but not its opposition to, bullfighting.[44]

In the March 10, 1966, edition of *L'Osservatore della Domenica*, Msgr. Ferdinando Lambruschini condemned bullfighting and other blood sports:

With pigeon-shooting should also be condemned all "Sports" based on purposeless cruelty toward animals. A classic example is the bull-fight, in which there is a crescendo of cruelty against the bull inflicted by the banderillos, which pierce it and draw blood in order to drive it to the utmost stages of fury and menace.[45]

Yet, bullfighting has also had its defenders within the church. The Jesuit publication *Christian Order* of February 1961 assured its readers that "the Church has not condemned bullfighting as immoral," that it "can be honestly and convincingly defended," and that the "physical fitness" and "courage and skill" of the matadors justify the torments inflicted on the bulls.[46]

### The Recent Popes and Animal Welfare

Although some of them have issued ambiguous or contradictory statements, many of the popes over the last few hundred years have spoken out against cruelty to animals.

Pope Paul II (1417–71), whose original name was Pietro Barbo, the Venetian who is thought to have introduced printing into Rome and is the patron of scholars, is said to have greatly loved animals. He is reported to have once bought and to have given freedom to a goat at Sutria, and to have grabbed chickens away from his servants and released them.[47]

Reverend Ambrose Agius lists most of the recent popes (with the period of their reign) as having "directly or indirectly blessed work for animal welfare": Paul II (1464–71), St. Pius V (1566–72), Pius IX (1846–78), Leo XIII (1878–1903), Pius X (1903–14), Benedict XV (1914–22), Pius XI (1922–39), Pius XII (1939–58), and John XXIII (1958–63). Indeed, Reverend Agius relates, "The highest Catholic officials have frequently and emphatically expressed themselves in favor of work for animal welfare, and no high official has delivered an opinion in the contrary sense."[48]

The contradictions in the Catholic Church are exemplified in two often recounted incidents involving Pope Pius XII. In one, he supposedly echoed the animal-machine theory of the Cartesians, saying that when animals are killed in a slaughterhouse or laboratory,

> their cries should not arouse unreasonable compassion any more than do red hot metals undergoing the blows of the hammer, seeds spoiling underground, branches crackling when they are pruned, grain that is surrendered to the harvester, wheat being ground by the milling machine.[49]

But at a November 10, 1950, meeting, in a statement to representatives of two hundred humane societies, reportedly written by him on his own typewriter, the pope said that animals should be treated kindly and with respect even if they are below human beings and meant for human use:

> The animal world, as all creation, is a manifestation of God's power, His wisdom and His goodness, and as such deserves man's respect and consideration. Any reckless desire to kill off animals, all unnecessary harshness and callous cruelty toward them are to be condemned. Such conduct, moreover, is baleful to a healthy sentiment and only tends to brutalize it.
>
> This said, one will also recognize that the Creator has given the animal to serve man (Gen. 1:28), who because of his intelligence is essentially superior to the entire animal world.[50]

The pope is also said to have told the slaughterhouse workers of Rome that they must do everything they can to minimize the suffering of animals about to be killed.[51]

Pope Pius has also been quoted as saying, "The animal creation has been loaned for the service of man. All wanton and unnecessary cruelty, all senseless killing is to be condemned. The church exists to establish and to guard these principles."[52] Certainly, there can be no question that, on balance, the late pope strongly condemned unnecessary cruelty to animals, even if he did not have as great a reverence for animals as some of his spiritual ancestors.

Other recent popes have also endorsed animal welfare work. On September 11, 1961, Pope John XXIII received a delegation from, and gave his blessing to, the National Catholic Society for Animal Welfare. The Vatican has said of the pope, "It is certainly not his wish that any dumb creature should be submitted to unnecessary hardship."

In August 1967, the Catholic Study Circle for Animal Welfare (CSCAW) submitted a petition to Pope Paul VI, asking for his support and "blessing on our efforts to forward a merciful and intelligent treatment of the animals created by God for His Glory."

On October 4, 1967, on the day of the Feast of St. Francis, the secretary of state of the Vatican, Cardinal Cicognami, received the CSCAW delegation and presented to them a letter on behalf of the Holy Father warmly praising, blessing, and endorsing their efforts.[53]

## Pope John Paul II

The current pope, John Paul II, has on several occasions strongly endorsed protection of animals and nature.

In a message on "Reconciliation" delivered at Assisi, Italy, on March

12, 1982, Pope John Paul II described St. Francis as an example to humankind of proper concern for animals:

> He looked upon creation with the eyes of one who could recognize in it the marvelous work of the hand of God. His voice, his glance, his solicitous care, not only towards men, but also towards animals are . . . a faithful echo of the love with which God in the beginning pronounced his "fiat" which had brought them into existence. How can we not feel vibrating in the Canticle of the Creatures something of the transcendent joy of God the Creator, of whom it is written that "he saw everything that he had made, and behold it was very good" (Gen. 1:31)?
>
> We too are called to a similar attitude. Created in the image of God, we must make him present among creatures "as intelligent and noble masters and guardians of nature" and "not as heedless exploiters and destroyers" (cf. Encyclical *Redemptor Hominis*, 15).[54]

On July 12, 1987, in Val Visdende, Italy, he addressed thirty thousand people in an open-air Mass in a pristine valley in the Dolomite Mountains, saying that Christians have a moral responsibility to preserve the environment. In a homily he stated that "respect of natural resources of our planet" must be a part of everyone's conscience.[55]

On November 16, 1989, Pope John Paul told a United Nations conference that "the protection of the natural environment" has become an important issue, that conservation was a "grave moral obligation," and that businesses should take a cut in profits to pay for measures to safeguard nature:

> An indiscriminate use of available natural goods, with harm to . . . the natural environment in general, entails a serious moral responsibility. Not only the present generation but also future generations are affected by such actions.
>
> Economic activity carries with it the obligation to use the goods of nature reasonably. But it also involves the grave moral obligation both to repair damage already inflicted on nature, and to prevent any negative effects which may later arise.

He stressed that "more careful control" was needed, "especially in regard to toxic residue, and in . . . excessive use of chemicals in agriculture."[56]

On December 5, 1989, Pope John Paul warned that the world was caught in an ecological crisis that violates human rights and "lays bare the depth of man's moral crisis." In the first papal document devoted entirely to the environment, the pope used unusually strong language to attack the destruction of nature throughout the world. In his annual message for the church's World Day of Peace, he criticized both industrialized and developing nations, saying that "countries in the process of industrializing are not morally free to repeat the errors made in the past by others, and needlessly continue to damage the environment through industrial pollutants, radical deforestation, or unlimited exploitation of non-renewable resources."

In this document, entitled "Peace with God the Creator, Peace with All Creation," the pope warned that the ecological collapse facing the environment was the concern of everyone and urged that "the right to a safe environment" be included in a revised version of the UN Universal Declaration of Human Rights.[57]

On May 9, 1990, addressing hundreds of business executives in Durango, Mexico, the pope condemned the pursuing of profits "at any price" at the expense of workers, social justice, and the environment. And at the end of a visit to a Mexican prison, the pope was presented with two doves in a wooden cage, which was opened, allowing the doves to fly away.[58]

Ironically, the pope's message has not always been fully understood by his hosts or followers. For example, on his early 1990 trip to Africa, when he visited Cape Verde's capital of Praia to say Mass, police are reported to have shot 792 stray dogs as part of the cleanup effort.[59]

## The Church and the Population Explosion

While John Paul II has been an extremely popular pope, he has come under criticism for maintaining the church's centuries-old opposition to artificial methods of birth control. Critics, including many Catholics, contend that this policy exacerbates the urgent problem of human overpopulation, which is causing environmental degradation, human misery, and massive poverty and starvation, affecting hundreds of millions of people, even a billion or more, around the globe. Many people argue that the best way to help the poor is to allow them, and teach them, to have fewer children through *effective* methods of birth control.

The seriousness of the human overpopulation crisis can hardly be exaggerated. As of mid-1990, the world's population of 5.3 billion was increasing at a rate of at least three people a second — 250,000 people a day, 90 to 100 million people a year. During the next century, the world's population will more than double, and perhaps triple. Although it took about three million years for the world's population to reach a billion, which it did around 1800, the next billion will be added in only about ten years.[60]

Some Roman Catholic leaders have recognized the harmful effects of the population explosion and advocated that it be dealt with by social and economic development, rather than by artificial contraception, sterilization, or abortion, all of which the church strongly condemns. The only techniques of contraception the church approves of are natural ones, such as the "rhythm" method, which relies on abstaining from sexual intercourse except during intervals of infertility during a woman's menstrual cycle.

There are no signs that the church's opposition to birth control will change in the foreseeable future, despite growing opposition within the church to such a policy. For example, in May 1990 Pope John Paul declared in Mexico, where the population is exploding at an alarming rate: "If the possibility of conceiving a child is artificially eliminated in the conjugal act, couples shut themselves off from God and oppose His will."[61]

And on Earth Day, April 22, 1990, Cardinal John O'Connor, the archbishop of New York, said in his homily at St. Patrick's Cathedral, "I do not think the total number of people in the world is an ecological and environmental problem." (Seeming to express misgivings about the celebration of Earth Day, he said its focus should not be "on snails and whales" but "on the sacredness of the human person," adding that "the earth exists for the human person and not vice versa.")[62]

## Environmental Victims in the Third World

In many underdeveloped nations, serious environmental problems, such as deforestation, pollution, pesticide poisoning, and, of course, human overpopulation, have caused immense harm to the local people. In response, some Catholic leaders in Third World nations have, in recent years, strongly condemned the abuse of people and the environment.

Bishops in the Dominican Republic have criticized the deforestation of so much of the country. And the Catholic Bishops Conference of the Philippines has endorsed a pastoral letter that assails the destruction of the Philippine forests, mainly by Japanese timber interests. The ten-page pastoral letter, read from all Catholic pulpits on March 13, 1988 (about 85 percent of Filipinos are Roman Catholic), says of protecting the environment, "It is now a matter of life and death.... Our forests are almost gone, our rivers are almost empty.... During monsoon rains, flash floods destroy everything in their path." The letter, endorsed by the country's ninety-nine bishops, warned that the "assault on creation is sinful and contrary to the teachings of our faith. God created this world, He loves it and is pleased with it.... He created man and woman and charged them to be stewards of his creation."[63]

Because people in the Third World often live so much closer to, and are dependent on, the land, they directly experience, and suffer from, the results of abusing the environment. Thus, conservation is more than an abstract concern for them. It is sometimes a matter of survival, and they can plainly see the interdependence of people and nature.

As America and the industrialized world continue to wreak havoc on their environments, the impacts on people — already showing up in the form of droughts, soil erosion, and health tragedies such as cancer, miscarriages, and birth defects — will become even more widespread and apparent.

*Chapter 8* _____

# The Protestant Churches: Addressing the Ecological Reformation

I do not believe a person can be a true Christian, and at the same time engage in cruel or inconsiderate treatment of animals.
— Rev. Norman Vincent Peale,[1]
June 5, 1958

Many of the major Protestant denominations in America, including the Methodists, Presbyterians, and Episcopalians, after decades of ignoring stewardship issues, have recently adopted official policies favoring protection for animals and the environment. Others, such as the Christian Scientists, the Quakers, and the Seventh-Day Adventists, have a long history of such teaching. However, these proclamations and policies have seldom been translated into the kinds of programs and action needed to address meaningfully the ecological crisis. And while some religious leaders and publications have worked against humane and conservation measures, other individuals and denominations have actively fought for progress in these fields.

### Failing to Speak Out

The few but fervent voices speaking out for animals and nature over recent decades have been remarkable in that, until the last few years, most Protestant leaders and denominations showed virtually no interest in ecological or humane matters.

In 1941, the British Reverend V. A. Holmes-Gore wrote: "It is noticeable that such humanitarian reforms that were made were seldom supported and hardly ever initiated by the Church.... There are a few noble ones within the Church who show real compassion, but we grieve to say that the Church as a whole has yet to learn the true meaning of mercy."[2]

The Right Reverend Robert McConnell Hatch, who has called conservation "a challenge to the churches," wrote eloquently in the 1960s of how the churches were ignoring a fundamental issue of the day: the ever-increasing destruction of the natural environment:

> One attends services at propitious times of year, such as Thanksgiving... in the hope of hearing a message on the need for conservation, or perhaps a prayer or hymn containing at least a suggestion that what is left of the earth's bounty cannot survive unless it is conserved, but usually one's disappointment is complete. Altars brim with fruits and vegetables... but little if anything in the service calls attention to the fact that much of the beauty of our land is being bulldozed into ugliness, that streams and rivers are being turned into sewers, and the air over our cities made unsafe to breathe.[3]

Reverend Hatch suggested that what was needed was "a warning in the forthright style of the Hebrew prophets against the assaults on our remnants of wilderness and unspoiled places" which are subject to destruction "if a dollar can be made from them": "As far as conservation is concerned, one would gather that much of the organized church is so self-enclosed that it cannot see what is happening outside its stained glass windows."[4]

Writing in the 1970s, the late humanitarian leader Dr. Frederick L. Thomsen pulled no punches in blaming institutionalized religion for the sad plight of animals throughout history and today, specifically citing the three dominant religions of the West — Catholicism, Protestantism, and Judaism — as the major culprits: "Religionists in general have deviated greatly from the humane traditions of the Bible.... The resulting deviations from Biblical traditions of humaneness have given rise to the greatest single obstacle in the way of effective humane education. They have made men cruel to animals in the name of religion."[5]

Thomsen particularly deplored the incredible cruelty to animals so pervasive in the "Bible Belt" of the southern United States, such as contests in which raccoons are torn apart by dogs. He blamed the influence of fundamentalist Protestant churches for permitting and even encouraging such abuses, many of which would take place for church fund-raising drives.

"The Clergy Speak for Animals," a booklet edited by the late C. Richard Calore and published by *Voice of the Voiceless*, a humane and religiously oriented magazine in Los Angeles, California, contains a collection of statements, quotations, and sermons by clergymen of various religions and denominations urging kind treatment of animals. In his foreword, Calore writes that "the purpose of this booklet is not to convey to the reader that clergymen as a group are merciful to animals":

On the contrary, my experiences have proved otherwise. It is indeed a rarity to hear a Catholic priest, a Protestant minister, a Jewish rabbi, or any other man of the cloth preach a sermon on our moral obligation to God's innocent and unprotected animals.... All too few clergymen ... have taken it upon themselves to champion the cause of God's helpless creation — a cause which religious leaders have sadly neglected.[6]

Russell E. Train, chairman of the World Wildlife Fund and the Conservation Foundation and former administrator of the U.S. Environmental Protection Agency, has also bemoaned the church's apathy on such issues:

For the past 30 years, I have been puzzled — to say the least — by what has seemed to me the almost total obliviousness of organized religion toward the environment. It has been nothing less than extraordinary.

Here we have had one of the most fundamental concerns to agitate human society within living memory — Here we have issues that go to the heart of the human conditions, to the quality of human life, even to humanity's ultimate survival.... Here we have problems that can be said to threaten the very integrity of Creation. And yet the church and other institutions of organized religion have largely ignored the whole subject.[7]

In light of all this, it is interesting, and perhaps not surprising, that a recent study on people's attitudes toward the environment found a direct correlation between church attendance and a negative attitude toward nature. The study at the Yale Forestry School found that the more a person attended church or participated in religious services, the more likely he or she would feel negative or hostile toward the natural environment, and the less likely he or she would have a concern for nature. In his lengthy study, Dr. Stephen Kellert also found that those who were less involved in formal worship had a greater concern for ecological values.[8]

And besides largely ignoring environmental and humane concerns, some Protestant religious traditions still involve abuse of animals and nature. The cutting down of pines or other evergreens for Christmas trees, unless they came from tree farms, results in the removal from the wild of millions of trees that clean the air, soak up carbon dioxide, produce oxygen, and provide habitat for birds, squirrels, and other creatures.

An especially cruel religious tradition is the practice of giving ducklings, chicks, and bunnies to children on Easter. Most of the animals are inevitably killed, crippled, or otherwise mistreated by the youngsters, and for weeks afterward humane societies are flooded with maimed and terrified baby animals.

Ironically, few devout Christian parents would participate in this tradition if they were aware of its pagan sexual origins and overtones.

The eggs and young animals — symbols of fertility — refer back to and stand for the sensuality and licentiousness associated with festivals celebrated on the vernal equinox — namely that of the pagan Anglo-Saxon goddess Eostre or Ostara, which appears to have given Easter its name.[9]

## James Gaius Watt

Some fundamentalist religious groups and leaders, as did the early American Puritans, still view the environment as something to be used, exploited, even destroyed as part of the deity's plan for the planet. One of the most prominent examples of one who used religion to justify the destruction of nature was President Ronald Reagan's secretary of the interior, James Gaius Watt.

Invoking holy scripture and his fundamentalist Christian beliefs, Watt set out to open up parks, refuges, and other protected federal lands to exploitation and despoliation and to halt programs to preserve wildlife, wilderness, forests, and other natural resources. Watt made clear his attitude toward the natural world: since the end was near, why try to preserve it?

At his 1981 Senate confirmation hearings, when asked how he planned to protect American forests, Watt replied, "I don't know how many future generations we can count on before the Lord returns."[10] And in citing divine sanction for his policies of giving developers and concessionaires access to federally controlled parks and natural resources, Watt stated, "My responsibility is to follow the Scriptures, which call upon us to occupy the land until Jesus returns."[11]

A charismatic Christian and member of the Aurora First Assembly of God in Denver, Watt seemed to view the earth as temporary, transitory, and not worth saving. *Rocky Mountain* magazine described the religious tradition forming "the core of his life and values" as follows:

This view holds that the earth is merely a temporary way station on the road to eternal life. It is unimportant except as a place of testing to get into heaven. In this evil and dangerous world, one's duty is to pass through unspotted by the surrounding corruption. The earth was put here by the Lord for his people to subdue and to use for profitable purposes on their way to the hereafter.[12]

John A. Hoyt, a former Presbyterian minister who is president of the Humane Society of the United States, has described a 1982 dinner table conversation he had with Watt:

With great sincerity, he expressed the conviction that we were living in a world and on a planet called Earth that would no longer be our home within a few short years. He professed then, and perhaps still does, that the "second coming of Christ" was imminent, and that, once that event had occurred, the earth would cease forever to be of importance to anyone, or at least to those who would be taken to a "home" beyond this place.[13]

After several years of battling environmentalists and following a series of gaffes and controversies, Watt became such an embarrassment to the Reagan administration that he was forced to resign his post on October 9, 1983. But he did so only after wreaking what many consider to be serious and permanent damage on some of America's most valuable wildlife and wilderness areas.

## The Biblical Roots of Our Ecological Crisis

By the late 1960s, the role of the church was widely seen as a negative influence on the growing conservation and humane movements. Indeed, it became fashionable in some historical and religious quarters to focus on Western religion in general, and the Bible in particular, as the cause for much of the past and present destruction and abuse of nature.

Those holding this viewpoint argue that monotheism, and the Judaic-Christian religious tradition, destroyed the respect for nature and its sanctity held by humans through the years. They blame Western religion for providing the justification for humans to exploit and abuse the planet at will.

One of the earliest and most prominent proponents of this school of thought was University of California history professor Lynn White, Jr. His views on the pernicious influence of religion on ecology gained widespread circulation in a much debated essay, "The Historical Roots of Our Ecological Crisis," published in the March 1967 edition of *Science* magazine. Calling "Christianity, especially in the Western form, the most anthropocentric religion the world has seen," White writes: "Christianity, in absolute contrast to ancient paganism, and Asia's religions . . . not only established a dualism of man and nature, but also insisted that it is God's will that man exploit nature for his proper ends."[14] White discusses how, in ancient times, there were religious restraints against ravaging nature:

In antiquity, every tree, every spring, every stream, every hill had its own *genius loci*, its guardian spirit. Before we cut a tree, mined a mountain, or damned a brook, it was important to placate the spirit in charge of that particular situation, and to keep it placated. By destroying pagan animism,

Christianity made it possible to exploit nature in a mood of indifference to the feelings of natural objects.[15]

White says that "Christianity bears a huge burden of guilt" for the human attitude that "we are superior to nature, contemptuous of it, willing to use it for our slightest whim. . . . We shall continue to have a worsening ecologic crisis until we reject the Christian axiom that nature has no reason for existence save to serve man."[16]

The great writer and humanitarian Joseph Wood Krutch (1893–1970), in his book *The World of Animals*, attributed to the early Hebrews the first tendencies toward desanctifying nature:

> We know that most primitive men were deeply concerned with the question of their relation to animals. To animals they often attributed a consciousness much like their own and they made of them ancestors, fellow creatures, or gods. Though they might live by hunting, they often found it desirable to placate their victims and sometimes offered formal apology for killing or eating them.
>
> The Hebraic tradition, on the other hand, tended to go to the other extreme. The reason perhaps was, not any impulse toward cruelty, but simply that the new monotheism was aware how easily deep concern with animals leads to animal gods and to polytheism.[17]

Julian Hartt, a Yale theologian, has written that Christian thought has helped "legitimize man's total exploitation of his environment" through an emphasis on one's life in the *next* world instead of this one.[18] The eminent English historian Arnold Toynbee, in a 1973 article, goes so far as to assert that it was monotheism and Western civilization's loss of awe for nature, prompted by Genesis 1:28, that has led to most of our contemporary problems:

> Some of the major maladies of the present day world — in particular the recklessly extravagant consumption of nature's irreplaceable treasures, and the pollution of those of them that man has not already devoured — can be traced back to a religious cause, and this cause is the rise of monotheism. . . .
>
> Monotheism, as enunciated in the book of Genesis, has removed the age-old restraint that was once placed on man's greed by his awe. Man's greedy impulse to exploit nature used to be held in check by his pious worship of nature.[19]

Theodore Hiebert, an Old Testament scholar at Harvard University, has written that this concept of a hierarchical world was just what the early Hebrew priests intended to convey when they authored the "seven-day" version of the creation story and made it the first book of the Bible (Genesis 1). Hiebert believes that the more egalitarian version of Adam and Eve's being placed in the Garden of Eden to "dress it and keep it" (Genesis 2) was actually written hundreds of years before the former account, and more accurately represents how the Lord intended for humans to relate to the environment.[20]

Professor Tom Regan, author of several books, including *The Case for Animal Rights*, call this human attitude of dominance "speciesism" and blames it for causing humans to be "responsible for an incalculable amount of evil, an amount of truly monumental proportions": "It is an arrogant, unbridled anthropocentrism, often aided and abetted in our history by an arrogant, unbridled Christian theology . . . that has brought the earth to the brink of ecological disaster."[21]

(Dr. Regan, of course, also recognizes how parts of the scriptures condemn abuse of animals, and once asked cogently, "Could a God that despises a 'proud look' [Prov. 6:17] be anything but outraged at the sight of a $25,000 mink coat?")[22]

There is some truth in what these critics say, for portions of the Bible have indeed been used to justify a variety of destructive activities. But it would be more accurate to say that it has been more a *mis*-interpretation, a distortion, a misunderstanding of the scriptures, rather than the text itself, that has caused these problems. In short, the problem is not what is written in Genesis, but rather the failure correctly to interpret or understand it. Indeed, the Bible repeats over and over again the opposite of the narrow and fallacious antinature interpretation.

The late scientist and author, Dr. René Dubos, in his 1972 book *A God Within*, strongly disputes White's thesis and points out that "ecological disasters are not peculiar to the Judeo-Christian tradition and to scientific technology": "At all times and all over the world, man's thoughtless interventions into nature have had a variety of disastrous consequences, or at least have changed profoundly the complexion of nature. The process began some ten thousand years ago, long before the Bible was written."[23]

Reverend Vincent Rossi, a founder of the Eleventh Commandment Fellowship in San Francisco, sees the real root of the problem as "the industrialization and secularization of society," which he considers to be "anti-Christian": "Contrary to the opinions of Lynn White and Arnold Toynbee, it was only when Western civilization 'liberated' itself from Christianity and its traditional doctrinal restraints that the door was opened for the ecological disasters of the present day."[24]

And even Lynn White proposes that religion, rather than science or technology, holds the answer to our ecological crisis, which, he says, will continue "until we find a new religion, or rethink our old one": "Since the roots of our trouble are so largely religious, the remedy must also be essentially religious, whether we call it that or not."[25] He even concludes his essay by writing, "I propose Francis of Assisi as a patron saint of ecologists."

## The Episcopal Church

While it is true that the churches in general have not, until very recently, been actively and effectively involved in humane and conservation issues, some denominations and individuals have been notable exceptions to this rule.

The Episcopal Church in America has produced several outstanding advocates for animals and the environment.* Reverend James E. Carroll, an Episcopal priest in Van Nuys, California, has written of "what I believe to be the Christian viewpoint in regard to the treatment of animals":

> The Church of God is concerned with all life, when she is true to the Divine vocation, and thus "all" includes the creatures of God's animal kingdom....
>
> The callous may escape the prosecution of human law, but he will never escape divine judgment, for he has abused the dominion which God gave him over the creatures, and there are few graver sins than this....
>
> A committed Christian, who knows what his religion is about, will never kill an animal needlessly. Above all, he will do his utmost to put a stop to any kind of cruelty to any animal. A Christian who participates in or gives consent to cruelty to animals had better reexamine his religion or else drop the name Christian.[26]

Another church leader who has been active in the humane movement has been the rector of Christ Church in Bay Ridge, Brooklyn, New York, Dr. Marion L. Matics. Reverend Matics has spoken out and worked on behalf of various animal welfare causes. An example of his forthrightness and courage in taking on powerful and entrenched interests was his blast at the medical research lobby, published in the May 1965 *Christ Church Chronicle*, urging the passage of legislation to help laboratory animals.

Each year, in October, in honor of St. Francis of Assisi's birthday, the Reverend Delmar S. Markle, of St. George's Episcopal Church in Bridgeport, Connecticut, would conduct a blessing of the animals, with the ceremony including over two hundred pets and their owners from

---

*The spiritual head of the 2.5 million American Episcopalians and of millions of Anglicans worldwide is the archbishop of Canterbury, who heads the state Church of England. The church has a long history of involvement in humane and conservation issues. See pp. 149–151.

all parts of the state. (After his retirement in 1965, the services were held in St. Peter's Roman Catholic Church.)[27]

One of the greatest environmental writers America has produced has been an Episcopal bishop, the Right Reverend Robert McConnell Hatch. In 1967, as the suffragan bishop of Connecticut, Reverend Hatch wrote eloquently of humankind's moral and religious duty to protect and respect the environment. In an article in the *Atlantic Naturalist*, he laid out the "cornerstones of a Conservation Ethic":

> The cause of conservation involves man's soul. It is a spiritual choice, grounded in ethics, and its roots are in the Bible. Conservation teaches the principles of wise stewardship. It is profoundly ethical because it counsels foresight in place of selfishness, vision in place of greed, reverence in place of destructiveness.
>
> The earth was made by God, and it belongs to God. The trackless forests, the rivers that wind across our continent, the marsh lands, the prairies and the deserts — all were made by Him. They belong to Him. Their riches come to us from Him.
>
> All of these things have been loaned to man as a trust. None of it really belongs to him. His days are as grass, and when the span of his life is over, he is the owner of nothing. He is called to be a steward of the riches of the earth, leaving them as a goodly inheritance to his children.[28]

In 1968, as the Episcopal bishop of Western Massachusetts, Reverend Hatch underscored the spiritual foundation of the conservation ethic. Writing in *Appalachia* magazine, he called conservation "a challenge to the churches," and pointed out that "there is nothing in the Bible to justify an arrogant exploitation of the earth or a callous indifference to what is left generations. On the contrary, gratitude, humility, and wise stewardship are in order."[29]

Indeed, as Hatch points out, there are selfish, hardheaded reasons for protecting nature — it is in humankind's self-interest to do so: "Man has begun to learn that he does not really stand alone but is part of an intricate web of life in which all the parts are related to one another and where the well-being of one part depends on the well-being of all."[30]

Reverend Hatch ends his article with an appeal for the churches to teach stewardship in the use of our natural resources:

> The churches should reiterate that man is not the real owner of anything, that he is here only as a steward, and that he will be judged by the way he treats what has been loaned to him. This not only involves the use of our land and resources for the sake of the present generation, but it also upholds the rights of those who will inherit the earth from us. If we leave them nothing but desecration, we shall be judged accordingly, and the

judgment will be a moral one. In its essence, conservation is a moral and spiritual matter.[31]

The Cathedral Church of St. John the Divine in New York has for years carried on a series of activities designed to foster concern for animals and the environment, including Lenten services dealing with "the passion of the earth" and ceremonies for "the blessing of the animals." The cathedral's dean, the Very Reverend Parks Morton, was instrumental in organizing a 1990 statement on the environment endorsed by 273 leading religious figures from around the world (see p. 168).

The Washington National Cathedral, in May 1990, co-hosted the "Caring for Creation" Conference (see pp. 171–174), at which the Reverend Dr. Stuart Phillips, an environmental consultant to the National Episcopal Church, observed: "In witness to the conviction that the Earth is the Lord's and the fulness thereof, and in the midst of general disregard and wanton destruction, we are reminded that as tenants of God's creation, we are to be life-bringers and care-givers of the environment."[32]

## The Christian Scientists

The Church of Christ, Scientist (the Christian Scientists) has a long tradition of promoting respect for nature and animals.

One of the basic books is *Science and Health with Key to the Scriptures*, by Mary Baker Eddy, founder of the religion. In this work, an underlying principle of the faith is set forth: "God is the life, or intelligence, which forms and preserves the individuality and identity of animals as well as of men" (p. 550).

In her analysis of the Book of Genesis, Mary Baker Eddy writes, "All of God's creatures, moving in the harmony of Science, are harmless, useful, indestructible. A realization of this grand verity was a source of strength to the ancient worthies. It supports Christian healing, and enables its possessor to emulate the example of Jesus."[33]

And a strong conservation ethic is contained in a brochure distributed by the Christian Scientists, "Cleansing Man's Environment," which includes articles and essays by several of the church's members. For example, in discussing humankind's dominion over animals, Erwin D. Canham points out that "it has been terribly misunderstood. Too frequently it has been assumed by men to be their right to despoil. An arrogant, aggressive, greedy, selfish, men-centered role has been asserted. This is not dominion. Man is not God. Dominion is obedience to God's law."[34]

## The Quakers

The Society of Friends (Quakers) has advocated compassion for other creatures since it was founded in mid-seventeenth century England (see p. 86).

A Quaker brochure entitled *Advice and Queries* states, "Let the law of kindness know no limits. Show a loving consideration for all God's creatures." The Society's official publication, *Christian Life, Faith and Thought in the Society of Friends*, quotes thusly from the well-known American preacher and abolitionist John Woolman (1720–72), who traveled throughout the colonies inveighing against slavery:

> I believe where the love of God is verily perfected and the true spirit of government watchfully attended to, a tenderness toward all creatures made subject to us will be experienced, and a care felt in us that we do not lessen that sweetness of life in the animal creation which the Great Creator intends for them under our government.[35]

An official statement on the Quakers' religious duty to animals includes the following admonitions:

> Kindness to animals should be explicitly proclaimed as a Christian duty. Suffering can be caused through callousness based often upon ignorance, and we must testify against such cruelty wherever we find it. . . .
>
> In recognizing the wonder and mystery of God's animal kingdom we increase our reverence for Him. We need to show a humble acknowledgement of the responsibility for animals with which God has entrusted us.[36]

One very active Quaker humanitarian was the French missionary Stephen Grellet (1733–1855) (originally known as Étienne de Grellet du Mobillier). He was a missionary minister and philanthropist who traveled throughout Europe and America reporting on and helping to improve conditions in poorhouses and prisons. He is best remembered by humanitarians for the statement attributed to him: "I expect to pass through this world but once; any good thing therefore that I can do, or any kindness that I can show to any fellow-creature, let me do it now; let me not defer or neglect it, for I shall not pass this way again."[37]

## Seventh-Day Adventists

Kindness to animals is also traditional in the health-oriented Seventh-Day Adventist Church. This Christian denomination believes that

Christ's second coming and the end of the world are close at hand. Like those of the Jewish faith, they observe Saturday as the Sabbath day.

In 1860, in Battle Creek, Michigan, the church was formally named; and its founder and prophetess, Ellen G. White, taught love for animals and a vegetarian diet in her various books on the religion and its doctrines.

Mrs. White, in her book *Counsel on Diet and Foods*, writes that it was not in accordance with God's plan "to have the life of any creature taken." She cites as evidence the fact that in the Garden of Eden, there was no death, and the Lord forbade humans from consuming meat up until the time of the Great Flood.[38] In *Ministry of Healing*, she adds a humane view to her advocacy of a vegetarian diet for health reasons: "Think of the cruelty to animals that meat eating involves, and its effect on those who inflict and those who behold it. How it destroys the tenderness with which we should regard these creatures of God."[39]

And in *Patriarchs and Prophets*, Mrs. White cites various passages in the Bible advocating kindness to animals, and she concludes that humans will be judged according to how they fulfill their obligations to animals: "It becomes man to seek to lighten, instead of increasing, the weight of suffering which his transgression has brought upon God's creatures."

## Jehovah's Witnesses

Jehovah's Witnesses, which began in America in the late nineteenth century and has spread across the globe, actively teaches and promotes conservation and kindness to other creatures.

Articles on the environment are often carried in *The Watchtower*, their semimonthly magazine printed in 108 languages with an average run of almost fourteen million. The July 1990 issue featured a cover story entitled "Ruining the Earth," describing the various threats to the planet's survival and concluding that:

> Yes, our planet is being abused, ruined. Its seas, drinking water, farmlands, and even its atmosphere are being polluted. . . . Surely, this alone would suggest that the time is near for God to intervene and "bring to ruin those ruining the earth" (Rev. 11:18).
>
> Reason tells us that God must soon act to save the earth from man's ruinous activities, and Bible prophecy confirms this. . . . Just as a landlord ejects a destructive tenant, so God will "eject" those who ruin his beautiful creation, the earth.[40]

Similar articles appear frequently in *Awake!*, the Witnesses' other semimonthly publication, over eleven million copies of which are published in fifty-four languages. Some recent cover articles include the following: "Pollution, the Relentless Killer"; "What Is Happening to Our Forests?"; "Africa's Wildlife: Still There — But for How long?"; and "Who Will Inherit the Earth?" The latter article exemplifies the Witnesses' teachings about ecology:

> When Jehovah created man, He put him in charge of the earth. He commissioned him to "cultivate and to take care of it" (Genesis 2:15). Instead man pollutes and destroys it. . . .
>
> Men today have become misfits, First they pollute themselves morally, then they pollute the earth literally. It is the moral pollution that renders them unfit in God's eyes to inherit the earth.[41]

Another representative issue was that of July 8, 1990, which carried a cover story entitled "Animal Research: Right or Wrong?" which examined the issue from both viewpoints. It was followed by "Bullfighting: Art or Outrage," which concluded: "The creator of the bull cannot look at this spectacle with pleasure. Although regarded by many as an art, it is really an outrage against divine principles."

### The Mormons

The early teachings of the approximately five-million-member Mormon Church strongly emphasize kindness to animals. Known as the Church of Jesus Christ of Latter-day Saints, it is now the dominant religious group in Utah.

Consider for example, the following writings of Joseph Fielding Smith (1838–1918), president of the Mormon Church from 1901 to 1918 (as compiled by John Paul Fox of the Humane Society of Utah):[42]

> It was intended that all creatures should be happy in their several elements. Therefore to take the life of these creatures wantonly is a sin before the Lord.
>
> There is no inference in the scriptures that it is a privilege of men to slay birds or beasts or to catch fish wantonly.
>
> The domination the Lord gave man over the brute creations has been, to a very large extent, used selfishly, thoughtlessly, cruelly. . . . Kindness to the whole animal creation is not only a virtue that should be developed, but is the absolute duty of mankind. . . . But with this dominion came responsibility to treat with love and consideration every living thing. . . .
>
> Man in his wanton disregard of a sacred duty has been reckless of life. . . . Man can not worship the creator and look with careless indifference upon his creations. . . . To all his creations we owe an allegiance of

service and profound admiration. . . . Love of nature is akin to the love of God; the two are inseparable.

Every soul should be impressed with reference to the killing of our innocent birds who live upon the vermin that are indeed enemies to the farmer and to mankind. It is not only wicked to destroy them, it is abominable.

Take not the life you cannot give. For all things have an equal right to live.

I have been surprised at prominent men — whose very souls seemed to be athirst for the shedding of animal blood — just for the fun of it.

Man should be more the friend and never the enemy of any living creature, the Lord placed them here.

Joseph Smith (1805–1844), who founded the Mormon Church in 1830 (and is the uncle of Joseph Fielding Smith), also preached humane treatment of animals:

God glorified himself by saving all that his hands had made, whether beasts, fowls, fishes, or men; and he will glorify himself with them.

Kindness to the whole animal creation and especially to all domestic animals is not only a virtue that should be developed but is the ABSOLUTE DUTY OF MANKIND. Children should be taught that nature in all forms is our heavenly Father's Great Book of Life.

Furthermore, he who treats in a brutal manner a poor dumb animal, at that moment disqualifies himself for the companionship of the Holy Spirit.[43]

Even poisonous snakes were accorded respect. An entry in Smith's diary for May 26, 1834, describes how they were treated when found in the encampment: "The brethren took the serpents carefully on sticks and carried them across the creek. I exhorted the brethren not to kill the serpent, bird or animal of any kind during our journey unless it became necessary to preserve ourselves from hunger."

The Mormons' theology on animals teaches that humankind is held responsible for treatment of every animal in its care. Joseph Smith's inspired version of the Bible, Genesis 9:11, states, "Blood of animals shall not be shed only for meat to save your lives; and the blood of every beast I will require at your hands." Commenting on the above paragraph, in his *First Two Thousand Years*, W. Cleon Skowsen writes: "God did not intend that the lives of animals should be subjected to cruelty and abuse. The proper treatment of the animal kingdom is part of the human stewardship. "

The Mormon scripture and Bible (*Doctrine and Covenants*, 49:21) also warns: "And woe be unto man that sheddeth blood or that wasteth flesh and hath no need." It also states that "Man has been entrusted with sovereignty over the animal kingdom that he may learn to govern as God Rules, by the power of love and justice, and become fit for his eternal destiny as a ruler of worlds" (*Doctrine and Covenants Commentary,* section 47, p. 361).

And David O. McKay, former president of the Mormon Church, put humankind's obligation to animals quite simply: "A true Latter-day Saint is kind to animals, is kind to every living thing, for God has created all.... In all teaching, the element of love for all of the creatures of the earth can be emphasized, and thus religion imparted."[44]

Brigham Young, the first governor of the Territory of Utah, who succeeded Joseph Smith as head of the Mormon Church in 1847, taught that animals are a sacred gift from God that we are obliged to respect:

> If we maltreat our animals, or each other, the spirit within us, our traditions and the Bible, all agree in declaring it is wrong.... The more kind we are to our animals, the more will peace increase.
>
> If the people could see as an angel sees, they would behold a great sin in neglecting the stock which the Lord has given them.
>
> It is the Lord who gives us the increase of cattle and sheep, yet many of the people treat them as a thing of nought.
>
> Let the people be holy, and filled with the spirit of God, and every animal and creeping thing will be filled with peace.[45]

*The Latter-day Saint Journal History* (1937) commands us to treat humanely the animals under our dominion:

> If we take animals into our possessions and use them for our service and our pleasure the least we can do is to furnish them food, drink, and shelter.... In the beautiful story of creation, it is said that God made animals and the birds and the creeping things of the earth — And this dominion places man under obligation to them and tells him that it is his duty to treat them humanely because the creator placed them in his charge and blessed them. The animals have a right to live, a right to whatever enjoyment they can get out of life — just as much right as you and I. Let us concede that right and for the sake of our natures and for their enjoyment and welfare, let us treat them with kindliness and get delight out of their beauty and service.

Hugh W. Nibley, a leader of the Mormon Church in Utah, has written: "Man's domination is a call to service, not a license to exterminate. It is precisely because men now prey upon each other and shed the blood and waste the flesh of other creatures without need that the world lieth in sin." And according to another Utah Mormon, George Q. Cannon (1827–1901): "These birds and animals and fish cannot speak, but they can suffer, and our God who created them knows their sufferings, and will hold him who causes them to suffer unnecessarily to answer for it. It is a sin against their creator." Cannon also believed that teaching children about animal welfare made them better citizens:

> Children who are trained to respect the rights of the lower animals will be more inclined to respect human rights and become good citizens. It has been observed that in places where special attention has been given in the public schools to the subject of kindness to animals, the percentage of crime has been lessened.[46]

The Mormon Church also has advocated a basically nonmeat diet as part of its reverence for life philosophy. This originated with church founder Joseph Smith, who in 1833 received a revelation of such a health code as divine will, emphasizing grain as the basis for one's diet. Meat could be eaten only rarely, such as in times of famine or extreme cold, when some animals would perish because of the weather.[47]

Unfortunately, many modern-day Mormons appear to have forgotten the spirit of the teachings of the founders of the church. Contemporary Mormon leaders no longer teach the humane and conservation precepts of the church, and some Mormon ranchers, sheep raisers, and cattle ranchers in Utah and the western United States do their best to kill off much of the local wildlife to prevent it from competing with them. (At the behest of western livestock interests, the US Departments of Interior and Agriculture have killed over one hundred thousand coyotes each year, as well as poisoning, shooting, and trapping thousands of bears, foxes, badgers, mountain lions, and prairie dogs, mainly on federal land leased for grazing. Even eagles were poisoned and shot by the thousands in the 1970s by sheep ranchers, and wild horses are still being eliminated from public lands to provide more acres of forage for livestock.)

But some Mormons are also working to reawaken and keep alive the humane tradition of their church. An example is a 1980 book, *Animals and the Gospel*, written by Scott S. Smith and Dr. Gerald Jones, providing quotations and humane teachings from the early church leaders. According to Smith,

> The decade after publication... saw a complete absence of mention of the subject in the Church's semi-annual conferences, probably because of the hysterical reaction of hunters to President Kimball's comments in 1978.... There are a couple of dozen modest admonitions to be kind to animals, mostly in lessons for children, a rather poor showing for an institution which has the strongest humane theology of any major western religion.

Nevertheless, Smith sees signs of hope that activists with the church will be able to rekindle some of its original policies on animals and the environment.[48]

## Reverend Billy Graham

One of the most influential and widely respected spiritual leaders in America today is the Reverend Dr. Billy Graham (b. 1918). In recent years, he has taken a strong stand on behalf of kindness to animals. But it is also true that he has infrequently spoken out on the subject, and has sometimes been ambivalent when he has done so, or has passed up opportunities to endorse humane teachings.

In 1975, two of Reverend Graham's newspaper columns responded to queries from readers in a manner that would please humanitarians. On June 11, he was asked by one follower: "I read your column daily, and watch you on television. But one thing I have never heard you preach on is kindness and responsibility to animals. Why?"

Reverend Graham responded:

> According to Bible teaching, all the animals of the earth were created good and pure (Gen. 1:25). . . . Man was given responsibility for the animal kingdom. However, God never intended their abuse.
>
> On occasion, I've alluded to kindness to animals. I believe it's a characteristic of the mature mind. In my youth in North Carolina, I learned to milk cows before dawn, and I discovered kindness paid off in their cooperative respect.
>
> The Christian viewpoint, of course, is one that prohibits cruelty, abuse, and even waste of this and other valued resources.

But Reverend Graham modified and weakened the impact of his humane message by suggesting that it was of secondary importance to saving human souls: "In a few places, the Bible does mention certain standards for the treatment of animals. . . . But such comments are not germane to the main thrust of the Bible's message, the plan for man's salvation. My ministry has been sharing that good news."[49]

On another occasion in 1975, Reverend Graham took a much stronger stand against mistreatment of animals when he was asked, "Does the Bible say anything about cruelty to animals?" He replied:

> Yes, the Bible teaches that we are not to abuse or punish animals in a cruel way. God has created them, and while mankind is given dominion over the animals, we are not to treat them cruelly.
>
> Actually, the Bible's emphasis is on the good treatment of animals, and not just the forbidding of cruel treatment. For example, not only were men to observe the Sabbath as a day of rest, but they were to allow their animals to rest on the Sabbath also (Exod. 20:10). A working animal was also to be fed properly: "Thou shalt not muzzle the ox when he treadeth out the corn" (Deut. 25:4). The Bible says, "A good man is concerned for the welfare of his animals, but even the kindness of godless men is cruel" (Prov. 12:10, Living Bible).

A person who is cruel to animals may have a selfish and insensitive nature, and the Bible says this is a spiritual problem.[50]

A June 27, 1973, letter, written on behalf of Dr. Graham by Reverend Ralph L. Williams, spiritual counselor of the Billy Graham Evangelistic Association, states:

Man should have humanitarian concerns and view all of God's creation with appreciation and delight.... God takes no pleasure in forms of cruelty to animals for they are subjects of His creation, and He will not hold men guiltless when this occurs. Inasmuch as God has given man dominion over the animals of the field, it seems that those domesticated for the purpose of food are in His plan for man to use. We do, however, regret the sporting nature of hunting. It is evident that God's earth has been deprived of many of the species in God's creative order due to the fact that man has chosen to decimate the animal population, thus upsetting the balance in nature.[51]

Recently, Dr. Graham said that Christians should "take a lead" in caring for the earth.[52]

Perhaps the greatest test of his real views will come when he helps decide the disposition of the many thousands of acres of undeveloped woods and forests, mountains, and other real estate holdings in North Carolina owned by his foundation. What a great example he would set if he set aside some of the most pristine areas, teeming with wildlife, as nature sanctuaries to be preserved so future generations could see what God's creation looked like before humans covered it over with asphalt, concrete, and housing developments.

## Other Voices of Reason

Many other Protestant clergymen, too numerous to all be mentioned here, have spoken out for animals and nature in recent decades. Some of the most memorable statements are discussed below.

In May 1957, Reverend Lloyd Putnam preached a Sunday sermon in recognition of Be Kind to Animals Week. Saying that "we have a small religion if it has no room for the rest of God's creatures," Reverend Putnam asks if many Christians do not suffer from "religious myopia":

If we see God's handiwork in all of creation, we will want to use our freedom to conserve, to appreciate, to protect all living things.... Is our view of God and His creation too small? Is our sense of responsibility too limited? Is our love too narrow?... Let us enlarge our religion that we may do our part in redeeming all of creation.[53]

Another plea for nature protection appeared in May 1970 in the *Lutheran Witness* in an article by Reverend Richard Koenig, pastor of Immanuel Church (in Amherst, Massachusetts), the University of Massachusetts, Amherst College, and Smith College. In his article, "Can We Save Mother Earth," Reverend Koenig observes:

> From the theological viewpoint, preservation of the environment is a God-given task of the highest importance for man....
> Nature is not man's to "conquer," as we so arrogantly like to say, but to be cared for. The language of conquest and exploitation is symptomatic of a serious departure from the Christian understanding of man's relation to nature.[54]

Indeed, as Richard A. Baer, Jr., has observed in *Conservation Catalyst*, "Modern Man's ravaging of his natural environment would have been viewed by the Biblical writers as essentially sacrilegious."[55]

Certainly, one of the most courageous incidents of modern-day Christians' defense of animals came in October 1975, when the Episcopalian Reverend Frederick F. Powers made headlines by taking on the gun lobby. Reverend Powers, rector of St. Giles Episcopal Church in Upper Darby, Pennsylvania, held feast day services for St. Francis of Assisi — which coincided with hunting season in Pennsylvania, a state with an estimated 2.5 million hunters — and prayed that "the hunter" would atone and change his ways. "The thrill of killing," said the Reverend, is "not good for Christians."[56]

Reverend Powers called sport hunting "wanton killing which reinforces the hunter's destructive instincts and violates respect for God's creation."[57]

### Albert Schweitzer

One of the greatest clergymen, humanitarians, and philosophers of our time was dedicated to the concept of "reverence for life" for all creatures. The French theologian and medical missionary Dr. Albert Schweitzer (1875–1965), who won the Nobel Prize in 1952, preached and lived by the humane ethic. A Protestant clergyman, physician, and music scholar, Dr. Schweitzer founded Lambaréné Hospital in French Equatorial Africa in 1913 and ran it for many years.

Schweitzer believed that "sympathy with animals, which is so often represented as sentimentality, [is] a duty which no thinking man can escape."[58] Dr. Schweitzer wrote eloquently of the need to show reverence for all forms of life:

A man's religion is of little value unless even seemingly insignificant creatures benefit from it. A truly religious man does not ask how far this or that life deserves sympathy as valuable in itself. Nor how far it is capable of feeling. To him, life as such is sacred. The countryman who has mowed down a meadow as fodder for his cows should take care that on the way home he does not, in wanton pastime, cut off the head of a single flower growing on the edge of the road, for in doing so he injured life without being forced to do so by necessity.

Schweitzer stressed the moral responsibility of humans to care for all forms of life: "We ... are compelled by the commandment of love contained in our hearts and thoughts, and proclaimed by Jesus, to give rein to our natural sympathy to animals. We are also compelled to help them and spare suffering as far as it is in our power."

A prayer written by Dr. Schweitzer summed up his feelings toward animals:

Hear our humble prayer, O God, for our friends the animals, for animals who are suffering; for animals who are overworked, underfed and cruelly treated; for all wistful creatures in captivity that beat their wings against bars; for any that are hunted or lost or deserted or frightened or hungry; for all that must be put to death. We entreat for them all thy mercy and pity, and for those who deal with them, we ask a heart of compassion and gentle hands and kind words. Make us, ourselves, to be true friends to animals, and so to share the blessings of the merciful.

Schweitzer went so far as to help insects that were in trouble and refused whenever possible to kill even poisonous snakes at the medical clinic.[59]

The ultimate result of humankind's careless destruction of nature, so apparent now, was understood decades ago by Schweitzer, who said, "Man has lost the capacity to foresee and to forestall. He will end by destroying the earth."[60]

(An inspiring collection of Schweitzer's writings is found in *Animals, Nature, and Albert Schweitzer,* by Ann Cottrell Free, published by the Humane Society of the United States and the Animal Welfare Institute, in Washington, D.C.)

## European Protestant Action

In Europe, particularly in the United Kingdom, many church leaders and denominations have for decades spoken out for animals and the environment.

The Anglican Church (the Church of England) has a long history of advocating kind treatment of animals. In 1970, the National Assembly of the Church of England issued a report stating:

> The Church Assembly is of the opinion that the practices of hare-coursing, deer-hunting, and otter-hunting are cruel, unjustifiable and degrading, and urges Christian people in the light of their Christian profession and responsibility to make plain their opposition to activities of this sort, and their determination to do all in their power to secure their speedy abolition.[61]

In 1971, the spiritual head of the church, the archbishop of Canterbury Michael Ramsey, commissioned a report by Anglican theologians entitled *Man and Nature*. Published in 1975, the report found that "the teaching of the mainstream of Biblical thought" was that "God has a redeeming purpose for the whole creation, for nature as well as man":

> For everything that God had made he judged to be good. Although it cannot be denied that man is very much at the center of biblical teaching on creation, this teaching does not hold that nature has been created simply for man's sake. It exists for God's glory, that is to say, it has a meaning and worth beyond its meaning and worth as seen from the point of view of human utility. It is in this sense that we can say that it has an intrinsic value. To imagine that God has created the whole universe solely for man's use and pleasure is a mark of folly.[62]

In 1977, at the annual meeting in London of the Royal Society for the Prevention of Cruelty to Animals (R.S.P.C.A), the archbishop of Canterbury, Dr. Donald Coggan, said, "Animals, as part of God's creation, have rights which must be respected. It behooves us always to be sensitive to their needs and to the reality of their pain."[63]

Also in 1977, the General Synod of the Church of England endorsed the effort to "prevent cruelty to animal life by the promotion of humane behavior, . . . so as to reduce pain, fear and stress inflicted upon animals by mankind whether relating to pet animals, wild animals, animals used in laboratory experiments, farm animals, performing animals or any other form of animal life." The synod urged all members of the Church of England to work for this objective and "to make life more tolerable for those creatures, and to safeguard species threatened with extinction, and generally to prevent ignorance, neglect, cruelty, degradation and commercial exploitation so far as animals are concerned."[64]

In January 1981, addressing the issue of animal welfare and humane farming methods, the recent archbishop of Canterbury, Dr. Robert Runcie, issued a statement saying:

> It is integral to our Christian faith that this world is God's world and that man is a trustee and steward of God's creation who must render up an

account for his stewardship. He must therefore exercise his "dominion" in conformity with God's will and purposes, not only in relation to himself but to the whole area of created life. Man is not an absolute owner of the earth which he inhabits.[65]

The Quakers have long taught kindness to animals. As far back as 1795, the Society of Friends (Quakers) in London adopted a resolution condemning sport hunting and stating, "let our leisure be employed in serving our neighbor, and not in distressing, for our amusement, the creatures of God."[66]

At the Society of Friends London Yearly Meeting in 1981, the following statement was adopted:

> Our stewardship of the world does not allow us to exercise an absolute right over animals. All animals should be treated as if they have rights and as if they suffer pain and stress similar to human experience and differing only in degree. We have a duty to consider the consequences of our influence on the environment and its effects on animals, taking great care to reduce the harmful effects. Some activities, like killing for sport and aspects of trapping or hunting, which involve cruelty in a slow death, are indefensible and we need to urge those who engage in these activities to reconsider their position.[67]

The Presbyterians and Methodists have also endorsed humane concepts. The General Assembly of the Church of Scotland (Presbyterian), on May 27, 1947, adopted the following pronouncement: "The General Assembly, recognizing kindness to animals and their protection from ill treatment as a practical application of Christianity, urge members of the Church to be active in this Christian duty, and commend to their support the work of the Scottish S.P.C.A." Earlier, on May 30, 1939, it was recommended that all ministers "devote all or part of a sermon on one Sunday in the year to the general subject of mercy and kindness to all living creatures."[68] And a 1978 report by the Church of Scotland stated, "Humane concern in the matter of animals must therefore be welcomed and fostered by the church."[69]

In Ireland, the General Assembly of the Presbyterian Church in June 1956 adopted a resolution recognizing the importance of animal welfare:

> the welfare of animals and their just treatment is an essential part of Christian responsibility, [and we] urge members of the Church to be active in this sphere of service, and commend to their support the work of the Societies for the Prevention of Cruelty to Animals throughout Ireland.

The assembly also recommended that this subject be taught and discussed before congregations and at Sunday schools and group meetings, especially during Animal Welfare Week and at other specified times.[70]

On July 13, 1951, a Methodist conference on the treatment of animals adopted a resolution representing the church's official policy and stating:

> God has, in His wisdom, placed animals under man's dominion, and he must so treat them as one who will have to give an account of his office to God. . . . The overriding consideration is, not only what we must refrain from doing, but what we can do positively to secure the well-being of those who, with ourselves, inhabit the earth, and fulfill the creative joy and purpose of Almighty God.[71]

The 1980 Methodist conference in London condemned factory farming, "cruel sports such as stag hunting and hare coursing," and unjustifiable animal experimentation, and concluded: "In all his dealings with the creatures who share creation with him, the proper function of the Christian man or woman is to serve as a steward under God."[72]

The famous Austrian Lutheran theologian, Dr. Jürgen Moltmann, of German's Tübingen University, warns that "the destruction of the environment which we perpetrate . . . will, with certainty, seriously endanger the survival of humanity at the latest in the twenty-first century." Saying that "the ecological crisis of nature today is, at the same time, a religious crisis of the human race," he asserts that "every assault on creation that cannot be made good is a sacrilege. The consequence is that those who perpetrate this excommunicate themselves. The nihilistic destruction of nature is applied atheism."[73]

Professor Moltmann proposes the adoption of a "General Declaration of the Rights of Nature," and a "Universal Declaration of Animal Rights," because:

> Before God, the Creator, we and our descendants and every living creature (Gen. 9:9–10) are equal partners of God's Covenant. Nature is not our property. . . . All living beings must be respected by humans as God's partners in the Covenant. . . . Whoever injures the dignity of animals, injures God.

Moltmann also argues that acts of "serious, irreparable destruction of nature are to be seen as 'crimes against humanity.' " As he told the May 1990 "Caring for Creation" Conference: "With all destruction of nature, humans destroy a piece of themselves. Whoever destroys nature, saws off the branch upon which humanity is sitting. The 'end of nature' is therefore also definitely the end of humanity."[74]

In many other instances, European church leaders and groups have recognized the Bible's teaching on nature and kindness to animals. An extensive discussion of this can be found in C. W. Hume's book, *The Status of Animals in the Christian Religion; God's Animals*, by Don Ambrose Agius;[75] *Christianity and the Rights of Animals*, by Andrew Linzey;[76]

and in *The Ark,* the regular publication of the Catholic Study Circle for Animal Welfare in London.[77]

## What Needs to Be Done

Given the improving but still largely inactive status of the Protestant churches in America and Europe concerning conservation issues, several leading figures have written of what needs to be done. What is really needed is a maturing of theology, according to the Reverend Andrew Linzey, a Church of England priest who teaches at the Center for the Study of Theology at the University of Essex in England and is author of *Christianity and the Rights of Animals:* "Archbishop William Temple said that theology is still in its infancy. How right he was. It took the churches 1,800 years to recognize that you can't love God and keep humans as slaves ... what we now have to learn is that we cannot love God and hate his non-human creatures."[78]

And conservationist Russell Train sees a reinvigorated church role as crucial to the survival of our civilization:

> The Church has the credibility and the historic mission of articulating and teaching values to society. The church should assume a major responsibility for teaching that we humans, individually and collectively, are part of the living community of the earth that nurtures and sustains us; that humanity as well as all life depends for its very being upon the healthy functioning of the natural systems of the Earth; that all living things, including humans, are interdependent; that we have the duty, collectively and individually, to care for God's creation and that in it lie all the creative possibilities for life now and in the future.
>
> After all, ecology is nothing more than Creation at work. It is now high time for the oldest human institutions of all, our religions, to make concern for nature — Caring for Creation — a central part of their doctrine and practice.[79]

As we move into the 1990s, that may, hopefully, be just what is happening.

*Chapter 9* _____

# The 1980s:
# A Revolution
# in Environmental Theology

The decade of the 1980s, particularly the latter part, has seen a virtual revolution in the way the religious community has begun to view, respond to, and involve itself in environmental issues. In just the last few years, major breakthroughs have occurred in the policies of major church groups toward preserving "God's creation" and in the number of religious people working on such issues. The present involvement of so many religious figures, in a field where they had for so long been conspicuous by their absence, is nothing short of amazing.

### Sowing the Seeds

The "greening of the churches" has been a long time in coming. While there have always been a few courageous individuals speaking out for conservation and animal welfare, the churches have, since at least the Middle Ages, been largely hostile or indifferent to such concerns.

By the late 1960s, a fledgling movement was afoot to get the mainstream churches involved in conservation and environmental causes, and an increasing number of clergy and religious thinkers began speaking out on these issues. For instances, Joseph Sittler, a well-known Lutheran theologian, declared that "reason says that destroying clean air is impractical. Faith ought to say it is blasphemous."[1]

The Methodist Church's General Board of Christian Social Concerns in Washington, D.C., was active in the 1960s in lobbying for passage of the Federal Humane Slaughter Act, and for a stronger law to reduce the suffering of animals used in medical and scientific laboratories.

One of the first church organizations to involve itself actively in environmental issues was the National Council of Churches (N.C.C.), a liberal consortium of American Protestant churches. In the fall of 1969, the N.C.C. established an Environmental Stewardship Action Team to work on ecological problems, and seventy-five religious thinkers formed an association called the Faith-Man-Nature Group. Indeed, all this novel activity prompted *New York Times* reporter Edward Fiske to write in January 1970: "The result is what may prove to be the most far-reaching new religious issue of the 1970s — the theology of ecology, or man's relationship to his environment."[2]

This prediction turned out to be somewhat premature — by about two decades. Today, environmentalists still ask where the churches have been during the major battles on wilderness, endangered species, Alaska lands, clean air and water, toxic chemicals, farmland preservation, and other issues that took place during the 1970s. Although many religiously oriented individuals and some organizations were to their great credit active, the churches have been largely absent. But in the 1970s, the seeds were sown that blossomed a decade later into a burgeoning of interest in the environment on the part of many church groups and leaders.

## The National Council of Churches

In March 1976, the N.C.C.'s Division of Church and Society began a project, headed by Katherine Seelman, to study and address the ethical implications of energy production and use. The result was the compiling of a "Church Energy Kit" distributed to churches, religious groups, and individuals throughout the nation.[3]

Working alongside the N.C.C. on energy and environmental issues was the Interfaith Coalition on Energy, sponsored by Baptist, Methodist, Jewish, Roman Catholic, Lutheran, Presbyterian, United Church of Christ, and other denominations. The coalition compiled a "Covenant for Conservation" with "the twelve commitments for energy conservation" based on "care and stewardship of resources."[4]

In 1979, the N.C.C.'s Energy Education Project published a booklet, *Energy and Ethics*, which observes: "The reality is that every thing and every one is connected with every other thing and every other one in the community of life.... The challenge is to each person...to help bring about justice for the whole of God's creation within all of nature and throughout all of history."[5] The booklet discusses the religious and moral implications of the nation's energy policy, calling pollution and environmental degradation sinful:

It is the province of the religious community to address the ethical questions underlying the energy crisis. Human beings can now use energy technologies to sustain or to destroy life, and to alter the nature of the human species....

The Old Testament declares that an essential part of the divine commission to humanity is to exercise "dominion" over the earth and to "till and keep it...." This means that all persons, since they are created in God's image, are responsible for the wise conservation of the Creator's gift of limited energy.

Humanity has often selfishly distorted the divine commission to exercise dominion into an unlimited license to exploit the material world and weaker persons. This perversion of dominion into domination is a sin and it is one of the underlying causes of the energy crisis....

The current energy situation can be seen as the result of the idolatrous and unjust ways in which humans have used, abused or neglected to use the limited sources of energy the Creator has made available for the well-being of the continuing creation.[6]

Recently, the N.C.C. set up an "Eco-Justice Working Group," which is distributing a booklet, *101 Ways to Help Save the Earth*, to 350,000 Protestant, Catholic, Jewish, and Unitarian congregations throughout the nation. Saying that "it is our common vision that humans are put on this earth to be its caretakers," the document lists "fifty-two weeks of congregational activities to save the earth." In the introduction, David Trickett, executive director of the Washington Theological Consortium, writes: "Our faiths make it clear to us that God is truly present with us.... But we should never be so proud as to think that this separates us from other creatures about which God also cares deeply."[7]

## Setting the Stage in the 1980s

The 1980s have seen many Christian leaders speak out on stewardship responsibilities, including no less a figure than Pope John Paul II, who has, on several occasions, condemned abuse of the environment (see pp. 125–127).

One influential writer and theologian who has long addressed environmental issues is the Reverend Wesley Granberg-Michaelson, an author, minister in the Reformed Church in America, and president of the New Creation Institute. He attracted considerable attention within the religious community in a November 1981 article subtitled "A Theology of the Environment" in *Sojourners*, a liberal Christian magazine. In this essay, he described the true nature of "dominion": "the Bible does not give humanity a sanction to dominate nature which justifies reckless, wasteful, or selfish exploitation of the environment":

The concept of humanity's dominion over other parts of creation occurs only in the context of humanity's creation in God's image. Thus, humanity exercises this dominion only as God would — God who creates, sustains, upholds, and is glorified in all creation.

Construing dominion to mean having all power over creation reflects the desire to be "like God" and the central fact of sin and the Fall. Sin began, after all, with humanity deciding to ignore God and do what it pleased with God's creation.[8]

Another influential article of the early 1980s was an essay by the Right Reverend Vincent Rossi, "The Eleventh Commandment: Toward an Ethic of Ecology." First appearing in *Sonflowers Discipleship Journal* in March 1979, it was reprinted in 1981 in *Epiphany Journal*, and has been much quoted and discussed since then.

In his essay, Father Rossi, director general of the Holy Order of MANS, a Christian brotherhood, attributes much of the blame for the destructiveness of our society to our abandonment of traditional religious principles:

The global environment is in unprecedented danger and we must act now to save it and ourselves. The ecological crisis must be seen as a spiritual or theological crisis. The world is sick because man has forgotten his proper and essential role as priest or mediator in creation. Man is religious by nature. Religion preserves and expresses the sense of the sacred for man. The natural world must be seen as sacred because it is the abode of God.

Man is now acting like a cancer in nature, not because religion has in the past allowed man to abuse nature, but because modern man has abandoned true religion in favor of a spiritless humanism without God and therefore without a center or a purpose outside itself.

Conversely, the solution to our ecological crisis is to rediscover our early awe for nature, which he calls a "living, sacred temple":

We must love nature for herself and also because she is a "handmaiden" of the Lord. We must return to a kind of *aboriginal* consciousness of nature, an atonement for nature so direct one could not open the earth or cut down a tree or kill an animal without a profound emotional response or a heartfelt prayer. Our awareness of nature must be directly attached to our own feelings, as it once was for primitive man.

Nature is a theophany.*Man must learn once again to see God everywhere in Nature. We must let the scales fall from our eyes, and discerning the Divine Presence in all things, love the earth and all nature as the visible Form of God.

---

*Theophany is the appearance or manifestation of the Deity.

Therefore, what is needed is an Eleventh Commandment that will restore humankind to harmony with nature:

THE EARTH IS THE LORD'S AND THE FULLNESS THEREOF: THOU SHALL NOT DESPOIL THE EARTH, NOR DESTROY THE LIFE THEREON.

This commandment, like the others, is so basic to our being that it cannot be ignored with impunity. To disobey it is to imperil, not only the earth, but also our own souls. To ignore it is to deny the sense of the sacred which is the very substance of our spirit and our existence. Of what good are all manner of churches and temples if man has so lost the intuition of the supernatural that he no longer can recognize all nature as the living temple of God? . . . To be God-fearing is to be nature-revering.

"What is needed," Rossi concludes, "is for men and women to feel *religious* about nature":

We need "monks" and "nuns" in the temple of the Earth, men and women who are willing to take a vow of obedience to God by serving nature, to make their lives a witness to the value of the Eleventh Commandment. . . . All creatures, great and small, must be seen as our neighbors. . . .

We . . . must love the earth as we love ourselves. We must open our hearts to the plight of all creatures, and find therein such a poignant brother-love for them all that we are moved to rise up with prophetic fire to condemn the desecration that is now going on. We have been commissioned by God to replenish the earth. We need no other justification or incentive to begin.[9]

Later, adopting this theme, a group was formed in San Francisco, called the Eleventh Commandment Fellowship, to promote ecological concern within the Christian community. One of the group's tenets is also taken from Father Rossi's writings, "to be Christian is to be ecologist," to which he added, "This is absolutely fundamental to an authentic Christian understanding of the relationship between Man and Nature."

### Reverend Andrew Linzey

Reverend Andrew Linzey, chaplain and director of studies at the Center for the Study of Theology at the University of Essex, has written extensively and knowledgeably on Christian theology and human obligations toward other life forms.

In Tom Regan's book *Animal Sacrifices*, Linzey explains why the doctrines of Christianity (as well as Judaism and Islam) require kind treatment of animals:

The created world exists both as a manifestation of his love and his intention to manifest his love within it. . . .

We see that the creation and its order, character, and design, insofar as they reflect the creator's intention, must be valuable to him. If creation has value to God, then it should possess value to humans.[10]

In an August 1989 article in *Animals' Voice* magazine, Linzey writes:

Animals are God's creatures. . . . Animals belong to God and exist primarily for God. God, in other words, rejoices in differentiated creation. . . . In Colossians 1:16 (RSV): in him *all* things were created, in heaven and on earth . . . *all* things were created through him and *for* him.[11]

Linzey asserts that a "basic doctrinal point" is that "God is the generous Creator of all life and all life exists principally for the glory of God. . . . The one moral principle" Linzey proposes to summarize this theology is that "it is wrong to be the cause of avoidable injury."

His 1987 book, *Christianity and the Rights of Animals*, argues that because all life was created by and belongs to the Lord, harm to any creature violates God's rights. Biblical evidence cited that animals have the same rights as humans includes the following:

- Humans were created on the same "day" as all other land animals, the sixth day.

- Humans received the same "blessing" as the "wild animals, cattle, and all reptiles."

- The Lord made the same covenant with humans (Noah and his descendants) as He did with "living things on earth of every kind."[12]

He concludes his book by asserting that *gradual* progress may be our best hope of improving the status of animals:

What we need is progressive disengagement from our inhumanity to animals. The urgent and essential task is to invite, encourage, support and welcome those who want to take some steps along the road to a more peaceful world with the non-human creation. . . .

What is important is that we all move some way on, if only by one step at a time, however falteringly. . . . If we can persuade an intensive farmer to refrain from de-beaking one hen, then at least some small burden of suffering is lessened in the world. The enemy of progress is the view that everything must be changed before some real gains can be secured. . . . But what is essential for this new world to emerge is the sense that each of us can change our individual worlds, however slightly, to live more peaceably with our nonhuman neighbors.[13]

## The North American Conference on Christianity and Ecology

Since 1980, the Au Sable Institute of Environmental Studies, in Mancelona, Michigan, has held forums on ecology and religion involving scholars and religious and environmental leaders from around the world.

Inspired in part by these forums, a watershed event occurred in August 1987, when five to six hundred people from all over the United States, Canada, Europe, and elsewhere gathered at the first North American Conference on Christianity and Ecology (NACCE).

The purpose of the conference was announced by one of its main organizers, Frederick W. Krueger of the Eleventh Commandment Fellowship in San Francisco, who pointed out that "the task before us is a large one, yet it must be done. What humanity is now doing to the air, water and earth is destroying the delicate fabric of the biosphere which supports human life. The Christian Church, taken as a whole, represents that last best hope for bringing healing to our beleaguered planet."[14]

The conference's prospectus further explored the theme of the churches' responsibility and power to influence events:

> The fact is, our society cannot continue on its present course without a confrontation with catastrophe. Yet . . . there have been few voices from the Christian tradition that have stood up to articulate a path that would lead us into a healing of the land. But the handwriting is now on the wall. Unless we are willing to make the drastic changes and sacrifices necessary to curtail our excessive consumption and despoliation of the land, we will not survive as a people — and we will inherit an end of our own making.
>
> Of prime importance in this predicament is the voice of the churches. No other voice has the potential to exert the degree of awakening and ecological repentance as the voice out of our Christian tradition.[15]

As Thomas Fox, editor of the *National Catholic Reporter*, described the gathering, which was held at the United Methodist Church's Epworth Forest Conference Center in North Webster, Indiana:

> A newly formed, broad-based Christian Coalition, citing the unprecedented threat to the planet's life systems and the relative disinterest of the continent's churches, pledged here to bring ecological concerns — and the spiritual dimensions of these concerns — into its members' faith communities.[16]

"The Christian Churches," as one person put it, "have belatedly entered the environmental movement."[17]

At the gathering, many leading Christian clergy and theologians delivered papers and addresses stressing the responsibility of the churches, and of all Christians, to work for the preservation and healing of the natural environment.

Father Thomas Berry, director of the Riverdale Center for Religious Research in New York, stressed that "concern for the fate of the earth is inherently a sacred concern.... The issues we are dealing with are the most awesome issues that the planet has ever experienced":

> Nothing comparable has ever been known in the entire story of the earth. Our industrial economy is closing down all the basic life systems of the planet. According to one estimate, what is happening is likely the greatest setback to the abundance and diversity of life on earth since the first flickerings of life some four billion years ago. This threatened impasse of life on earth involves an extensive diminishment in our religious experience, our intellectual insight, our emotional sensitivities and our aesthetic creativity. No phase of the human can be effectively saved without saving the integral functioning of the entire planet.[18]

Father Berry, a Catholic priest and one of the leading proponents of a spiritually based environmental ethic, pointed out that humans' religious tradition, along with much else, is threatened by the destruction of the environment:

> Christianity and the entire range of human religious experience is dependent on the survival of the ecosystems of the planet. Our sense of the divine itself is dependent on our perceptions of the natural world around us. We have such a sublime sense of the divine because of the grandeur of the divine as revealed in our natural surroundings. In so far as these are damaged, our sense of the divine is damaged in a corresponding degree.[19]

And David Haenke, a co-founder of the conference and of the Christian ecology movement, spoke of "the astounding creation that is the earth":

> The more we study and understand the creation, with all of our ways of knowing from the scientific to the spiritual, the more we see its astounding perfection, even in its tiniest manifestation, far beyond anything that we ourselves could create. In the myriad interconnections of its ecosystemic elements, we see a totality that is far beyond what we can even begin to comprehend.... It is no wonder that such a work can only be that of God.[20]

Poet and farmer Wendell Berry from Kentucky stressed that "the ecological teaching of the Bible is inescapable.... God made the world. He thinks the world is good. He loves it. It's his world. He has never relinquished title to it. And he has never revoked the conditions ... that oblige us to take excellent care of it." Berry said that the "Bible supports a moral economy," one that shows "reverence for the Maker and does not harm the making." He further observed that "we think that God's granting us dominion over the earth gives us a license to exterminate. To 'have dominion over' means to serve."[21]

In his paper "Toward a Christian Ecological Consciousness," Dr. Hans Schwarz, from Regensburg University in West Germany, asserted that "the world...was designed good and entrusted to human care," and failure to show reverence for the earth and other life forms is a sin:

> We must agree with Albert Schweitzer that we should not make a sharp distinction between higher and lower forms of life. No life should be destroyed if such destruction can be avoided. This does not only apply to animal life but to plant life as well. Even picking a flower without necessity is a sin against life....
>
> The earth...is a gift which has been entrusted to us, so that we can enjoy it and take good care of it. The failure to conserve the land is not only a misuse of God's gift but a sin, not only against humans and animals but against God.

Schwarz concluded that protecting the earth is essential to the perpetuation of future generations:

> Since we have neither created the earth nor acquired it from its creator, we cannot assume that we have an absolute right to it.... Since our lifetime is shorter than that of the earth, and since successive generations are always depending on the preceding ones, the earth should be kept in trust for future generations. Since life cannot be sustained without the earth on which it moves, we cannot assign an unequivalent priority to human life. Ultimately all life belongs to God who sustains us in and through the land.[22]

Another of the conference's organizers, its vice chair Professor Calvin B. DeWitt of the University of Wisconsin–Madison, delivered a paper entitled "Responding to Creation's Degradation." He observed that "Judaism and Christianity include teachings that are at their base ecological, and supportive of a sustained habitation of Earth. These ancient teachings provide the basis for Christian Stewardship":

> From the scriptures, much is learned about stewardship: people do not own the Earth; all creatures have intrinsic value; endangered species are worthy of preservation; every creature, the land, and all Creation needs its sabbaths of fulfillment; and, people of the Earth should engage in a loving keeping of the Earth and its creatures.

Writing that "ecology is the business of all who claim Earth as home," Professor DeWitt, a director of the Au Sable Institute, provided the conference with a "Jewish and Christian confession — a statement on a sustainable planetary ecology to which believers can subscribe":

> The organization and integrity we observe in Earth and the biosphere is a reflection of the goodness and integrity of the Creator, through whom everything was created, is sustained and is harmoniously held together.
>
> Through God's providence, all of His creatures interact with each other and their environments in a stream of creation history, so beautiful and proclaiming of His might and power that through it all people can know something of God's eternal power and divine majesty.[23]

Before adjourning, the conference approved and issued a statement urging Christian churches to become involved in the struggle to save the earth:

> The earth is in danger. While an ecological crisis of unprecedented proportions looms before all creation, our society continues down a path of excessive consumption and despoliation of the land. The North American Conference on Christianity and Ecology asks the Christian community to take on the burden of rescuing the earth from degradation, to join ongoing efforts so that the present ripple of spiritual-ecological concern will be amplified into a mighty wave of compassion, protection, healing and revitalization of the earth.

Or, as this call-to-arms was put in the conference's prospectus, (paraphrasing Reverend Vincent Rossi): "We have been commissioned by God to 'replenish the earth.' What other justification or incentive do we need to begin?"[24]

## The World Council of Churches

The World Council of Churches (W.C.C.), a politically left-liberal group with influence in countries throughout the world, has also recently become active in conservation and humane issues. The W.C.C., based in Geneva, Switzerland, is the world's largest Christian ecumenical organization, with over two hundred member churches representing Protestant and Orthodox traditions around the globe.

A recent W.C.C. statement observed that: "The whole earth and all of its people are threatened with destruction. We confess that this results from human failure to discharge faithfully the responsibilities of stewardship."[25]

Another and very important W.C.C. document, "Liberation of Life," drafted in September 1988, goes so far as to call on "human beings to abandon domination and exploitation . . . [of] the rest of creation . . . and live with other creatures in peace and justice":

An ethic for the liberation of life . . . demands respect for every creature. . . .
The need to preserve species is for the sake of the creatures themselves and
at the same time for the sake of the human purposes. . . . Indeed . . . even
when respect for animals does not coincide with human benefit, it is still
required by Christians.[26]

The statement stressed the intrinsic worth of all creatures and their value
to human well-being:

The Noah story highlights God's concern for the preservation of species.
The value of all creatures in and for themselves, for one another, and
for God, and their interconnectedness in a diverse whole that has unique
value for God, together constitute the integrity of creation. . . . [27]

Indeed, our violence against one another and against the rest of
creation threatens the continuation of life on the planet.

Within the message of Jesus we find a profound deepening of the
importance of our treatment of one another and especially of the weak
and oppressed. "Truly, I say to you as you did it to one of the least of these
my brothers and sisters, you did it to me" (Matt. 25:48). Primarily this
refers to our treatment of human beings, but on the lips of the Jesus who
speaks of God's care for the grass of the field and the fallen sparrow, these
too are included among "the least of these."[28]

Specific examples of animal abuse cited include "wasteful, needlessly
duplicative . . . scientific use of animals; the 'sport' of hunting; and the
killing of members of rare and endangered species"; such animal entertainments as rodeos, bullfights, cock and dog fights, and even circuses
and marine mammal exhibitions and shows. The compulsory dissection
by students of frogs and other animals is condemned as causing "not
only the unnecessary pain and death of countless numbers of animals,
but also the moral damage done to our children."

The W.C.C. report states that "the ethic of the liberation of life is a
call to Christian action":

Christians are called to act respectfully toward "these, the least of our
brothers and sisters." This is not a simple question of kindness, however
laudable that virtue is. *It is an issue of strict justice.* In all our dealing
with animals, whether direct or indirect, the ethic for the liberation of life
requires that *we render unto animals what they are due, as creatures with an
independent integrity and value.* Precisely because they cannot speak for
themselves or act purposely to free themselves from the shackles of their
enslavement, the Christian duty to speak and act for them is the greater,
not the lesser.[29]

At this W.C.C. conference, renowned professor of philosophy at
North Carolina State University Dr. Tom Regan presented a paper de-
lineating human moral responsibilities toward other life forms: "We

are chosen by God...to be as loving in our day-to-day dealings with the created order, as God was in creating that order in the first place."[30]

The W.C.C. report ends with this conclusion: "If we destroy other species and the ecosystem, human beings cannot live.... Other creatures, both species and individuals, deserve to live in and for themselves and for God. Therefore we call on Christians as well as other people of good will to work toward the liberation of life, all life."

Among the Recommendations included in the document are the following:

1. Avoid cosmetics and household products that have been cruelly tested on animals. Instead, buy cruelty-free items.

2. Avoid clothing and other aspects of fashion that have a history of cruelty to animals, products of the fur industry in particular. Instead, purchase clothes that are "cruelty-free."

3. Avoid meat and animal products that have been produced on factory farms. Instead, purchase meat and animal products from sources where the animals have been treated with respect, or abstain from these products altogether.

4. Avoid patronizing forms of entertainment that treat animals as mere means to human ends.

This document is remarkable not just because it was developed by the world's largest interdenominational Christian organization, the W.C.C., but because it is the most far-reaching animal protection position to emerge from a worldwide Christian religious body.

"Liberation of Life" will not become an official statement of the W.C.C. until it is fully debated and accepted by its Central Committee. But the document does represent the final report of the delegates present at the September 1988 W.C.C. meeting held in Annecy, France, the Conference on Creation Theology and Environmental Ethics.[31]

In March 1990 population biologist L. Charles Birch, a vice chairman of the W.C.C. and a longtime advocate of humane stewardship, was named a co-winner of the prestigious $580,000 Templeton Prize for Progress in Religion. Dr. Birch, an Australian "eco-philosopher," has long taught that the churches have a responsibility to preach conservation of nature and respect for other life forms. In July 1979 he argued at a W.C.C. conference in Cambridge, Massachusetts, that all creatures should be valued for their "capacity for feeling," condemned as "unethical" factory farming methods, and stated that "the animal rights movement should be supported by all Christians."[32]

## Eastern Orthodoxy

In September 1989, the patriarch of the Greek Orthodox Church and ecumenical leader of 250 million Eastern Orthodox Christians issued a statement of major importance urging action to protect the environment. In this document, published in 1990 by the World Wide Fund for Nature International, Patriarch Dimitrios I stated that "this Ecumenical Throne of Orthodoxy...watches with great anxiety the merciless trampling down and destruction of the natural environment,...with extremely dangerous consequences for the very survival of the natural world created by God."

> In view of this situation, the Church of Christ cannot remain unmoved. It constitutes a fundamental dogma of her faith that the world was created by God the Father, who is confessed in the Creed to be "maker of heaven and earth and all things visible and invisible."
>
> The Church continuously declares that Man is destined not to exercise power over creation, as if he were the owner of it, but to act as its steward, cultivating it in love and referring it in thankfulness, with respect and reference, to its Creator.
>
> Unfortunately,... man has lost the sense of sacredness of creation and acts as its arbitrary ruler and rude violator....
>
> But creation "groans and travails in all its parts" (Rom. 8, 22), and is now beginning to protest at its treatment by the human being. Man cannot infinitely and at his pleasure exploit the natural sources of energy. The price of his arrogance will be his self-destruction, if the present situation continues.

Declaring the first day of September of each year "to be the day of the protection of the environment," with "prayers offered...for all creation," the document goes on to state,

> We paternally urge on the one hand all the faithful in the world to admonish themselves and their children to respect and protect the natural environment, and on the other hand all those who are entrusted with the responsibility of governing the nations to act without delay taking all necessary measures for the protection and preservation of natural creation.

An accompanying statement, "Orthodoxy and the Ecological Crisis," says, "We cannot continue plundering God's creation without reaping the results of its eventual destruction." It cites unappreciated examples of nature's value: "Who on earth would look at a pink, minute forest flower and guess that the rosy periwinkle is responsible for virtually eradicating childhood leukemia?"[33]

The paper goes so far as to criticize powerful interests in Greece, saying that "developers both large and small, who dump raw sewage into our once crystal-clear seas and who build haphazardly on our beaches are attacking not only those of us who were content with living in harmony with nature, a nature that is fast vanishing, but are attacking so many aspects of creation as a whole."

And the document announces the introduction of an organic farming project to be launched at the monastery at Ormylia, northern Greece, that "fully embodies the need to celebrate and preserve nature while engaging in sound ecological practices designed to protect that very environment."

The statement's section on "Biological Diversity" eloquently describes how "the variety of species is essential to the process of God's purpose in creation":

Biological diversity — the sum of God's creation now on earth — is an intricate web of interdependence, with no single part more important than the whole. Like a chain, the severing of even a single link — such as the destruction of a habitat or the extinction of a plant or animal — can have untold consequences for the links which remain.

## The Moscow Statement on Science and Religion

The decade of the 1990s began auspiciously, with leaders of virtually *every major world religion* signing a statement recognizing the religious implications of the ecological crisis and urging that steps be taken to solve it.[34]

In January 1990, at the Global Forum of Spiritual and Parliamentary leaders held in Moscow, U.S.S.R., renowned scientist and author Dr. Carl Sagan presented a statement signed by thirty-two leading scientists, "Preserving and Cherishing the Earth," appealing for a joint commitment in science and religion "to preserve the environment of the earth." The document, referring to "crimes against creation," pointed out that

the historical record makes clear that religious teaching, example, and leadership are powerfully able to influence personal conduct and commitment. As scientists, many of us have had profound experiences of awe and reverence before the universe. We understand that what is regarded as sacred is more likely to be treated with care and respect. Our planetary home should be so regarded. Efforts to safeguard and cherish the environment need to be infused with a vision of the sacred.

The appeal was endorsed by some 270 leading spiritual leaders from eighty-three nations — archbishops, cardinals, patriarchs, lamas, chief rabbis, mullahs, grand muftis; the presiding bishops of all the Christian churches of China, and of the Episcopal, Lutheran, Methodist and Mennonite Churches in the U.S.A.; professors of theology, seminary presidents, cathedral deans, and heads of religious orders worldwide; and indigenous religious leaders from five continents.

The response was organized by the Reverend Theodore M. Hesburgh, President Emeritus, Notre Dame University; the Reverend Leonid Kishkovsky, President, National Council of Churches, U.S.A.; Sheikh Ahmed Kuftaro, Grand Mufti of Syria; the Very Reverend Parks Morton, Dean, Cathedral of St. John the Divine; and Elie Wiesel, the Jewish writer and Nobel laureate.

The document affirmed these leaders' belief that "the environmental crisis is intrinsically religious":

> All faith traditions and teachings firmly instruct us to revere and care for the natural world. Yet, sacred creation is being violated and is in ultimate jeopardy as a result of long-standing human behavior. A religious response is essential to reverse such long-standing patterns of neglect and exploitation.

## Other Voices Crying for the Wilderness

In the 1980s, other Christian leaders have come forward to call attention to the urgency of our ecological crisis and its spiritual implications. At the World Wildlife Conference on religion and nature, held on September 29, 1986, in Assisi, Italy, representatives of the five major religions — Buddhism, Christianity, Hinduism, Islam, and Judaism — met and issued statements on each of their faiths' commitment to preserving other creatures and the natural environment.*The meeting, held at the birthplace of St. Francis, the patron saint of ecology, was organized in large part by Prince Philip, the Duke of Edinburgh.

At the conference, the Christian perspective was presented by Father Lanfrancho Serrini, minister general of the Franciscan Order, who affirmed that

> man's dominion cannot be understood as license to abuse, spoil, squander or destroy what God has made to manifest his glory. That dominion cannot be anything else than a stewardship in symbiosis with all creatures.... Every human act of irresponsibility towards creatures is an abomination. According to its gravity, it is an offense against that divine wisdom which sustains and gives purpose to the interdependent harmony of the universe.

---

*These statements are discussed in the chapters on these faiths.

The American Baptist Churches have issued a policy statement on the dangers of global warming, cutting of forests, and destruction of the atmosphere's protective ozone layer. The document urges all Baptists to get involved in protecting the environment and "pursue a lifestyle that is wise and responsible in light of our understanding of the problems."[35]

The Southern Baptist Convention decided to focus its 1991 national seminar in Fort Worth, Texas, on environmental problems. Writing in *SBC Today*, Robert Parham observed, "We need a serious discussion about earth care. For too long we have ignored this important biblical witness, and we cannot overlook this issue in the 1990s.... Christians must correct the problem."[36]

The Reverend J. Andy Smith III, director of the National Baptists' program for Social and Ethical Responsibility in Investment, recently wrote in an article for the Interfaith Center for Corporate Responsibility:

> Disruption of the peaceable relationship between creature and creation is sin. Actions of individuals and corporations contribute to that disruption. The church, as the community of God's stewards, has a vocation ... to work to change practices causing the disturbance. Therefore, the alliance of churches with environmentalists ... is a natural one.[37]

Citing scriptural references applicable to today's situation, Reverend Smith writes that "the relationship is embodied in an everlasting covenant to which the prophet Isaiah refers (24:5–6)":

> The Earth lies polluted under its inhabitants; for they have transgressed the laws, violated the statutes, broken the everlasting covenant. Therefore, a curse devours the Earth and its inhabitants suffer for their guilt; therefore, the inhabitants of the Earth are scorched and few are left.[38]

In 1987, the United Church of Christ formed its Christian Concern for Animals Committee, "to promote awareness and concern for the beasts of God's Creation with whom we share this world." Later, in April of 1990, a conference was organized "to consider the issue of Christian responsibility for the animal creation" and to sponsor a "Christian Concern for Animals Pronouncement," to be submitted to the 1991 General Synod.[39]

A majority of the seventy-three United Methodist conferences have environmental offices, which work on such issues, and the bishops of the Methodist Church sent pastoral letters to their thirty-eight thousand American churches asking them to participate in Earth Day 1990.[40]

A brochure distributed by the Catholic charitable organization The Christophers, entitled "What on Earth Can I Do?" contains useful tips on fighting pollution and working for conservation. The brochure observes that the gifts of creation have been given to us to nurture, to protect, to preserve; these gifts also preserve, protect, and nurture us. In our day-to-day lives, there is much we can do to act as responsible stewards of God's handiwork. . . . We must recognize that we have no right to divest the Creator of His creation; we are but stewards of his creation. And we must see that God has given us the power, through Jesus . . . to effect a change for the better.[41]

Beginning in 1987, the United Nations Environment Program (UNEP) has sponsored an "Environmental Sabbath" and urged congregations throughout the world to observe it through sermons and services designed to "transform our fundamental relationship with the earth from one of destruction to one of redemption." The Environmental Sabbath is held on the weekend closest to World Environment Day (June 5), and UNEP publishes a regular "Environmental Sabbath — Earth Rest Day" newsletter on the event.[42]

Daniel Martin, a Roman Catholic missionary priest who works with UNEP, believes that religion must find a way to "resanctify nature" and help people learn to "cherish" the earth. He has helped organize the International Coordinating Committee on Religion and the Earth (ICCRE), which will be holding a series of interfaith conferences on religion and ecology.[43]

Church groups that invest in corporations have also pressured many such firms to be more sensitive about how their polices affect the environment. An example is the "Valdez Principles," a set of ten ethical guidelines for shareholders and companies, named after the Exxon *Valdez* oil tanker that ran aground in September 1989, causing a disastrous oil spill in Prince William Sound in Alaska. The Valdez Principles have been endorsed by the Interfaith Center on Corporate Responsibility, an association of some 250 Christian institutions with about $25 billion in investments, including the National Episcopal Church, YWCA National Board, and Maryknoll Fathers and Brothers.[44]

Throughout the nation, concern for animals and the environment is spreading. In Berkeley, California, Ministries for Animals (formerly the International Society for Religion and Animal Rights, founded in 1985), an interreligious organization devoted to a spiritually based ethic of animal welfare, publishes *ANIMA/L* magazine, a publication containing articles, prayers, poetry, letters, reviews, and a variety of information on this subject. Headed by Joan Beth Clair, the group works with, and publishes material on, all the major religions.[45]

In Selden, New York, Christians Helping Animals and People, headed by Frances Arnetta, distributes information on similar concerns, including a brochure explaining why Christians should be concerned about animals.[46]

Scientist James Lovelock, author of the "Gaia" hypothesis that the earth is a living organism, says, "To see and feel the earth this way ...gives substance to the Christian concept of stewardship, and turns our hearts and minds towards what should be our prime environmental concern, the care and protection of the earth itself."[47]

Even in America's conservative rural heartland, this new message of environmental stewardship is being heard. On March 23, 1990, Melvin A. Schmidt, pastor of the First Mennonite Church in Bluffton, Ohio, preached a sermon that he described as "the most important single thing [I have] ever done," discussing "the overwhelming importance of the task that God has given the church to do in these closing days of the twentieth century, which may also turn out to be the closing days of the human race":

> The human being, a part of God's creation, has arrogantly usurped God's place by living in such a way that the earth is being destroyed. As part of the creation, we human beings have no more right to decide upon the earth's destruction than we had to decide upon the earth's creation.

Pastor Schmidt argues that "it is time for us to recognize that there is no hope for the survival of the human race unless and until our theology gives us a reason for saving the earth":

> I believe that the earth and the survival of the human race matter very much in the heart of God....
> When we know that the formation of this planet took billions upon billions of years, it is incredibly arrogant for the human family to use it up, burn and destroy this delightful little corner of the solar system within a few hundred years of industrial and agricultural activity.

"We are emptying the pantry that feeds us," he writes, "and we are making war on the land that sustains our lives." Finally, Pastor Schmidt concludes that if the earth is to be saved, "we need another copernican revolution ..., the totally heretical idea that God's love does not revolve around us alone, but around the entire created order."[48]

Canon Jeff Batkin, of St. John's Episcopal Cathedral in Jacksonville, Florida, agrees, saying, "We are stewards of God's creation, and we had better start paying attention to it or we're going to be cast out of the garden one more time."[49]

## Cooperation on "Caring for Creation"

Recent years have also witnessed the beginning of meaningful cooperation not just among religious groups, but also between them and conservation and animal protection organizations, to promote interest in and action on ecological concerns. Many leading conservationists and religious figures from various denominations throughout the country came together in mid-1990 to discuss ways to organize church involvement in ecological issues.

In May 1990, Dr. Donald B. Conroy, a Catholic priest and theologian who is president of the North American Conference on Religion and Ecology (NACRE), convened a meeting of hundreds of religious and environmental leaders from around the world to discuss "Caring for Creation." Based in Washington, D.C., NACRE is attempting to involve the religious community with the mainstream environmental movement. NACRE is working to persuade religious leaders and congregations to speak out on environmental issues, adopt a more environmentally oriented life-style, make their churches "centers of environmental consciousness," and "sway the American Conscience" as some religious figures did during the civil rights movement.

Reverend Charles A Perry, provost of the Washington (National) Cathedral, one of the planners and hosts of the conference, said that its purpose was "to help move the environment into a focal point for our nation's churches, temples, and mosques ... and to advance the environmental cause and place it on the agenda of our nation's religious leaders."[50]

Among those conservationists attending or addressing the conference's predominantly religious-oriented delegates were Britain's Prince Philip; Environmental Protection Agency (EPA) administrator William Reilly; scientist Carl Sagan; Worldwatch Institute president Lester Brown; World Wildlife Fund president Russell Train; and US Senator Albert Gore (D.-Tenn.), who told the gathering, "If we believe that 'The Earth is the Lord's, and the fullness thereof' (Ps. 104), and we heap contempt on the Creation, that implies a lack of faith or respect in the Deity."

One of the principal sponsors of the NACRE conference was the Humane Society of the United States (HSUS), whose president, John A. Hoyt, is a former Presbyterian minister. HSUS, America's largest animal protection organization, has established and/or affiliated itself with two important religious-oriented groups working to bring a spiritual perspective to conservation and animal issues.

One is the Center for Respect of Life and Environment in Washington, D.C., an affiliate of HSUS headed by the highly respected author, columnist, and animal expert Dr. Michael Fox, who writes of "the evil that has desacralized Earthly Creation and the natural world," resulting in a "cycle of suffering and destruction since our fall from grace and banishment from Eden":

> From the spiritual and ethical perspectives of older religious traditions, this fall is our separation from the natural world, the Earth Mother of us all, and from the Great Spirit whose original instructions we no longer follow.... We have broken the covenant to dress and to keep the Garden of Eden in all its beauty and vitality, and we now stand witness to an Earth crucified and a dying planet.... Our salvation and redemption lie in reconsecrating the Earth, in resanctifying all of creation ... by living in respect ... of all living things.[51]

In endeavoring to carry out its objectives, the Center distributes books, brochures, and educational films and programs. Among the Center's programs is its sustainable agriculture project, which seeks to halt current farming practices that cause tremendous cruelty to farm animals, massive soil erosion, depletion and contamination of ground water, and the pollution of air, water, food — and people.[52]

Another group affiliated with and supported by HSUS is the Interfaith Council for the Protection of Animals and Nature (ICPAN), which "is composed of people of various religious faiths who are interested in the preservation of God's creation; that is, the natural environment and the other creatures with which we share this planet." ICPAN promotes the thesis that "the health of the earth's ecology, and the welfare of humanity, are inextricably linked." ICPAN distributes various greeting cards and educational materials, including a booklet on the ecological theme of the Bible, "Replenish the Earth: The Bible's Message of Conservation and Kindness to Animals."[53]

HSUS and its affiliates distribute a variety of information and material on animals, ecology, and religion, including an "action packet" telling individuals, organizations, and congregations how they can get involved and be effective. The kit can be obtained from HSUS at 2100 L Street N.W., Washington, DC 20037.

The International Network for Religion and Animals (INRA) in Silver Spring, Maryland, founded in 1985 by Virginia Bourquardez, carries out a variety of interfaith educational and religious activities. Its programs are designed to "bring religious principles to bear upon humanity's attitude toward the treatment of our animal kin ... and, through leadership, materials, and programs, to successfully interact with clergy and laity from many religious traditions." INRA's executive director, United Church of Christ Reverend Dr. Marc A. Wessels, recently wrote in the group's semiannual newsletter:

> As a Christian clergyman who speaks of having compassion for other creatures and who actively declares the need for humans to develop an ethic that gives reverence for all of life, I hope that others will open their eyes, hearts and minds to the responsibility of loving care for God's creatures.[54]

Much of the cooperation between the religious and environmental communities has been coordinated by the highly respected environmentalist Jan Hartke, who served as National Religious Liaison for Earth Day 1990 and is now a vice president of the Humane Society of the United States. As director of the Global Tomorrow Coalition, a consortium of major conservation groups representing over eight million Americans, Hartke was a keynote speaker at the first North American Conference on Religion and Ecology. Hartke says that "since that time, I have been amazed at the speed with which the churches and synagogues have developed the connective themes and stewardship, ecological justice, and caring for creation. . . . The meteoric rise in interest that I have witnessed has been astonishing."[55]

## Can the Churches Save Our Planet?

Indeed, church involvement in ecological problems is burgeoning. On November 27, 1989, *U.S. News and World Report* magazine published a major article entitled "The Greening of the Church: The Clergy Are Beginning to View Ecological Concerns as Central to Their Mission." This was also the theme of a February 28, 1990, *USA Today* article headlined "Worshippers Join Fight to Save the Earth": "In the USA's churches and synagogues, people with their minds on heaven are increasingly worried about Earth. In the pulpits and pews, seminaries, and denominational headquarters, clergy and laity are mobilizing to protect the environment."

The importance of the church's role can hardly be exaggerated. A Gallup poll shows that 40 percent of Americans, some 100 million people, attend church or synagogue. This means that, with the nation's 350,000 congregations (mostly Protestant) having access to four in ten Americans on an average weekend, organized religion has enormous potential to influence people's behavior and beliefs.[56] And virtually all American Christian denominations have called upon their adherents to work to preserve the natural environment. How strongly this message is emphasized remains to be seen.

Worldwide, there are an estimated 1.75 billion Christians (as of early 1990), a third of the world's population, including 963 million Roman Catholics, 324 million Protestants, 180 million Eastern Orthodox, and 54 million Anglicans.[57] Thus, if the world's Christians undertook a serious effort to adopt and promote stewardship principles, the impact could be tremendous.

Les Ann Kirkland, who organizes people to fight pollution in Plaquemine, Louisiana, says: "The Church may be the only institution that can save the earth from destruction, and it needs to wake up to this fact.... The Churches must get involved.... People are dying. The world is dying, and all Christians are called to take action as earthly stewards."[58]

Father Albert Fritsch, S.J., a Jesuit priest who helped organize the above-mentioned North American conference and is author of *Environmental Ethics,* has also spoken of the urgency of the situation: "The time is short; the matter has the utmost urgency. Our earth is suffering enormous stresses.... We must announce to the world that it is imperative that we act to save the earth and its inhabitants. We may not have another chance."[59]

# The Religious Basis for Vegetarianism

Through the ages, many theologians have argued that people who love animals should not eat them. Indeed, such proponents of vegetarianism are able to muster impressive scriptural support for such views, in addition to the enormous health, humane, and environmental benefits that accrue from such a diet.

There is a strong tradition of vegetarianism among many of the great religions of the world, which are discussed elsewhere in this book. But this chapter will focus on the vegetarian heritage of the Christian faith.

## The Biblical Evidence

In the beginning, before the Fall, all the creatures of the earth were vegetarians. In Genesis 1:29–30, the Lord says,

> Behold, I have given you every herb yielding seed, which is upon the face of the earth, and every tree . . . to you it shall be food; and to every beast of the earth, and to every fowl of the air, and to every thing that creepeth upon the earth, wherein there is a living soul, [I have given] every green herb for food.

Genesis 3:18–19 tells us that after Adam and Eve were expelled from the Garden of Eden, their diet was expanded from fruit, nuts, and grains to include whole plants and bread: "and thou shalt eat the herb of the field. In the sweat of thy face shalt thou eat bread, till thou return unto the ground." It was only after the Great Flood, when the world's vegetation was largely destroyed, that humans were given permission to consume animals, and some theologians argue that this was only a temporary expedient.

The Mosaic law contains harsh prohibitions against eating certain portions of flesh which, if strictly observed, would effectively ban the consumption of meat. Leviticus 3:17 states unequivocally, "It shall be a perpetual statute throughout your generations in all your dwelling, that ye shall eat neither fat nor blood." Leviticus 7:22–27 is even more explicit and unyielding in banning the eating of such flesh; there, the Lord tells Moses to instruct the Israelites: "And ye shall eat no manner of blood, whether it be fowl or of beast in any of your dwellings. Whosoever it be that eat any blood, that soul shall be cut off from his people." Although blood can be mostly drained from the major arteries of an animal, it cannot be removed from the capillaries, as is obvious from a "rare" piece of steak or roast beef. Thus, the prohibition against consuming blood, if followed strictly, would prohibit the eating of flesh entirely.

The best-known apparent vegetarian in the Bible is Daniel, who refused to "defile" himself with the king's food. As the first chapter of the book of Daniel tells us, Daniel and his three friends, who followed a vegetarian diet of "pulse" (i.e., peas, beans, lentils, porridge, and cereals), ended up much healthier than the other youths that ate King Nebuchadnezzar's food and ten times smarter than the "magicians and enchanters" in the land:

> Their countenances appeared fairer, and they were fatter in flesh. . . . God gave them knowledge and skill in all learning and wisdom. . . . And in all matters of wisdom and understanding, that the king inquired of them, he found them ten times better than all the magicians and enchanters that were in all his realm.

The Book of Isaiah contains numerous passages condemning meat-eating and prophesying a day when people and animals will adopt a vegetarian diet, including his vision of the time when "the wolf shall dwell with the lamb, and the leopard shall lie down with the kid" (11:9, 65:25). In 66:3, Isaiah even equates the killing of animals with murder, saying that "he that killeth an ox is as if he slew a man."

The Books of Amos, Jeremiah, Psalms, and Proverbs also contain numerous passages that appear to condemn meat-eating and to advocate a vegetarian diet.[1]

One of the most intriguing aspects of the New Testament is the question of whether Jesus and some of his followers were vegetarians. While the evidence is ambiguous, the proponents of this theory do not lack data that can be cited in support of it. In the Book of Isaiah, which contains passages prophesying the coming of the Messiah, there is a suggestion that he will be a vegetarian: "Behold a virgin shall conceive and bear a son. . . . Butter and honey shall he eat, that he may know to refuse the evil, and choose the good." Nowhere in the New Testament is Jesus depicted as eating meat or flesh of any kind (although on two occasions after his death and resurrection he is said to have eaten fish). If the Last Supper was a Passover meal — as many believe — there is, interestingly, no mention of the traditional lamb dish. The question of whether or not Jesus was a vegetarian is a topic of much discussion and debate; it is discussed later in this chapter (see pp. 180–182).

At the time of Jesus, and during the first century of the Christian era, abstention from meat-eating was widely practiced by various Jewish and Christian sects. Among these were the Essenes, an ascetic Jewish sect that lived near the Dead Sea and had many communities in Israel, including Jesus' home town of Nazareth, in the province of lower Galilee. There was also the Gnostics, an early Christian sect, and the Nazarenes, originally a pre-Christian sect of Syrian Jews. The term came to refer to Christians of Jewish origin who retained many of the traditional Jewish practices, and still later to all Christians.[2]

Many early Christian leaders were vegetarians and advocated kindness to animals, including the church fathers Tertullian (160?–230?), the Latin ecclesiastical writer; the Greek theologian Clement of Alexandria (150 or 160?–220 or 240?); and St. John Chrysostom (345?–407), the Greek church father who became bishop (patriarch) of Constantinople in 398.[3]

Clement has written, "It is far better to be happy than to have your bodies act as graveyards for animals. Accordingly, the apostle Matthew partook of seeds, nuts and vegetables, without flesh."[4] One of the earliest Christian documents is the *Clementine Homilies*, a second-century work purportedly based on the teachings of St. Peter. Homily XII states, "The unnatural eating of flesh meats is as polluting as the heathen worship of devils, with its sacrifices and its impure feasts, through participation in which a man becomes a fellow eater with devils."[5]

St. Jerome (340?–420), one of the four doctors of the church and the translator of the Greek Bible into a Latin version called the Vulgate, advocated a meat-free diet, although he himself does not appear to have completely followed his own advice. He once wrote that he was not a follower of Pythagoras and Empedocles "who do not eat any living creature," but ended by commenting, "And so I too say to you: if you wish to be perfect, it is good not to drink wine and eat flesh."[6]

### Returning to Meat-Eating

In later years, the Christian church gradually abandoned its vegetarian roots; one account of this process is described by writer Steven Rosen in his book *Food for the Spirit*:

> The early Christian fathers adhered to a meatless regimen ... [and] many early Christian groups supported the meatless way of life. In fact, the writings of the early Church indicate that meat eating was not officially

allowed until the fourth century, when the Emperor Constantine decided that his version of Christianity would be the version for everyone. A meat eating interpretation of the Bible became the official creed of the Roman Empire, and vegetarian Christians had to practice in secret or risk being put to death for heresy. It is said that Constantine used to pour molten lead down their throats if they were captured.[7]

Other vegetarian martyrs included members of the Albigensian sect — a Catharist religious group in southern France in the twelfth and thirteenth centuries. As related by Dudley Giehl in *Vegetarianism as a Way of Life*, a group of them was put to death by hanging in 1052 in Goslar, France, because they refused to kill a chicken. A thirteenth-century document instructed members of the sect on dietary obligations accordingly: "Moreover, you will make this commitment to God: that you will never, knowingly or of your own will, eat cheese, milk, the flesh of birds, or creeping things, or of animals prohibited by the Church of God."[8]

And some prominent religious leaders have kept the vegetarian tradition alive in Christianity. One of the most prominent theologians of eighteenth-century England, William Paley (1743–1805), believed that killing animals for food could not be justified. Paley, who held the posts of archdeacon of Carlisle and subdean of Lincoln, is perhaps best known for his lectures that were published in 1785, *The Principles of Moral and Political Philosophy*, which were used as the ethical textbook at Cambridge University. In this work, Paley called the excuses so often used for killing animals "extremely lame" and refuted these rationalizations, especially those involving fishing.[9]

Reverend Basil Wrighton, chairman of the Catholic Study Circle for Animal Welfare in London, wrote in 1965 that a vegetarian diet is consistent with, and in fact required by, the tenets of Christianity. He concludes that the killing of animals for food, in addition to violating religious precepts, brutalizes humans to such an extent that warfare and violence against other humans become inevitable.[10]

As late as 1966, the Roman Catholic Church required Catholics to observe certain fast days and to abstain from meat on Fridays, in commemoration of Jesus' crucifixion. But in that year, the U.S. Catholic Conference restricted meatless Fridays just to the season of Lent.[11]

## Christian Vegetarians in America

The vegetarian movement in America was spearheaded by Christian clergymen, including Reverend William Metcalfe (1788–1862), a leader of the Bible Christian Church and author of *Bible Testimony on Abstinence from the Flesh of Animals as Food*. Metcalfe and his Bible Christians became the core of the vegetarian movement in America, teaching that the Bible forbids the eating of flesh. Metcalfe was the presiding officer at the founding in America of the Vegetarian Society in New York City in 1850, and its first meeting attracted such influential adherents as journalist Horace Greeley and women suffragettes Susan B. Anthony and Amelia Bloomer.

One of Metcalfe's converts was Sylvester Graham (1794–1851), a Presbyterian minister who originated Graham Crackers. He regained his health through a vegetarian diet and became an advocate of using unrefined, whole-wheat "Graham" flour from which Graham Crackers were made. In 1876, a vegetarian facility, the Battle Creek (Michigan) Sanitarium was founded by Dr. John Harvey Kellogg (1852–1943) under the sponsorship of the Seventh-Day Adventists. It was here that the health and breakfast food industries originated. Another Christian vegetarian was General William Booth (1829–1912), the Methodist preacher and independent revivalist who founded the Salvation Army.[12]

Today, several religious groups in the United States advocate and/or practice vegetarianism to one degree or another, including the Trappist monks, Seventh-Day Adventists, the Shakers, and the Rosicrucian Fellowship. There is a strong tradition of abstaining from meat in the Mormon Church and among Christian Scientists.

Concerning the latter, it is the tradition of kindness to animals and the emphasis on good health that have led many Christian Scientists to adopt a meatless diet. The basic doctrines of the Church of Christ, Scientist are set forth in *Science and Health with Key to the Scriptures*, by Mary Baker Eddy, the founder of the religion. In her analysis of Genesis and the creation, she refers to Isaiah's vision of the Millennium (11:6, "the wolf also shall dwell with the lamb"), and writes that "tenderness accompanies all the might imparted by Spirit. The individuality created by God is not carnivorous."[13]

Today, an increasing number of Christians are giving up meat, as they come to realize the enormous cruelty to animals and damage to the environment and human health that is caused by a meat-centered diet.

Father Thomas Berry, a Catholic priest, writer, and founder of the Riverdale Center of Religious Research in New York, says that "vegetarianism is a way of life that we should all move toward for economic survival, physical well-being, and spiritual integrity."[14]

## Was Jesus a Vegetarian?

The historical debate over Jesus' humane teachings and vegetarian ideals apparently goes back centuries, to the very beginning of Christianity. As summarized by author Keith Akers in *A Vegetarian Sourcebook*:

> Historians have identified the vegetarian faction in early Christianity....
> They were the Ebionites, or the Jewish Christians. The Ebionites required
> abstinence from meat, maintained their loyalty to Moses, and tried to be
> both good Jews and good Christians. They had their own version of the
> Gospel, which is now largely lost to us except in fragments.... The earliest
> Jewish Christians were vegetarian, and it is quite likely that vegetarianism
> was a primary tenet of the Christian Community immediately after the
> death of Jesus. If it is at all meaningful to speak of a historical Jesus, then
> it is quite probably that Jesus himself was a vegetarian.[15]

The Edenite Society in Imlaystown, New Jersey, a Christian vegetarian group, publishes and distributes a number of books and brochures promoting a humane philosophy and life-style based on scriptural evidence. The group's main thesis, discussed and documented at length in its literature, is that numerous passages in the original New Testament have been changed, added, or removed to make it consistent with the beliefs and desires of certain editors or "correctors" appointed by the ecclesiastical authorities.

At first, say the Edenites, the original Essene texts of early humane Christianity, written in Hebrew, were hellenized and translated into Greek, with many changes being made in the process. Then the Greek text itself was substantially altered.

It is a historical fact that, in the summer of 325 C.E., the Emperor of the Holy Roman Empire, Constantine I, or Constantine the Great (280?–337), convened a meeting of several hundred bishops at Nicaea, across the Bosphorus straits from Constantinople, to take control of, and settle arguments within, the Catholic Church. [16] The Edenites cite several religious scholars to assert that at this council, the original Christian Bible was significantly altered to change or delete Jesus' humane teachings on animals. For example, the Edenites contend that references to Jesus and his followers as vegetarians and as having condemned meat-eating were deleted in order to attract more people to Christianity, and to appease pagan converts and the appetite of Constantine and the bishops for meat.

Among the books published by the Edenites is *Jesus Was a Vegetarian — Why Aren't You?* and *The Humane Gospel of Jesus,*[17] the latter being a translation of what is purported to be the original gospels as preserved by the Essenes. The work describes Jesus and the community in which he was raised (as recounted in the Dead Sea Scrolls) as loving birds and animals and practicing a humane life-style and vegetarian diet. Jesus is portrayed as teaching kindness to animals and condemning hunting, the eating of fish and meat, and other cruelties to various creatures.

The Edenites describe at great length how the Dead Sea Scrolls "conclusively prove" that the Essenes schooled Jesus and John the Baptist, originally recorded the gospel of the apostles in Hebrew, and, as the earliest of Jesus' Jewish followers, adhered to a humane life-style.

Obviously, the Edenites' provocative thesis can neither be conclusively proved nor refuted, but there is no question that vegetarian and humane ideals motivated many Jews and Christians at the time of Jesus, just as they do so today.

## The Moral Benefits of Vegetarianism

In the final analysis, there are compelling moral and spiritual reasons, apart from scriptural ones, to abstain from meat.

The raising, transporting, and slaughtering of food animals entails enormous mistreatment and suffering of literally billions of creatures each year, in addition to the massive damage to the environment. Indeed, raising livestock is more destructive in depleting topsoil, groundwater, and energy resources than all other human activities *combined*, as well as causing enormous environmental damage such as clearing of forests, destruction of wildlife habitat, and pollution of rivers and lakes. And the consumption of meat and dairy products, especially red meat and whole fat products high in saturated fat and cholesterol, is linked to high rates of cancer, heart disease, strokes, and other potentially fatal health disorders.[18] (The best and most comprehensive recent book on this subject is John Robbins's *Diet for a New America*.)

Therefore, refraining from eating meat helps prevent cruelty to animals and promotes protection of the environment and the health of one's body, "the temple of the Lord." For all these reasons, a vegetarian diet is one good way of maintaining a life-style consistent with the humane and ecological spirit of the Scriptures.

# Chapter 11

# Judaism:
# The Jewish Tradition
# of Kindness

The teachings and laws of Judaism strongly emphasize kindness to animals and reverence for nature. This humane attitude is exemplified by a Hebrew proverb that holds that "the kind man first feeds his beasts before sitting down to the table," and by a rabbinical law that ordains, "A good man does not sell his beast to a cruel person." According to the *Encyclopedia Judaica*,

> Moral and legal rules concerning the treatment of animals are based on the principle that animals are part of God's creation towards which man bears responsibility. Laws . . . make it clear not only that cruelty to animals is forbidden but also that compassion and mercy to them are demanded of man by God. . . . In later rabbinic literature, . . . great prominence is also given to demonstrating God's mercy to animals, and to the importance of not causing them pain.[1]

This dictionary sums up the rabbinical law by saying, "The principle of kindness to animals . . . is as though God's treatment of man will be according to [man's] treatment of animals." And the *Universal Jewish Encyclopedia* observes:

> The Jewish attitude toward animals has always been governed by the consideration that they, too, are God's creatures . . . [and] the obligation to respect and consider the feelings and needs of these lower creatures. . . . The non-canonical . . . writings strongly urge kindness toward animals, declaring that one who harms an animal harms his own soul.[2]

Indeed, kindness to animals has become the basis of a whole code of laws in Judaism, whose importance is exemplified by the tenet that "to relieve an animal of pain or danger is a Biblical law, superseding a Rabbinic ordinance (the Sabbath Observance)."[3]

These obligations are embodied in the Hebrew concept known as *tsa'ar ba'alei hayim* — the commandment to prevent the "sorrow of living creatures," or "the suffering of animals." In fact, an entire section devoted to this concept appears in the Talmud, the collection of rules and doctrines that form the basis of Jewish law.

The Talmud stresses the obligations humans have to animals, saying: "As the Holy One, blessed be He, has compassion upon man, so has He compassion upon the beasts of the field. . . . And for the birds of the air."[4] As put by Dr. Richard Schwartz, associate professor at the College of Staten Island and author of *Judaism and Vegetarianism*, "In Judaism, one who does not treat animals with compassion cannot be regarded as a righteous individual."[5] Respect and veneration for the land, for trees, and for nature in general are fundamental tenets of Judaism, and various ordinances forbid abuse and pollution of the environment.

### Jewish Law Requires Humaneness

Jewish law is remarkably strict in its requirement that animals be treated properly. The *Code of Jewish Law* clearly states that "it is forbidden, according to the law of the Torah, to inflict pain upon any living creature. On the contrary, it is our duty to relieve the pain of any creature, even if it is ownerless or belongs to a non-Jew."[6]

The medieval Hebrew work *Sefer Chasidim* (or *Sefer Hasidim, The Book of the Pious*) reflects the traditional Jewish attitude of humane regard and compassion for animals: "Be kind and compassionate to all creatures that the Holy One, blessed be He, created in this world. Never beat nor inflict pain on any animal, beast, bird, or insect. Do not throw stones at a dog or a cat, nor kill flies or wasps."[7]

Concerning the Lord's giving people "dominion" over the animals (Gen. 1:28), Jewish scholars say that this should be interpreted as stewardship, wherein humans are obliged to show concern for what has been left in their care. As explained by Rabbi Abraham Isaac ha-Kohen Kook, the first rabbi of pre-statehood Israel:

> There can be no doubt in the minds of every thinking man that the concept of dominion as expressed in the Torah does not in any way imply the rule of a haughty despot who tyrannically governs his people and his servants for his own personal selfish ends and with a stubborn heart. Heaven forfend that such a repulsive form of servitude be forever integrated (sealed) in the world of the Lord, whose tender mercies are on all His works and of whom it is said, "He shall build a world of kindness."[8]

The renowned Jewish rabbi, physician, philosopher, and scholar Maimonides (Rabbi Moses ben Maimon, also known as Rambam, 1135–

1204) emphatically taught kindness to animals. Considered the greatest of all rabbinic scholars and authorities on Jewish law, Maimonides served as court physician to Saladin, the sultan of Egypt, and as rabbi of Cairo. In his famous book, *Guide for the Perplexed,"* he wrote, "There is no difference between the worry of a human mother and an animal mother for their offspring. A mother's love does not derive from the intellect but from the emotions, in animals just as in humans."[9] He also believed that animals must enjoy some form of eternal life in the hereafter to make up for their suffering on earth.[10]

Judaism's classic approach to animals and nature has been summarized by Dr. Jacob S. Raisin in *Popular Studies in Judaism:*

> In Judaism, man owes certain duties not only to God and his fellow men, but also to his fellow animals. Kindness to animals is with the Jews no mere sentimentality; like charity, it is part and parcel of justice, of righteousness, of piety. They advocate it as a religious injunction to be obeyed not for the sake of economic or material benefits. They feel that sympathy with the weak and dependent of any species reflects back, and promotes . . . peace and happiness among human species. Above all, they believe that the best service one could render Him is in being kind to His handiwork.[11]

## Conservation and Respect for Nature

Appreciation for the sanctity of nature has always been an important part of the Jewish tradition. The sixteenth-century philosopher Elijah de Vidas wrote in *Beginning of Wisdom,* "Of all the ways of awakening inner reverence in man, the best is the contemplation of the works of God. Their transcendent greatness must inspire awe."[12]

A 1923 book of prayers, *Blessings & Praise,* says that "both the mighty universe above him, and humble nature below him, speak into man's heart. He must hearken to both voices. From the eternal stars, let him learn patience and reverence for God's greatness. From the world beneath his feet, let him learn kindness and love."[13] The book offers a prayer that we may learn from nature: "Teach us how to reverence thy greatness, and unto those who reverence us, how to be merciful, how to stand unafraid amidst all thy wonders, and, learning from thy tenderness, how to be gentle to all thy creatures. May the heavens declare unto us thy glory."[14]

There are even special blessings that are to be recited when one beholds the beauty of lofty mountains, beautiful animals or birds, trees blossoming in spring, rainbows, and shooting stars. The Talmud requires that when devout Jews see a lovely animal, they must recite the special blessing, "Blessed art thou, O Lord our God, King of the Universe, who created beautiful animals in his world" (Berachot 9). And before tasting fruit, Jews recite a prayer called the B'racha, "Blessed art thou, O Lord our God, Ruler of the Universe, who creates the fruit of the tree." A similar blessing for the "fruit of the vines" is recited on holidays before sipping sacramental wine.[15]

The authoritative Jewish commentary on the Bible setting forth ethical values, known as the Midrash, even says that appreciation for the environment is required if one is to lead a full and good life: "A wicked man while alive is thought of as dead because he sees the sun shine and does not say the blessing, 'who creates light,' the sun sets and he does not recite the blessing, 'who brings night.' "[16]

As Dr. David Geffen of Jerusalem writes in the *Atlanta Jewish Times:*

> The concept known as *bal tashchit* — "Do not destroy" — has a special significance in Jewish tradition. . . . We are constantly being warned in our faith that the capricious, thoughtless, wasteful destruction of the elements and creatures of the earth is wrong. "Do not destroy" has been the watchword down through the centuries to prevent the misuse of our natural treasures. These and all other ingredients of nature were considered essential for life itself. Therefore, each individual Jew was responsible for them and had to protect them. We should remind ourself daily of our responsibility to all aspects of creation. May we show care and concern for the beauty of nature about us. . . . Then and only then will we have truly understood God's command to us — to guard the world and all it contains.[17]

Dr. Geffen points out that ancient Jewish law prohibited the artificial diversion of the normal flow of a river. This contrasts with our modern-day practice of damming up rivers and gouging out stream beds to "channelize" them for agricultural purposes, thereby destroying many natural areas.

Early Jewish law also prevented pollution of waterways by mandating that sewage be buried in the ground, not dumped into rivers. In ancient Jerusalem, dung heaps and garbage piles were banned, and refuse could not be disposed of near water systems.[18] The Israelites wisely protected their drinking water supply and avoided creating hazardous and unhealthy waste dumps, lessons our modern, polluted civilization would have done well to heed. The Book of Deuteronomy (23:13–15) even requires that armies waging war abroad properly dispose of their human waste by burial.

The rabbis of old Jerusalem also dealt with the problem of air pollution from wheat chaff by requiring that threshing houses for grain be built no closer than two miles from the city. In order to prevent foul odors, a similar ordinance existed for graves, carrion, and tanneries, with tanneries sometimes being required to be constructed on the edge of the city downwind from prevailing air currents.[19]

Garbage was not allowed to be dumped within the city, to avoid attracting vermin; and kilns and furnaces were banned within the city limits to prevent fumes and smoke from polluting the air, soil, and buildings. Wood from certain types of rare trees could not be burned at all, and the Talmud cautioned that lamps should be set to burn slowly so as not to use up too much naphtha. The biblical injunction to allow land to lie fallow every seven years (Lev. 25:3–7), of course, permitted the soil to replenish itself.

Trees are accorded special, revered status under Jewish law, which is exemplified by Psalm 92:12–15:

The righteous shall flourish like the Palm tree; he shall grow like a cedar in Lebanon. Those that be planted in the house of the Lord shall flourish in the courts of our God.

They shall still bring forth fruit in old age; they shall be full of sap and richness; to declare that the Lord is upright. . . .

One important source of rabbinic teachings — the Koheleth Rabbah — tells how the Lord instructed Adam to care for trees:

At the time that the Holy One, Blessed Be He, created the first man, He took him and had him pass before all the trees of the Garden of Eden, and said to him: See my works, how fine and excellent they are! Now all that I created was created for you. Think about this and do not harm or desolate the world: for if you harm it, there will be none to fix it after you."[20]

Saplings are still planted in the countryside to celebrate the New Year of the Trees, *Tu B'Sh'vat* (or *Rosh Hashana La Elanot*). This festival falls on the full moon of the month of *Sh'vat*, corresponding roughly with February. It was first celebrated in the sixteenth century, when Jewish mystics known as the Kabbalists of Safed observed the holiday with a joyous ceremony to honor all of nature.[21]

Commenting on the prohibition against killing or cutting down fruit trees when besieging a city, found in Deuteronomy 20:19–20, the Zohar — a book of mystical interpretations of the Torah — states that "if you cut down a tree before its time, it is as if you have destroyed a living soul." The great Jewish scholar Maimonides interpreted this verse of Deuteronomy to mean that in besieging the city of an enemy, one could not divert the waters of a river to prevent it from reaching the trees of a city, since this would result in their dying.[22]

Rabbi Barry Freundel of Washington, D.C., writes that this injunction shows that "clearly ecological concerns are well rooted in Jewish tradition":

Wanton environmental destruction is certainly prohibited for anyone if it is prohibited for soldiers under the pressure of war and battle. . . .

R. Nachman of Bratslav . . . declared as tantamount to murder the act of cutting down a tree for no appropriate purpose. . . .

Just as Adam was put in the Garden of Eden "*L'avdah Uleshomrah*" — "to work it and watch over it," so too we are required to watch over, preserve, and protect God's world.[23]

As part of the Interfaith Coalition on Energy, the Union of American Hebrew Congregations (Reform) issued a statement endorsing conservation: "The principles of our Jewish tradition stress mankind's responsibility to care for God's earth and to safeguard its resources, thus fulfilling our trust to generations yet unborn. We concur that a central priority of our national energy policy must be conservation."[24]

In September 1986, Rabbi Arthur Hertzberg, vice president of the World Jewish Congress, described how "these teachings of concern for all living beings and, indeed, for all of nature, for the whole of the environment" give humans certain obligations:

The rebirth of nature, day after day, is God's gift, but humanity is the custodian of this capacity of the earth to renew itself. As we consume any one of the products of divine bounty, we must first say the appropriate grace. The world is His, and we are but sojourners. At very least, we must leave the palace of our Host no worse than we found it.

Speaking for Judaism at the World Wildlife Conference on religion and nature, held in Assisi, Italy, Rabbi Hertzberg observed that our own future may depend on our treatment of the environment:

All humanity are our brothers and sisters. All animals are in this world because God willed them, as He willed us. He is the architect and builder of the universe, of all living forms on this planet. He promised Noah after the Flood that he would never destroy this world again — but we can. We keep turning forest into desert, by despoiling nature for our immediate advantage. We do not really think of the consequences for our children and grandchildren.

The destructive capacity of humankind has thus grown to diabolical proportions in our own century. Let us resolve together, this day, that we will work to make our love and compassion exceed, and master, our naked power. Then, "the earth will be full of the knowledge of the Lord, as the waters cover the sea." (Isaiah 11:9)[25]

## The Writings of the Talmud

The strict rules requiring kindness to animals and respect for nature are elaborately enunciated in the systemized collection of ancient laws, doctrines, and rabbinic writings of Judaism known as the Talmud. These doctrines constitute the basis of religious authority for traditional Judaism and are considered to be of supreme importance.

As Dr. Joseph Herman Hertz (1872–1946), the late chief rabbi of the British Empire, points out, "In the Talmud, kindness to animals becomes the basis of a whole code of laws."[26] What makes this humane orientation even more significant are the times in which it was written; as biblical commentator Joseph Morris (1848–1930) observes, "This sympathy for the dumb animals is all the more remarkable because the terrible scenes in the Roman arena are only too clear an indication of the inhumanity which prevailed in the civilized world during the Talmudic period."[27]

The Talmud states that Moses and David, two of the greatest leaders of the Jewish people, were able to become the heads of the Israelites only after proving themselves as shepherds (Baba Mezia 85a).

The Talmud even shows the wisdom to appreciate the lowliest, most obscure of creatures, many of which are largely considered pests: "Thou thinkest that flies, fleas, mosquitoes are superfluous, but they have their purpose in creation as a means of a final outcome. . . . Of all that the Holy One, Blessed be He, created in His world, He did not create a single thing without purpose" (Shabbat 77b).[28]

(Indeed, we now know that insects play an important and necessary role in nature's balance, by among other things providing food for birds, fish, reptiles, and amphibians. Probably 95 percent of the insects are harmless or even beneficial to humans, such as predatory insects who kill and eat the "pest" species. And without insects such as bees and butterflies to pollinate our crops and flowers, our world would have drastically less food and beauty.)

One passage from the Talmud declares that if human beings had not been taught the laws of propriety, they might have learned them from the animals: honesty from the ant, which does not steal the stores of other ants; decency from the cat, which covers its excrement; manners from the cock, which courts the hen by promises and duly apologizes when he is not able to fulfill them; cheerfulness from the grasshopper, which sings although it knows it is fated to die; piety from the stork, which guards the purity of its family and is kind to its fellows; and chastity from the dove (Eruvin 100b).[29] Another passage interprets the cry of each animal as representing all of them being engaged in a constant song of praise to God.[30]

Rabbi Arthur Hertzberg has summarized these teachings as follows:

"Whoever is merciful to all creatures is a descendant of our ancestor Abraham" (Bezoh 32b). In the sacred writings of Judaism, Jews are described over and over again as "merciful people, the children of merciful people" (Yebamot 79a, Shabbat 133b). The Talmud even tells us (Shabbat 151b) that heaven rewards the person who has concern and compassion for the rest of creation, but this assurance of reward is not the major moral thrust of Jewish teaching. Our tradition emphasizes that Jews are commanded to do what is moral, "not for the sake of receiving a reward" (Abot 1:3). The good is necessary even when it does not redound to our immediate, personal benefit.[31]

Indeed, the Talmud states that the first of three qualities distinguishing the Jewish people is compassion (Yebamot, 79a), and nowhere is this restricted just to humans.[32]

### Biblical Obligations of Kindness

The devout Jews' obligation to treat animals kindly is dealt with at length by Dr. J. H. Hertz, who as the chief rabbi of the British Empire edited a definitive commentary on the holy scriptures, *The Pentateuch and Haftorahs*. This book is considered an authoritative interpretation of the doctrines of Judaism, and it clearly spells out the obligations humans have to protect animals and the environment.

Commenting on God's promise to preserve Noah (see p. 24) and all that were with him in the ark (Gen. 8:1–5), this book states that "The animals are expressly included in the kindly thought of God."[33]

On the story of Rebekah at the well (Gen. 24:14; see p. 23), where she suggested giving water to the camels of Eliezer, it is noted: "Her doing so would be evidence of a tender heart. Kindness to animals is a virtue upon which Judaism lays stress."[34]

On the fourth commandment's including cattle in the rest required on the Sabbath (Exod. 20:10), the commentary notes: "It is one of the glories of Judaism that, thousands of years before anyone else, it so fully recognized our duties to the dumb friends and helpers of man."[35]

In Leviticus 25:3–7, the Lord commands Moses not to farm the land every seventh year, but to rest it and leave what grows for, among others, the cattle and wild animals. Apart from being good conservation and farming practice to allow the land to replenish itself, this also provided for the animals, as this commentary observes: "The Divine promise in this verse is in accordance with the uniformly tender regard for animals throughout Scripture. They were part of God's creation, and as such were comprehended in His pity and love."[36]

Concerning the story of Balaam's whipping his ass (Num. 22; see p. 36), when the angel of the Lord says to him, "Wherefore hast thou smitten thine ass these three times?" (vs. 32), the commentary states:

> This verse is a classical text for the preaching of humane treatment of animals. "There is a rule laid down by our Sages, that it is directly prohibited in the Torah to cause pain to an animal, and that rule is based on the words 'Wherefore hast thou smitten thine ass?' " (Maimonides).

The book goes on to explain that in saying "I have sinned" (vs. 34), Balaam was referring to his "cruelly beating the animal." Balaam knew that divine punishment could be averted only by penitence ... (Midrash)."[37]

## Caring for Domestic Animals

Jewish law requires that close attention be paid to the needs of pets and livestock. It is even ordained in the Talmud that a person must provide for his animals *before* he eats or drinks (Gitten 64). This is based partly on Deuteronomy 11:13–15, in which the Lord promises the Israelites that if they "hearken diligently unto my commandments, ... I will give grass in thy fields for thy cattle, and thou shalt eat and be satisfied." This duty to give nourishment to an animal first is so important that a rabbinic commandment may be interrupted to determine if this has been fulfilled (Orach Chayim 167:6; Talmud, Berachot 40a).[38] According to Rabbi Arthur Hertzberg, "This is no casual statement: it was pronounced as binding law by the greatest rabbinic authority of later centuries, Maimonides" (Yad ha-Hazakah; Avadim 9:8).[39]

The Talmud also states that one should not have an animal unless one can properly feed and care for it (Yerushalmi Keturot 4:8, 29a; Yevanot 15). Another Hebrew teaching is that "a good man does not sell his beast to a cruel person" (*Sefer Hassidim* 13c, #142, p. 64).[40]

The medieval rabbis spoke repeatedly of one's obligation to provide homeless animals with food and shelter, and of the wickedness of overloading beasts of burden and tormenting dogs, cats, or horses.[41] Rabbinical literature also says that one should not live in a city where the bark of a dog is not heard, or the neighing of a horse, perhaps on the theory that people who will not tolerate animals would not make good neighbors.[42] It is also forbidden to live in a town which has no garden or greenery (Kiddushin 4:12).[43]

Jews are even required to help animals that do not belong to them, including those of an enemy. This duty to prevent the suffering of an animal is based directly on the biblical text, and so carries the authority of the Torah (Bava Metzia 32b). For example, Exodus 23:5 commands that "if thou see the ass of him that hateth thee lying under its burden, you shall help him lift it up." According to Rabbi Solomon Ganzfried in *The Code of Jewish Law* (vol. 4, chap. 191),

> When horses, drawing a cart, come to a rough road or a steep hill, and it is hard for them to draw the cart without help, it is our duty to help them, even when they belong to a non-Jew, because of the precept not to be cruel to animals, lest the owner smite them to force them to draw more than their strength permits.[44]

So very important is the requirement to help animals in distress that it overrides the ordinances prohibiting work on the Sabbath (Shabbat 128b).

The twelfth-century work the *Sefer Hasidim* warns against the use of spurs on horses, which cause pain and injuries to the animals. Even though horses were then the only means of transportation, Rabbi Yehuda the Chassid (the "pious") forbade Jews who rode horses from using spurs.[45]

According to Rabbi Arthur Hertzberg, kind treatment of animals may help ensure the welfare of human society:

> The essential thrust of these teachings is that animals, even the most powerful among them, are ultimately helpless before people. We rule their kingdom, as God rules ours. The way that we exercise our power over the rest of God's creatures, over those who ultimately cannot defend themselves against us, must be the way of love and compassion. If it is not, then we ourselves have made the choice that the strong can do what they like to other living beings — and to each other. If such policies prevail, the world will soon be destroyed — by us.[46]

### Blood Sports Condemned

Jewish law strongly disapproves of blood sports involving animals. Bullfighting is specifically condemned: "Whoever sits in a stadium (as a spectator) spills blood" (Avodah Zarah 1). This injunction originates from the days of the Roman Empire, when the masses were entertained by gladiatorial contests in which men and animals fought to the death. The Talmudic sages did not differentiate between the human and animal victims, but forbade attendance at *all* such contests. Later, Jewish law condemned all games using animals, which would today apply to cockfights and dogfights.[47]

Hunting is also strongly disapproved of. Maimonides vehemently condemned hunting and wrote that "those who go to hunt [animals] and kill birds . . . violate the commandment that forbids us to wantonly destroy" God's creation.[48]

Hunting was also condemned by the great Jewish legal scholar and martyr Rabbi Akiba ben Joseph (c. 50–132 C.E.), who was flayed alive by the Romans and is one of the ten martyrs mentioned in Jewish penitential prayer. Rabbi Akiba ruled that it was forbidden to kill a wild animal unless it was given a fair trial, like a human being, before a court of twenty-three judges. Although this may not have been meant to be taken literally, it does demonstrate the Jewish view of the sanctity of all of God's creatures.[49]

Rabbi Ezekiel Landau, a noted eighteenth-century scholar in Austria-Hungary, was once asked by some Jewish estate managers if Jewish law allowed sport hunting, and he responded:

> In the Torah, the sport of hunting is imputed only to fierce characters like Nimrod and Esau, never to any of the patriarchs and their descendants. . . . I cannot comprehend how a Jew could even dream of killing animals merely for the pleasure of hunting . . . when the act of killing is prompted by that of sport, it is downright cruelty.[50]

The Talmud (Chulin 60b) discourages hunting, especially for "sport," and places it in the category of cruelty to animals.[51] The Talmud even discourages associating with hunters (Avodah Zorah 18b), based on the passage in Psalm 1:1 "not to stand in the way of sinners." Similarly, Proverbs 6:16–17 tells us that "the Lord hates . . . hands that shed innocent blood."

The Jewish dietary laws forbid the consumption of animals that have been killed by hunters, even if they are kosher animals. However, kosher animals that are trapped but uninjured may be eaten if the creature is slaughtered in the ritual manner.[52]

Similarly, Jewish law stipulates that fish cannot be hooked, only netted, because hooks cause pain and injury to the fish. In fact the word "hook" is mentioned in the Bible only as a symbol of cruelty or as a device of torture used by foreigners.[53]

The only hunters who appear in the Bible, Nimrod (Gen. 10:9) and Esau (Gen. 5:27) are portrayed as unattractive figures. Esau is described as not very bright, being vulnerable to manipulation, and as having actually been "hated" by the Lord. His character is disparagingly contrasted with that of his twin brother, Jacob: "Esau was a cunning hunter, a man of the field; and Jacob was a quiet man, dwelling in tents" (Gen. 25:27). This contrast is often alluded to and emphasized in the Midrash and rabbinic commentaries, according to Rabbi M. David Weiss.

Esau is also scorned for foolishly selling his birthright to Jacob for some bread and a pottage of lentils (Gen. 25:28–34). Ironically, the fate of Esau the hunter was that his land was taken away and turned over to the animals as a wilderness. In Malachi 1:2–3, the Lord says, "I loved Jacob, but Esau I hated, and made his mountains a desolation, and gave his heritage to the jackals of the wilderness."

## Kindness to Food and Farm Animals

One of the most important Jewish laws dealing with animals requires that they be allowed to rest on the Sabbath, as is ordained in the Ten Commandments (Exod. 20:8–10; 23:12; Deut. 5:14). A full chapter in the Talmud (the fifth chapter) and in the sixteenth-century code of Jewish law, the *Shulhan Arukh* (*Orah Hayyim* 305), discusses the prohibitions against working animals on the Sabbath.[54] Commenting on this requirement, Rabbi J. H. Hertz notes, "Care and kindness to cattle are of such profound importance for the humanizing of man that this duty has its place in the Decalogue (the Ten Commandments). The Rabbis classed cruelty to animals among the most serious of offenses."[55]

Rashi (d. 1105), the famous medieval French-Jewish Talmudic scholar and commentator on the Bible, has written that the duty to let animals rest on the Sabbath means that they must be free to roam in the fields on this day.[56] Such a requirement is not, and could not be, fulfilled under the factory farming techniques that supply almost all American meat and dairy products. This, and the very crowded, confined, and inhumane ways in which most American food animals are kept, raises the question of whether or not such meat and dairy products can be considered kosher, regardless of how the creatures are slaughtered (see pp. 196–199).

Other strict rules are intended to ensure that farm animals are treated humanely. Different types of animals cannot be used to plow together or work jointly on the same task, as this might cause the weaker animal to suffer or be overworked (see Deut. 22:10). According to the Talmud, "you may not allow one task to be done together by animals of two species. You may not allow them to carry the smallest thing together, even if it be only a seed.... You may not sit in a wagon drawn by animals of differing species" (Yoreh De'ah 297b).

Similarly, animals may not be muzzled during threshing, because they should be able to enjoy the fruits of the earth they are helping to reap. This rule is based on Deuteronomy 25:4, "Thou shalt not muzzle the ox when he treadeth out the corn." The *Code of Jewish Law* (vol. 4, chap. 186) punishes by whipping anyone who prevents an animal from eating while it works. According to the Talmud, this can only be done when it would be harmful to the animal to allow it to eat.[57] As Rabbi Hertz explains this injunction: "This prohibition applies to all animals employed in labour, and not to the ox alone. . . . It is a refinement of cruelty to excite the animal's desire for food and to prevent its satisfaction."[58]

Although early Jewish law permitted the raising and slaughtering of farm animals (some say as a concession to human weakness and to the barbaric practices of the biblical era), Jewish law requires that the creatures be treated as gently and compassionately as possible. Rabbi Abraham Kook has written that the restrictions on eating meat, such as the kosher laws, are intended to keep alive a spirit of reverence for life among meat eaters, so that someday they may return to the vegetarian diet humans had before the Great Flood.[59]

Indeed, the abhorrence of shedding blood is reflected in various Jewish laws and traditions. For example, shoes made from leather cannot be worn on the holiest of Jewish days — Yom Kippur, the Day of Atonement — on the grounds that one should not ask for mercy if one has not shown it. A noted authority on Jewish law, Rabbi Moses Isserles, has observed: "How can one put on (leather) shoes, a piece of clothing for which it is necessary to kill a living thing, on Yom Kippur, which is a day of grace and compassion, when it is written, 'His tender mercies are over all His works'" (Ps. 145:9).[60]

Likewise, the blessing of She-heh-eyanu (a festive benediction of thanksgiving to the Lord for allowing one to arrive at a special occasion), cannot be recited before slaughtering an animal. Nor can it be said when one puts on leather shoes or clothes with fur or other animal hides. This prohibition applies because one should not feel enjoyment over something that involves an animal's suffering; and one cannot destroy God's works and then bless God for having created them. Nor can the greeting of Tithadesh ("may you be renewed in your garment") be said when donning fur or leather shoes.[61]

In dealing directly with food and farm animals, mercy and compassion are required. The Code of Jewish Law (book 4, chap. 191, p. 84) specifically states that "it is forbidden to tie the legs of a beast or of a bird in a manner as to cause it pain." And rabbinical law permits Jews to ask non-Jews to milk cows for them on the Sabbath (since unmilked cows suffer from the pressure of the milk), and allows one to unload a burden from a working animal on the day of rest.[62]

In Leviticus 22:27–28, it is forbidden to kill a newborn goat, sheep, or ox until it has had at least seven days of warmth and nourishment from its mother: and "ye shall not kill it and its young both in one day." Commenting on his passage, Maimonides has observed:

> It is prohibited to kill an animal with its young on the same day, in order that people should be restrained and prevented from killing the two together in such a manner that the young is slain in the sight of the mother;

for the pain of animals under such circumstances is very great. There is no difference in this case between the pain of man and the pain of other living beings.[63]

In 1988, the late Rabbi Moses Feinstein issued an authoritative "responsa" stating categorically that Jewish law forbids the raising of animals under inhumane conditions to produce white veal. (Most veal calves are kept in small crates and deprived of nourishment to make them anemic and render their flesh tender and pale.) Describing as "wicked" people who raise animals by causing them unnecessary pain, Rabbi Feinstein stated,

> It is forbidden to cause suffering to an animal by feeding it food which it does not enjoy and which causes pain when it is eating, and also which causes it to suffer illness from which it will suffer pain. There is a prohibition against causing pain to animals in such a fashion simply for the sake of deceiving people to imagine that the meat is better.[64]

Presumably the rabbi's ruling would apply to other agricultural practices as well, such as forcibly stuffing geese with food to overfatten them and produce *paté de foie gras*.

## Kosher Slaughter: Tradition or Cruelty?

The rituals originally prescribed for kosher slaughter of animals were intended to minimize or eliminate the pain and suffering of the animal. Yet today, these age-old techniques are considered by many to be extraordinarily outdated, cruel, and in no way consistent with their original purpose. This dispute has created great controversy within the Jewish community and with humane groups, especially since kosher slaughter is usually exempt from state and federal humane slaughter laws.

The orthodox Jewish method of ritual slaughter, called *Schechitah*, contains requirements that the knife (a *challef*) be very sharp and without notches, and that it be carefully examined before being put to use. This, theoretically at least, benefits the animal, since it should help provide the least painful method of death when it is used to sever the jugular vein with one stroke.

Maimonides has observed that a primary purpose of this law is to ensure a relatively humane death for the animal: "The Law enjoins that the death of the animal should be the easiest. It is not allowed to torment the animal by cutting the throat in a clumsy manner, by pole-axing, or by cutting of a limb while the animal is still alive."[65] (In ancient times, hacking a limb off a living animal was common, for as long as the creature was alive, the meat would not spoil.)

As Chief Rabbi J. H. Hertz has written, "The Rabbinical regulations concerning *Schechitah* . . . are in part due to a desire to prevent the slightest unnecessary suffering to the animal." He goes on to aver that "the Jewish method of slaughter is one continuous cut with the sharpest of knives, applied by a skilled operator. Such cut severs all the great blood vessels of the neck, and produces *instantaneous* insensibility in the animal."[66]

Yet, many people see it as ironic that while a major purpose of the kosher slaughtering technique is to minimize pain and suffering to the animal, this ritual is exempt in most countries from governmental humane slaughter laws and regulations. In the United States, ritual killing for Jews and Moslems was exempted from the humane slaughter legislation passed in 1958. Humanitarians, including many Jews, consider the *preslaughter handling* of the animals to be very painful and traumatic to the creature and in no way consistent with Jewish law.

The way the kosher process works is that the animal — be it a cow, calf, chicken, or another — is shackled and hoisted upside down by a chain wrapped around a hind leg. This allows the neck to be fully outstretched and exposed for the shochet's (ritual slaughterer's) blade. According to Gerald Carson's graphic description, "dangling, struggling, and screaming, the beast is positioned for the knife, often with an iron clamp in the nostrils or human fingers rammed into the eyes to insure control."[67]

In nonritual slaughtering, the animal is stunned or knocked unconscious before being killed. But the kosher method requires that the animal remain *fully conscious* so that the blood will drain quickly from the body. The result is a bellowing, distressed animal, hung upside down, kicking and thrashing violently as the meat handlers immobilize the creature for the bleeding. Since some of the cows weigh as much as 1,350 pounds, they have to be suspended by an additional ring clasped around the nose to stretch the neck for the cutting.

According to Temple Grandin, a designer of a more humane kosher livestock handling system, up to four thousand cows, calves, and sheep are shackled and hoisted in US kosher plants *every day*. This represents about 10 percent of large beef animals, but 90 percent of veal calves and sheep.[68]

Ironically, since the 1960s a restraining pen has been used in some plants that allows the animal to be elevated off the floor without shackling and hoisting. Improved and more humane kosher slaughter methods are now required and used in Canada, New Zealand, and parts of Europe. And many US plants voluntarily use automatic restraining chutes, to hold and move a partially boxed animal along a conveyor belt to the shochet. Only *after* the cutting is the animal hoisted upside down to drain the blood out.[69]

Ms. Grandin designs such improved conveyor systems, as well as handling facilities for ranches, auction markets, feedlots, and packing plants, and offers free consulting services to any kosher meat processing plant that will use the more humane restraining system. But kosher plants have hardly rushed to embrace her methods. According to her, the reason plant managers do not switch over to a more humane system is financial rather than spiritual: "There is no religious reason. The big kosher houses are not ready to spend the money (up to $50,000) to retool. They will spend the money to counter animal rights activists."[70]

Ms. Grandin also points out that the more humane equipment has safety advantages as well, since thrashing and kicking animals can cause serious head, back, and knee injuries to workers. Moreover, the method prevents injuries to the animals, such as broken legs, that can make the meat unkosher.[71]

Indeed, many non-Orthodox Jews feel that because the hoisting of the terrified animal causes tearing of muscles and tendons, hemorrhaging, and broken legs or pelvis, the *intent* of shechitah is violated by causing excessive suffering and injury. Therefore, it is argued, *ritual slaughter actually renders the meat nonkosher!* It can also be asserted that because of the cruel and inhumane conditions under which the overwhelming majority of food animals are factory-farmed, the meat cannot be considered kosher *no matter how the animals are slaughtered!*[72]

According to Rabbi Sidney J. Jacobs, author of *The Jewish Word Book*,

The bottom line is that there can be no "humane" procedure when slaughter is involved, nor can factory farming ever be made merciful. Ironically, the dilemma of Jewish ritual slaughter could be resolved by switching to a vegan diet, the grain-based diet set forth in Genesis.[73]

Repeated attempts over the years by humane organizations — including the Jewish Committee for Humane Slaughter, headed by Max Schnapp in Brooklyn, New York — to eliminate and outlaw the unnecessary suffering of kosher animals have been rebuffed by Orthodox religious authorities, who insist they are upholding the laws and traditions of Judaism. But the advocates of humane slaughter charge that a small group of ultra-Orthodox rabbis, in violation of Judaism's tenets and heritage, care more for economics than compassion.

The critics of ritual slaughter find great irony in the fact that devout Orthodox Jews, out of devotion to God's teachings, will go to great lengths to observe to the letter the ancient, thousands-of-years-old biblical dietary laws, even to the extent of keeping separate sets of dishes for meats and milk products. When accidental mixing of the dishes occurs, the "contaminated" ones are destroyed. Yet, humanitarians charge that the Orthodox ignore the unnecessary suffering their ritual slaughter techniques cause to millions of God's creatures each year, and that a small group of them resists any changes that could alleviate this suffering.

As pointed out by Rabbi Jacobs, "The use of holding pens, which would satisfy U.S. laws and meet Jewish requirements, has long been advocated by humane groups, and, equally long, ignored by the Orthodox Jewish establishment which controls Jewish ritual slaughter." He attributes the lack of progress in using holding pens to "a combination of seeming indifference by Orthodox Jewish authorities, and evasive tactics by packers of 'kosher' meats."

Rabbi Jacobs also notes that criticism of ritual slaughter has been used as propaganda by Nazis and other anti-Semites. This, in turn, has resulted in advocates of humane slaughter being "smeared with a wide brush of anti-Semitic intent by otherwise reasonable spokespersons in the Jewish community," making it difficult for productive discussions to occur between the groups involved.[74]

The conflict here seems to stem from two sets of seemingly sincere and well-intentioned groups, both claiming to be working for the fulfillment of the Jewish law mandating kindness to animals. One group persists in clinging to the letter of the ancient rules promulgated to minimize suffering, which represented the best-known techniques of that time. But these methods are today outmoded and actually *promote* suffering rather than alleviate it, as the lawgivers intended. Since everyone more or less agrees on the original intent of the law, it is unfortunate that an agreement cannot be reached that would preserve most of traditional ritual while sparing the animals so much unnecessary suffering.

## Vegetarianism among Jews

There is a growing aversion to meat-eating among many Jews, for health reasons, and because of the extraordinary amount of suffering to which animals are subjected during their raising, in the transportation to the slaughterhouse, and while they are being ritually killed.

Although meat-eating is not prohibited, there is a strong tradition within Judaism against the consumption of animal flesh. The Talmud asserts that early humans were vegetarians, between the times of the creation and the Great Flood, after which the available plant life was destroyed.[75] Indeed, in the Garden of Eden, the Bible's portrayal of utopia, humans were commanded to be vegetarian, with the Lord saying: "Behold, I have given you every herb yielding seed, which is upon the face of the earth, and every tree, in which is the fruit of a tree yielding seed — to you it shall be for food" (Gen. 1:29). Moreover, such biblical passages as Isaiah 11:69 ("and the lion shall eat straw like the ox . . . and none shall hurt or destroy in all God's holy mountain") suggest that all creatures will be vegetarians when the still-awaited messianic era arrives and the Kingdom of God is established on earth.

In *The Nine Questions People Ask about Judaism,* Dennis Prager and Rabbi Telushkin write, "Keeping kosher is Judaism's compromise with its ideal vegetarianism. Ideally, according to Judaism, man would confine his eating to fruits and vegetables and not kill animals for food."[76] And Rabbi Simon Glazer's *Guide to Judaism* states,

> It appears that the first intention of the Maker was to have men live on a strictly vegetarian diet. The very earliest periods of Jewish history are marked with humanitarian conduct towards the lower animal kingdom.... It is clearly established that the ancient Hebrews knew, and perhaps were the first among men to know, that animals feel and suffer pain.[77]

When the great Jewish warrior and military hero Judas Maccabaeus (d. 160 B.C.E.) led his revolt against the Syrians, one reason for the uprising was the Syrian ruler's attempt to extirpate the Jewish faith and force Jews to eat forbidden flesh. Part II of the book of Maccabees (5:27) points out that Judas Maccabaeus and his followers fled to the mountains, where they lived on plant foods "in order that they might not be polluted like the rest."[78]

The Jewish historian and general Josephus (37–100? C.E.), in *The Life,* mentions some Jewish priests brought to trial in Rome who ate only nuts and figs to avoid meat that was used in heathen rituals.[79]

By the first century C.E., various Jewish and Christian sects made a point of abstaining from meat, including the Essenes, the Nazarenes, and the Ebionites, the last being Christians of Jewish origin. After the Jewish revolt and the destruction of Jerusalem by the Romans in 70 C.E., Jewish vegetarianism went into decline with the defeat and dispersal of the Jewish people.[80]

The *Encyclopedia Judaica* states:

> According to rabbinic tradition, interpreting the Biblical record, mankind was not allowed to eat meat until after the Flood.... Once permitted, the consumption of meat remained surrounded with many restrictions. According to the rabbis, the Hebrew word for "desireth" in the verse, "when the Lord thy God shall enlarge thy border and thou shalt say: 'I will eat flesh,' because thy soul desireth to eat flesh" (Deut. 12:20), has a negative connotation; hence, although it is permitted to slaughter animals for food, this should be done in moderation.

And the *Universal Jewish Encyclopedia* (p. 330) points out that "many Jewish sects were strict vegetarians, and the Talmud recommends that meat be eaten only when one has an overwhelming desire for it" (Hul. 84a).

Jewish law has a definite bias against eating food made from animals. According to Professor Richard Schwartz, author of *Judaism and Vegetarianism*, a special blessing is said before eating such vegetarian foods as fruits, vegetables, bread, and wine; but there is no special blessing for meat or fish. Indeed, since Orthodox Jews have a blessing for almost all beneficial things, including different blessings for various types of food, it is significant that there is no blessing for meat, and that the flesh of a creature that has been slaughtered cannot be blessed.[81]

Dr. Schwartz has also enunciated "three important Torah principles which strongly point toward vegetarianism":

1. *Tza-ar Baa-lir Chayim* — the pain of any living creature. This tradition of compassion and kindness toward animals is completely at variance with modern factory methods of raising animals for slaughter.

2. *Bal Tashchit* — Do not destroy. The Sages of the Talmud extended this to apply to anything which may be of use to anyone.... "Whoever ... does away with food in a destructive manner violates the prohibition of *bal tashchit.*" This prohibition is based on the belief that "the Earth is the Lord's." We are to be co-workers in helping preserve and improve the world. We are prohibited from wasting anything that has value. Meat diets are extremely wasteful. It takes twenty pounds of grain protein to produce a pound of edible beef protein in a feedlot. About 80 percent of the grain produced in this country is fed to livestock.

3. *Pikuach Nefesh* — Regard for Human Life. This involves the duty to save human life.... So important is this that one *must* (not may) violate the Sabbath, eat forbidden foods, and even eat on *Yom Kippur* if it will help to save life. There has been much evidence connecting a meat-centered diet to various diseases, including heart trouble and cancer.... A number of studies have shown that a well-chosen vegetarian diet can drastically reduce the risk of heart attack, stroke, and related circulatory disease, which account for over half of all U.S. fatalities annually.

He also points out that since many more people could be supplied with food if the wasteful practices involved in raising livestock were abandoned, "doesn't the principle of *pikuash nefesh* ... apply to (saving) starving people?"[82]

The Talmud says that eating the hearts of animals will make one forget what one has learned.[83] We now know, of course, that organ meats are high in saturated fat and cholesterol, which taken in excess can clog the arteries to the brain and help cause senility. The Talmud also recommends that eating meat be avoided unless one has an overpowering desire for it.[84]

Today, an increasing number of Jews are following the tradition of the early Jewish sects that were vegetarian. Perhaps the best-known contemporary Jewish vegetarian is the Nobel Prize–winning author and storyteller Isaac Bashevis Singer (b. 1904)), who often writes of the plight of persecuted animals. Singer has written eloquently of the obligation of humans to avoid meat:

> The longer I am a vegetarian, the more I feel how wrong it is to kill animals and eat them. I think that eating meat or fish is a denial of all ideals, even of all religions. How can we pray to God for mercy if we ourselves have no mercy? . . .
> As long as people will shed the blood of innocent creatures, there can be no peace, no liberty, no harmony between people. Slaughter and justice cannot dwell together.[85]

Singer wrote the foreword for Dudley Giehl's highly acclaimed book, *Vegetarianism as a Way of Life*, and Giehl quotes Singer as drawing a contrast between our asking God above for compassion, and our lack of it for those creatures under us: "We are all God's creatures — that we pray to God for mercy and justice while we continue to eat the flesh of animals that are slaughtered on our account is not consistent."[86]

This view is reflected in many of Singer's stories of Jewish life and culture, one of which, "The Fast," has the town slaughterer questioning his own hypocrisy: "How can one pray for life in the coming year, or for a favorable writ in Heaven, when one was robbing others of the breath of life?"[87]

Other well-known Jewish vegetarians include S. Y. Agnon (1888–1970), the Israeli author and Nobel laureate in literature, and the legendary Austrian writer and poet Franz Kafka (1883–1924).[88]

Professor Richard Schwartz has noted that legislation outlawing meat-eating was introduced in the Israeli Knesset (Parliament) — unsuccessfully — by Mordecai Ben Porat. He argued that the state's fragile economy was being damaged by the cost of fighting diseases associated with eating meat.[89] According to Dr. Schwartz, the recent chief rabbi of Israel, Schlomo Goren, is a strict vegetarian. And the first chief rabbi of the modern state of Israel, Abraham Isaac Kook, was also a vegetarian, who advocated such a diet in an essay entitled, "A Vision of Vegetarianism and Peace."[90]

Kook's successor as chief rabbi, the late Isaac ha-Levi Herzog, wrote that "Jews will move increasingly to vegetarianism out of their own deepening knowledge of what their tradition commands. . . . Man's carnivorous nature is not taken for granted or praised in the fundamental teachings of Judaism. . . . A whole galaxy of central rabbinic and spiritual leaders ... has been affirming vegetarianism as the ultimate meaning of Jewish moral teaching."[91]

Several Jewish organizations are currently working to persuade Jews to adopt a vegetarian diet. Jewish Vegetarians, in Baltimore, says of its members, "We feel ourselves to be part of an ancient people and a living tradition — one whose ethical principles, we believe, point towards vegetarianism."[92] This group distributes recipes, literature, contact lists, and other information on vegetarianism and works to "promote that viewpoint within the Jewish Community, as well as to represent Jewish people and values within the vegetarian community."

The International Jewish Vegetarian Society is an organization that works to "promote the compassionate and healthful way of life, and help counter the worldwide war against creation." It publishes a five-page quarterly the *Jewish Vegetarian*, and has offices or chapters in Jewish communities "from Australia, to Scotland, to South Africa," as well as Canada and the United States, and in Jerusalem, Haifa, and Tel Aviv in Israel. Its philosophy is that "the pristine teachings of Judaism are a complete philosophy for vegetarian living, and therefore a special responsibility devolves on us to take a leading role in the campaign against factory farming and the international trafficking in sentient creatures."[93] Founded in London in 1964 by Philip Pick, the IJVS is still headquartered there and recently established in Israel a home for orphaned and deprived children.[94]

The Jewish Vegetarian Hotel in Woodridge, New York, has been catering to vegetarians since 1920, and in 1987 it hosted the Jewish Vegetarian Convention, attended by people from all over the United States.[95]

Roberta Kalechofsky, head of Micah Publications and Jews for Animal Rights, in Marblehead, Massachusetts, publishes various works on Judaism and animal welfare.[96] Among these is her *Haggadah for the Liberated Lamb*, a guide for "a vegetarian (Passover) Seder that celebrates compassion for all creatures."[97]

## The Kindness of the Patriarchs

Jewish history and tradition are full of stories about the concern of Jewish leaders for animals. The Midrash relates that Moses was chosen to lead the Israelites only after he had proven himself as a shepherd by going after a stray lamb, and, upon seeing that it was exhausted, tenderly carrying it back home on his shoulders. The incident supposedly occurred while Moses was tending the sheep of Jethro in the wilderness of Midian. In this version, Moses found the little lamb drinking from a brook, and he said to it, "Had I known that thou wast thirsty, I would have taken thee in my arms and carried thee thither." Whereupon a heavenly voice replied, "as thou livest, thou are fit to shepherd Israel."[98]

Another version of this story ends with the Lord saying to Moses, "Because thou hast shown mercy in leading the flock, thou will surely tend my flock, Israel."[99] In a variation of this beautiful legend, which has been paraphrased by the English poet Samuel Taylor Coleridge (1772–1834), Moses returns the lamb to the fold, upon which a voice from heaven cries out, "Thou art worthy to be my people's pastor."[100]

A similar story is told of King David, who is said to have been deemed worthy to be a leader of his people because he showed kindness and knowledge in caring for his sheep. When working as a shepherd, David would let the smaller sheep graze before the larger ones. In this way, the very young and smaller animals could eat the tender grass; the old sheep would graze next, getting the ordinary grass; and finally the young, stronger sheep would take the tough grass.[101]

Other patriarchs of the Jewish people have demonstrated their care and concern for animals. In Genesis 24:11–20, Abraham's servant judges Rebekah to be worthy of becoming the wife of Isaac because of her kindness to animals (see p. 23). And Jacob, in Genesis 33:12–14, refuses to accompany his brother Esau on a journey because the pace of the trip would be stressful and injurious to his children and to his animals. Instead, Jacob says he will adopt a more leisurely pace, since "the children are tender, and the flocks and the herds giving suck are a care to me; and if they overdrive them one day, all the flocks will die. . . . I will journey on gently, according to the pace of the cattle that are before me and according to the pace of the children."

## Jewish Folklore of Kindness to Animals

Jewish folklore, handed down through the centuries, contains numerous stories demonstrating the importance of showing kindness to animals.

A famous Talmudic tale tells of a great rabbi and scholar who, after failing to help an animal in distress, was made to suffer from a toothache for thirteen years! The rabbi, Judah the Prince, was studying the Torah in front of a Babylonian synagogue in Sephoris, when a frightened calf on the way to slaughter passed by him, as if pleading, "Save me!" (In another version, it ran up to him, bleating for protection.) But Rabbi Judah said to the calf, "What can I do for you? For this you were created" (or, "Go, that is thy destiny"). For this, he was punished with thirteen years of continual pain.

Then one day, the rabbi's daughter was about to kill "a creeping thing" (a weasel) but he interceded to save it, saying to her, "My daughter, let the animal live, for it is written, 'and his tender mercies are over all his works' " (Ps. 145:9). (A variation on this story has the rabbi stop his housekeeper from throwing out a litter of kittens or weasels she has found, telling her one should show compassion to animals just as the Lord does.) As a result of his preventing an act of cruelty and unkindness to animals, the rabbi regained his health, and his pain vanished.[102]

And legend has it that Rabbi Israel Salanter, one of the nineteenth century's most respected rabbis, once missed a religious service on the eve of Yom Kippur — the holiest of the Jewish holidays — where he was to chant the sacred opening prayer, the Kol Nidre. A search party was sent out to find him, and finally located the rabbi in the barn of a Christian neighbor. On his way to services, the rabbi had found the neighbor's calf lost and entangled in some brush; so he freed it "and led the animal home through many fields and over many hills. His act of mercy represented the rabbi's prayers on that Yom Kippur evening."[103]

There is also the story of a Rabbi Abramtzi, who was so compassionate he would not walk on a grassy field lest he trample it down, and carefully avoided stepping on grasshoppers and other insects. He fed stray dogs and in winter put out bread crumbs for the birds. It is said that "when sparrows and other birds began to feed on the bread, he could not remove his gaze from them and his face would light up with joy like that of a little child."

The rabbi loved to be and pray in the woods, saying, "The field and the forest are the most beautiful and finest of the Houses of the Lord." Once while traveling home in a wagon on a Friday, he missed making it home by Sabbath in order to spare the exhausted horses from being over-exerted. So with his coachmen, he spent Sabbath in the forest, saying, "The Lord will look after us, supply us with our wants, and guard us against evil."[104]

Another nature lover, Rabbi Tanhum ben Hiyya has said: "The falling of the rain is greater than the giving of the Law, for the giving of the Law was a joy only to Israel, while the falling of the rain is a rejoicing for all the world, including the cattle and the wild beasts and the birds."[105]

Martin Buber (1878–1965), the Jewish scholar and philosopher, writes in his *Tales of the Hasidim* of Rabbi Zusya, who was once on his way to raise money to ransom some people being held prisoner. Arriving at an inn with many birds in a cage and seeing that the birds yearned for their freedom, the rabbi opened the cage and released them. When confronted by the furious innkeeper and asked why he had done this, the rabbi cited Psalm 145:9 ("His tender mercies are over all his works"). The innkeeper then beat the rabbi and threw him out of the inn, "and Zusya went on his way serenely."[106]

A famous eighteenth-century rabbi, Shneor Zalman of Ladi, delighted in taking walks with his grandson and stopping to enjoy the birds singing. When the grandson asked why such an important and busy rabbi would spend so much of his time listening to the songs of birds, the rabbi replied that one "can hear in the voice of every bird and beast the voice of God."[107]

The humane laws of the Talmud once even led a farmer to convert to Judaism. A religious Jew who owned a cow and took very good care of it lost all his money and possessions and had to sell his cow to a non-Jewish farmer. The farmer plowed all week with the cow, but on the Sabbath the cow was accustomed to resting and would not work. The farmer returned the cow to the Jew and asked for his money back, and the Jew explained to him about the law requiring that animals be allowed to rest on the Sabbath. The more the farmer heard about Jewish law, the more interested he became in it, eventually studying the Torah and converting to Judaism. He took as his new name "Yohanan ben Toraita" — son of the cow — in honor of the cow that observed Sabbath and inspired him to become a Jew.[108]

More recently, there is the touching story of Itzhik Rosenberg, a Jewish farmer in Slovakia during World War II, who, while being carried away by the Nazis to the death cars, cried out to his neighbors to feed his animals for him, since he would no longer be able to do so.[109]

There are many, many other such stories, too numerous to relate, that demonstrate the importance attached to this Jewish tradition of kindness to animals. Such tales have become an integral and important part of Jewish folklore, history, and culture, reflecting the significance in Judaism of this humane tradition.

## Contemporary Jewish Writings

Contemporary Judaism has reaffirmed humankind's responsibility to protect the environment. In 1970, the Union of America Hebrew Congregations (UAHC), comprised of Reform Jewish congregations, issued a publication stressing the spiritual roots of humankind's obligation to preserve the earth and its resources. Entitled *The Crisis of Ecology: Judaism and the Environment*, the booklet, by Albert Vorspan, observes that "Jewish tradition makes it clear that man's dominion over nature does not include a license to slaughter indiscriminately or to abuse the environment":

> "You shall not destroy" is the basis of the Talmudic law which prohibits willful destruction of natural resources, or any kind of vandalism, even if the act is committed by the owners of the property themselves. One must not destroy anything that may be useful to others. "The earth is the Lord's and the fullness thereof" (Psalm 104) implies that man is the steward of nature, obliged to cherish and preserve it.

*The Crisis of Ecology* quotes rabbinical writings on the traditional Jewish view of this obligation:

> Of everything God created, nothing was created in vain, not even the things you may think unnecessary, such as spiders, frogs, or snakes. . . . Man was not created until the sixth day, so that if his pride should govern him, it could be said to him "Even the tiniest flea preceded you in creation."

And since the earth was created by the Lord, humans are required to care for and preserve it.

> Why did God appear to Moses in the lowly bush? To teach us that nothing in creation is without God's holy presence, not even the commonest bush. . . . When God created man, He showed him everything in the Garden of Eden and said to him: "See my work, how good it is, know that everything which I have created, I have created for you. And now take care, lest you spoil and destroy my world. For if you spoil and destroy it, no one will rebuild it after you."

*The Crisis of Ecology*, citing numerous biblical references, emphasizes that the fates of humans and nature are intertwined:

> Judaism has never seen man as separate and apart from nature, as the licensed plunderer of a planet; Judaism calls on us to cherish and revere all that has been created in sacredness. In Jewish tradition, man and his world are one, inseparable and inviolable. Man and his world — both good and dependent on each other.[110]

Indeed, what is at stake in our obligation to protect our environment is no less than the survival of the human race. In Deuteronomy 30:19, the Lord enjoins humankind: "I have set before thee life and death, the blessing and the curse; therefore choose life, that thou mayest live, thou and thy seed." As *The Crisis of Ecology* concludes, "whether man, in our generation, has the will to choose life will determine the destiny of the human race."

Other recent Jewish publications have recognized the humane tradition of Judaism. A New York monthly, *The Jewish Spectator*, in June 1969 published a strong editorial laying out specific applications of the humane aspect of Jewish law:

> Cruelty to animals is forbidden by Jewish law and the modes and varieties of the humane treatment of animals are defined, described, and legislated in *all* Jewish law codes. . . . Cruelty to animals is known . . . as *tza'ar ba'aley hayim* — pain inflicted on living creatures. This is a grave sin according to Jewish law.

Concerning the annual Canadian-Norwegian baby seal kill, in which some 180,000 nursing baby harp seals were being clubbed to death in front of their mothers, the editorial said flatly: "The savagery of skinning baby seals alive and within sight of their mothers is a dual sin, as Jewish laws define it: it is inflicting torture upon the young animal and great emotional suffering upon the mother." The editorial ended with the observation that "human selfishness and the desire to profit from animals must be subordinated to the dictates of humane ethics.... Fur coats bespeak 'status,' but they are tainted by gratuitous cruelty to animals — and not only to harp seals."[111]

(The editorial's critical reference to fur coats was particularly bold for a Jewish newspaper, in light of the fact that the American retail fur industry, headquartered in New York City, is composed in large part of people of the Jewish faith. In recent years, the fur trade has come under strong attack from conservationists, since the demands of the industry have played a major role in bringing to the brink of extinction many species of wildlife, such as tigers and cheetahs. And tens of millions of fur-bearing animals are caught in leg-hold traps each year in the United States and Canada, suffering enormous pain in order to supply pelts to furriers. But it should be pointed out that while many furriers are Jewish, so are many leaders and active workers in the humane and conservation movements, including this writer.)

Perhaps the most forthright recent statement on Judaism's commitment to conservation and compassion is "The Jewish Declaration on Nature," drafted by Rabbi Arthur Hertzberg in his capacity as vice president of the World Jewish Congress. Delivered in September 1986 at the World Wildlife Conference in Assisi, Italy (the home of St. Francis), the declaration enunciated the theme that "the righteous Jew...can live in this world...without encroaching on the rights of other people, or of any of God's creatures":

> Now, when the whole world is in peril, when the environment is in danger of being poisoned and various species, both plant and animal, are becoming extinct, it is our Jewish responsibility to put the defense of the whole of nature at the very center of our concern.

Rabbi Hertzberg concluded his address with a parable about the fragility of our planet:

> Our ancestor Abraham inherited his passion for nature from Adam. The later rabbis never forgot it. Some twenty centuries ago they told the story of two men who were out on the water in a rowboat. Suddenly, one of them started to saw under his feet. He maintained that it was his right to do whatever he wished with the place which belonged to him. The other

answered him that they were in the rowboat together; the hole that he was making would sink both of them (Vayikra Rabbah 4:6).

We have a responsibility to life, to defend it everywhere, not only against our own sins but also against those of others. We are all passengers together in this same fragile and glorious world. Let us safeguard our rowboat — and let us row together.[112]

In October 1989 the Jewish Theological Seminary of America, the academic and religious center of Conservative Judaism, based its New Year's message on protecting the environment. Citing Leviticus 25:23, "the land is mine, you are my tenants," the message listed such problems as oil spills, pesticides, and holes in the ozone layer, and asked, "What are we doing?" It also quoted the *Qohelet Rabbah*, "Think upon this, and do not corrupt and desolate my world. For if you corrupt or desolate it, there is no one to set it right after you."[113]

And in the spring of 1990, the seminary produced a one-hour television documentary for NBC entitled, "The Earth Is the Lord's: Ecology as a Religious Concern." The thesis of the program was that "if human beings are to preserve an environment in which future generations can survive, . . . we must learn . . . to be stewards of the universe, and not seek simply to dominate it, no matter what the cost."

## Nature and Animals in Jewish Worship Services

Jewish prayer books used in worship services contain numerous references to humankind's obligations to respect other creatures and the natural environment.

In reform Judaism, the services in the *Union Prayerbook* for Rosh Hashonah — the Jewish New Year — contain the following prayers showing reverence for nature and animals and an appreciation for humankind's stewardship responsibilities:

Praised be Thou, O Lord our God, ruler of the world, by whose law the shadows of evening fall and the gates of morn are opened. In wisdom Thou hast established the changes of times and seasons and ordered the ways of the stars in their heavenly courses. Thou didst lay the foundations of the earth and the heavens are the work of thy hands.[114]

Our God, and God of our fathers, may thy kingdom come speedily, that every creature may know that Thou art its Creator, and every living being exclaim: The Lord, the God of Israel, ruleth and His dominion endureth forever.[115]

May we never forget that all we have and prize is but lent to us, a trust for which we must render account to thee.[116]

Thou rulest the world in kindness and all thy creatures in mercy.[117]

O Lord, our God, let thy presence be manifest to us in all thy works, that reverence for Thee may fill the hearts of all Thy creatures.[118]

Similar passages, clearly and unequivocally expressing a strong humane and conservation ethic, are contained in the services for Yom Kippur (the Day of Atonement), the holiest day in Judaism.

A traditional Yom Kippur prayer reminds Jews of the Lord's dominion over every creature: "Thou visits the soul of every living thing, appointing the measure of every creature and decreeing their destiny."[119] Other portions of the Yom Kippur service contain similar themes:

He has given us dominion over the works of His hands, so that, as faithful stewards, we may dispense wisely for the good of all His creatures. . . . God is the Lord of all the earth, the creator and owner of the land, and all that is thereon. For the heaven and the earth are His, and we are but day-laborers and sojourners before him.

Great and Holy God, who inhabitest eternity, Thine everlasting arms uphold the universe and support the lowliest of Thy creatures.

The Lord is good to all, and His tender mercies are over all His works. . . . Thou openest Thy hand and satisfiest the desire of every living thing.

Every living soul shall praise Thee; the spirit of all flesh shall glorify Thy name. . . . Thou rulest the world in kindness and all Thy creatures in mercy.

Let all living creatures praise and glorify Thy name, O God.

When I behold the heavens, the work of Thy hands, the countless hosts of stars which Thou hast set in the firmament; when I consider the wonders of the universe and endeavor to comprehend the excellence of Thy majesty, I am overwhelmed by Thy greatness and power. . . . Yet upon the earth with all its abundance and beauty, with forests filled with song, with mountains reared like pillars, with roaring billows of the sea; with all the mysteries of the boundless depths and the immeasurable heights, Thou hast placed man to proclaim Thy grandeur and to voice the longing of all beings for Thee.[120]

The new, revised version of the *Union Prayerbook*, entitled *Gates of Repentance* and used by many Reform congregations, also contains many prayers and statements on behalf of animals and nature for the New Year and the Day of Atonement:

You create the world, Your child, anew at every moment.

Again the birds chirp their joy before you.

Praised be the One whose compassion covers the earth and all its creatures.

### WE STAND IN AWE OF CREATION

We stand in awe of all created things,
the power within them that gives them form,
the ancient law that rules them all:
fish of the sea, birds of the air,
the quiet stone and the beating wave,
all woven from a single loom.
We stand in awe of all created things.

The Lord is good to all; His compassion shelters all His creatures.

God of all ages, Ruler of all creatures, Lord of all generations; all praise to You. You guide the world with steadfast love, Your creatures with tender mercy.

God of beginning, God of the end, God of all creatures, Lord of all generations: With love you guide the world, with love You walk hand in hand with all the living.[121]

There is also an interesting prayer giving a provocative interpretation of the Genesis account of the Creation:

Then Isaac asked the Eternal: King of the world, when You made the light, You said in Your Torah that it was good; when You made the expanse of heaven and earth, You said in Your Torah that they were good; and of every herb You made, and every beast, You said that they were good; but when You made us in Your image, You did not say of us in Your Torah that humanity was good. Why, Lord? And God answered him: Because you I have not yet perfected, because through the Torah you are to perfect yourselves, and to perfect the world. All other things are completed; they cannot grow. But human kind is not complete; you have yet to grow. Then I will call you good.[122]

There is even a prayer of forgiveness for sinning against God "for poisoning the air, and polluting land and sea."[123]

The prayerbook services for Yom Kippur in Conservative Judaism also stress God's love for, and human responsibilities to, the natural world:

Never turn aside from any fellow creature.

He is the world's and every creature's Lord.

In Thy hand is the soul of every living thing, and the breath of all mankind. The soul is thine, and the body is Thy creation; have compassion on thy handiwork, Yea, both soul and body are Thine.

Therefore, O Lord our God, let Thine awe be manifest in all Thy works, and a reverence for Thee fill all that thou hast created, so that all Thy creatures may know thee.[124]

Jewish congregations often dispose of old and worn out sacred books not by burning or throwing them away, but by burying them in a "genizah" ceremony. The reading from one of these ceremonies stresses its ecological aspects: "Books are made of paper, which comes from wood, which comes from trees, which comes from nature, which is a symbol of God. It is like a chain that never ends. . . . Old book, you've served us faithfully. It's time to rest now in peace." Then the boxes of old books are lowered into a deep well or hole where they will be "allowed ultimately to dissolve into dust." This Jewish tradition of burying old Bibles, scrolls, and prayer books is also consistent with avoiding having God's sacred name destroyed or wiped out.[125]

In fact, because this book contains the name of the Deity, Jewish law may consider it a sacred text that is subject to certain rules. It should therefore not be disposed of by destruction, burning, or throwing away, but should be passed on to a friend or a library.

## Wildlife Conservation in Israel

The government of Israel has a strong wildlife and nature protection program; many critically endangered animals mentioned in the scriptures are being bred and are repopulating the Holy Land; and unique natural areas of great beauty and biblical significance are being preserved.

Israel — the land that gave birth to the religions of Christianity, Islam, and Judaism — was once teeming with wildlife: swift desert antelopes and deer, leopards and cheetahs, wild goats and sheep, wolves, eagles, storks, herons, hippopotami, ostrich, and even elephants and perhaps the mythical "unicorn" all flourished here.[126]

At one time, lions were common in Israel. Their dens were the thickets of Jordan (Jer. 49:19) and the Syrian and Negev deserts (Isa. 30:6), even the hills of Jerusalem; and they still occurred in the Negev in Crusader times. 1 Samuel 17:34 tells how the young David, inexperienced at warfare, urged King Saul to let him go fight Goliath the Philistine by telling how he, as a shepherd, had killed bears and lions.

The Middle East of today bears scant resemblance to the paradise of plants and animals described in the Old Testament, the "good land" that Deuteronomy 8:7 tells us was "a land of brooks of water, of fountains and depths that spring out of valleys and hills." Thousands of years ago, humans began to destroy and alter the natural environment of this "land of milk and honey."

The Book of Kings describes the cutting of the stately cedars of Lebanon by King Solomon and Hiram, King of Tyre (or Phoenecia). Israel was further denuded when, during World War I, the Turks occupying the region in the reign of the Ottoman Empire cut down most of the remaining trees and used them to fuel the Turkish railroad.[127] This destruction of habitat, combined with overhunting and the countless wars and armies that have moved across the area since the dawn of recorded history, have caused the extinction in Israel of many of the animals of the Bible.

Israel's attempt to build a modern-day "Noah's Ark" has been carried out by the country's Society for the Protection of Nature in Israel (SPNI) and the government's Nature Reserves Authority. For years, this effort was led by one of Israel's national heroes, retired Major General Avraham Yoffe, a former tank commander with a distinguished war record. Stories about Yoffe's war exploits are legendary and have become part of Israeli folklore.

Once, during a fierce tank battle his command was fighting with the Egyptians in the Sinai desert, Yoffe halted his tanks and ordered a cease fire long enough to allow a rare bird — a cream-colored courser — to cross his path and move out of harm's way. On another occasion, Yoffe ordered an entire army encampment to pull up stakes and move to another location in order to prevent a field of rare wildflowers from being trampled and destroyed. Within two days after the end of the 1967 Six-Day War, Yoffe had marked off areas captured from Syria, Egypt, and Jordan as nature preserves, with hunting and destruction of habitat forbidden.[128]

One of the Nature Reserves Authority's most important projects was the setting up of a ten-thousand-acre wildlife preserve called Hai-Bar (Hebrew for wildlife), located in southern Israel in a rocky plain not far from the border with Jordan and near the location of King Solomon's famous copper mines. At Hai-Bar the Israelis have established an open, natural sanctuary, where some of the biblical animals that are now faced with extinction are free to roam, graze, and — hopefully — "be fruitful and multiply." Many of the approximately 120 species mentioned in the Old Testament are already extinct in Israel and throughout most of their original range. Since some of these species seem doomed in the few areas in which they remain, Israel's attempt to establish breeding herds may be their only hope for survival.[129]

Among the rare animals being bred at Hai-Bar are several that remain only in small numbers (if at all) in the Arab nations and are still in danger of being killed off there, such as the addax and the oryx. One of the most striking residents of Hai-Bar, the addax (addax nasomaculatus) is a graceful desert antelope whose dual spiraling horns reach a length of three feet.

A close relative of the addax is the Arabian oryx (oryx leucoryx), a magnificent desert antelope whose long, straight, needle-sharp horns may have given birth to the legend of the unicorn referred to in Deuteronomy and elsewhere. Like the addax, the oryx migrates across the desert, following the meager rain showers. This animal once roamed throughout the Holy Land, but appears to have been completely wiped out there by the mid-nineteenth century. By the early 1970s, it survived only in the desert of the Saudi Arabian peninsula, mainly Oman, where, although "protected" by law, it was still hunted down, despite the fact that only one to two hundred at most were left. It is now considered extinct there, or virtually so.[130]

The ostrich — which was common in the Mideast during biblical times — is also being restocked at Hai-Bar. The largest of all living birds, standing six to eight feet tall and weighing up to three hundred pounds, the ostrich is mentioned at least eight times in the Old Testament. The Book of Job (39:13–18) mentions the myth that ostriches hide their heads in the sand if threatened by an enemy and refers to the ostrich's enormous speed, which can reach 50 m.p.h. for the first half mile, saying the bird "scorneth the horse and his rider."

Also part of the Israeli conservation program are wild asses, Syrian bears, scimitar-horned oryx, and ibex. Even wolves, leopards, and cheetahs survive in small numbers in Israel, mainly in remote, sparsely inhabited desert regions.

The Israeli Air Force (IAF) has even adopted regulations limiting training flights to avoid collisions with migrating birds. Israel forms a major axis for the migration route for millions of birds flying back and forth between nesting sites in Europe, Asia, and Africa. During a two-day period in October 1984, SPNI observers counted some 220,000 birds of prey flying over Israel! By avoiding migration routes and seasons as much as possible, the IAF has greatly reduced the number of birds killed by aircraft.[131]

Although only about the size of the state of Maryland, Israel has, within its tiny borders, an amazing variety of terrains and climates, from its northern alpine region, where snow falls on Mount Hermon, to the subtropical climate of the oases around the Dead Sea, to the burning desert sands in the south, to the Mediterranean climate of its beaches and coral reefs. These climatic variations can support a wide assortment of animal and plant life, which is one reason there are so many species mentioned in the Bible. Protected areas set aside by the Nature Reserves Authority encompass high mountains, fields of flowers, pools and waterfalls, desert oases, dripping springs, deep ravines and red sandstone canyons, limestone cliffs, coral reefs and bays, forests, ancient ruins, prehistoric caves, palm trees, papyrus plants, great thickets, huge carob and oak trees, wild plum and Syrian pear trees, miles of desert gravel surfaces, dry desert riverbeds that flow and flood from time to time, patches of white acacias (the famous fig tree of the Book of Amos), and marshes, swamps, and valleys, including the world's lowest depression, the Dead Sea.

Amid such splendor and beauty, it is no wonder that Moses said before his death (Deut. 33:13):

> Blessed of the Lord be His land; for the precious things of heaven, for the dew, and for the deep that coucheth beneath, and for the precious things of the fruit of the sun.... And for the tops of the ancient mountains, and for the precious things of the everlasting hills, and for the precious things of the earth and the fulness thereof, and the good will of Him that dwelt in the bush.

But Israeli environmentalists face many of the same obstacles as do environmentalists in other countries. Powerful agricultural interests still promote the draining of swamps, the use of deadly pesticides, and the extermination of bats, foxes, and other wildlife. And in the summer of 1990, near the town of Carmiel, Housing Minister Ariel Sharon had twenty thousand trees that were planted by the Jewish National Fund uprooted to make room for apartments for Soviet immigrants.

The Israeli conservationists are committed to save their fabled animals and natural areas, which remind us of what the biblical landscape was once like, and show us a major source of inspiration for many of the Bible's prophets.

## Jewish Animal Protection Groups

In addition to those groups mentioned in the section on Jewish vegetarianism, several individuals and organizations are actively involved in promoting and spreading information on Jewish law concerning conservation and kindness to animals and were the sources for much of the material in this chapter.

The Hebrew word for "life" is CHAI, which also stands for Concern for Helping Animals in Israel. This group, headed by Nina Natelson and headquartered in Alexandria, Virginia,[132] was established to assist animal welfare efforts in Israel, a truly monumental task. According to CHAI:

> Americans familiar with Israel's excellent treatment of wildlife assume that similar conditions are true for domestic animals.... The truth, however, is the opposite.... Starving stray cats and dogs can be seen on the streets of cities and town throughout the country.... The few, small animal shelters in Israel are inadequate.... They receive no financial support from the national or municipal governments, are run mostly by volunteers, and survive entirely on donations from the public.[133]

CHAI is hard at work trying to improve the situation in Israel:

Assistance is urgently needed to expand and modernize the few small and inadequate animal shelters in Israel.... The municipalities in Israel presently control cat and dog overpopulation by putting strychnine poison in food left in the streets. Death by strychnine poisoning takes approximately 1 1/2 to 2 hours (but sometimes up to 10 hours). The animals die of asphyxiation during convulsions.... Pets, as well as the starving strays who consume the poisoned food,... often die before the eyes of the children who own them.[134]

CHAI also helps shelters inspect the often pitifully overworked, underfed, and abused horses, donkeys, and mules used by street vendors. (Israel has a general anticruelty law, but it lacks enforcement provisions.) And CHAI's public education programs, using films, slideshows, and written materials, helps promote sympathetic attitudes toward animals in the schools and elsewhere. This effort is particularly important, since most immigrants to Israel came from Middle Eastern nations with no tradition of animal welfare.

Unfortunately, the Israeli government has not shown any real concern for these problems and has even obstructed efforts to ameliorate them. When CHAI tried to donate an animal ambulance to the Israeli S.P.C.A., the Ministry of Finance blocked the vehicle's entry by demanding a $20,000 payment as customs duty, even though ambulances for humans enjoy a duty-free status. Despite appeals from twenty-five US senators and representatives and numerous others, including the Union of Orthodox Jewish Congregations, the Finance Ministry prevented the delivery of the ambulance that would have taken care of countless sick, stray, and injured animals.

A recent CHAI project has been protesting the Israeli army's use of dogs to carry tear gas bombs and explosives, strapped around their bellies, into tunnels where terrorists may be hiding. The explosives are then detonated by remote control, maiming or killing the dogs.[135]

CHAI has also initiated lawsuits in Israel charging cruelty to animals against a researcher who sews the eyelids of kittens shut in sight deprivation experiments; against Tel Hashomer Hospital for allegedly "keeping monkeys in cages so small they cannot stand up for over two years"; and against a medical school for "opening the skulls of not fully anesthetized cats to demonstrate epileptic seizures to students over the objections of the students."[136]

Another group, Jews for Animal Rights, headed by Roberta Kalechofsky in Marblehead, Massachusetts, describes its mission as "to disseminate the knowledge and values of *Tsa'ar ba'ale hayim*" ("you may not cause sorrow to a living creature"):

This tradition is as old as Judaism itself, and it obliges Jews to attend to the present atrocities being committed against animals.... It is the aim of JAR to . . . recover the original Jewish instinct — that the earth is sacred because God created it, and that a Jew cannot divide God the Creator from the works of His Hand. It is the work of JAR to make this a living insight again.[137]

A group known as *Shomrei Adamah* (Guardians of the Earth), headed by Ellen Bernstein in Wyncote, Pennsylvania, describes its goal as "reintegrating nature and ecology with our Jewish practice, ritual, and prayer. . . . We believe that we live in a unique and critical time in history. We believe that our tradition offers us a way to live in peace with our earth. And we believe that as Jews, we can make a difference in the healing of our planet."[138] The group uses ceremonies like the New Year of the Trees to "re-awaken us to a sense of awe and wonder at the preciousness of the planet we usually take for granted":

Our tradition has taught us: Do not needlessly destroy any living thing. It is tragedy, then, that over the last 2000 years we Jews have become separate from the land and the natural cycles of life. Our estrangement from our earthly roots has meant a profound spiritual and psychological loss for our people. And our failure to advocate for the ecological principles inherent in our Torah has meant a loss to civilization of an ethical system that embraces the earth and all creation. Such an ethical system can prove invaluable to us today in grappling with the environmental problems of this age.[139]

Working with these Jewish groups are two nondenominational organizations that promote these concepts among all religions: the International Network for Religion and Animals (INRA), based in suburban Washington, D.C. (in Silver Spring, Maryland), and headed by Virginia Bourquardez;[140] and the Interfaith Council for the Protection of Animals and Nature (ICPAN), an affiliate of the Humane Society of the United States based in Atlanta, Georgia.[141] (Both groups are discussed above; see p. 173.)

# PART THREE

# *Religions of the East*

# Chapter 12

# Hinduism: The Kinship of All Creatures

Hinduism, primarily a religion of India (nominally adhered to by some 80 percent of the nation), is more than just a creed: it is a total culture, a way of life based on the belief in the unity of all creation. Hindus, like Buddhists, see humankind not as an entity separate from animals, but rather as an integral part of the universe that includes all living creatures.[1]

Although Hinduism is well known for considering cows to be holy, in Hindu doctrine, *all* living creatures, including insects, plants, and trees, are thought to enjoy a kinship with one another and to be worthy of respect and life. This, of course, leads to an appreciation for nature and for the sanctity of "mother earth" and all of her children.[2]

A proverb sums up the ideal Hindu view of the sacredness of life: "Do not kill any animal for pleasure, see harmony in nature, and lend a helping hand to all living creatures." The German philosopher Arthur Schopenhauer (1788–1860) once wrote, "I know of no more beautiful prayer than that which the Hindus of old used in closing their public spectacles: 'may all that have life be delivered from suffering.' "[3]

## The Humane Doctrines of Hinduism

The term "Hinduism" refers to the social and religious system that has developed among the people of India since the third century C.E. This culture encompasses a wide and complex range of practices and beliefs, based on its set of ancient and sacred scriptures called the Vedas. The only firm obligation of devout Hindus is to abide by the rules of their caste, which will ensure that their next life will be a happier one.[4]

One of the tenets of Hinduism that compels kindness to animals is

221

the belief in metempsychosis, the transmigration of souls, or reincarnation, which in India is known as *samsara*. Under this concept, souls are reborn into another life form, with rebirth following rebirth. The status of one's next life, whether one enters into a higher or lower existence, is determined by the law of *karma*, which holds that one's future existence is shaped by the deeds and thoughts of the present life. Every deed of one's life shapes one's soul and is weighted against every other deed, to determine one's destiny.[5]

In the final analysis, the about-to-be reincarnated soul must find a form into which it can fit according to the eternal laws of the universe. An early explanation of the law of karma described it as follows:

> Those who are of pleasant conduct here — the prospect is, indeed, that they will enter a pleasant womb, either the womb of a Brahmin, or the womb of a Kshatriya, or the womb of a Vaisya.*But those who are of stinking conduct here — the prospect is, indeed, that they will enter either the womb of a dog, or the womb of a swine, or the womb of an outcast.[6]

The first of the law books of early India was a collection of rules of how to conduct one's life, drawn up around 200 B.C.E. by Hindu priests.[7] Known as the Code of Manu, it gives a later and more precise analysis of karma:

> In consequence of many sinful acts committed with his body, a man becomes in the next birth something inanimate, in consequence of sins committed by speech, a bird, and in consequence of mental sins he is re-born in a low caste.... Those who committed mortal sins, having passed during large numbers of years through dreadful hells, obtain, after the expiration of that term of punishment, the following births. The slayer of a Brahmin enters the womb of a dog, a pig, an ass, a camel, a cow, a goat, a sheep, a deer, a bird.... A Brahmin who steals the gold of a Brahmin shall pass a thousand times through the bodies of spiders, snakes, lizards, of aquatic animals.... Men who delight in doing hurt become carnivorous animals; those who eat forbidden foods, worms; thieves, creatures consuming their own kind.... For stealing grain, a man becomes a rat; ... for stealing a horse, a tiger; for stealing fruits and roots, a monkey; for stealing a woman, a bear; for stealing cattle, a he-goat.[8]

The code also relates that "he who injures innocuous beings from a wish to give himself pleasure, never finds happiness, neither living nor dead." And another passage states that "he who does not willingly cause the pain of confinement and death to living beings, but desires the good of all, obtains endless bliss. He who injures no creature obtains

---

*The three high orders of the Indian caste system.

without effort what he thinks of, what he strives for, and what he fixes his mind in."[9]

One of the six systems of orthodox Hindu philosophy is the technique of mental discipline known as the Yoga system. The classic *Raja Yoga* of Patanjali includes a vow to abstain from harming living things, known as the practice of *ahimsa*.[10]

This doctrine of *ahimsa* — not harming living creatures — is supposedly adhered to by devout Jainists, Buddhists, and Hindus, and the laws of Manu indicate that vegetarianism is part of this concept. In his book *Vegetarianism as a Way of Life*, Dudley Giehl cites several of these injunctions:

> He who permits [the killing of an animal], he who cuts it up, he who kills it, he who buys or sells [the meat], he who cooks it, he who serves it up, and he who eats it, [all should be considered as] slayers.
>
> Meat can never be obtained without injury to living creatures, and injury to sentient beings is detrimental to [attaining] heavenly bliss; let him therefore shun meat.
>
> Having well considered the [disgusting] origin of flesh and the [cruelty of] fettering and slaying corporeal beings, let him entirely abstain from eating flesh.[11]

Yet, paradoxically, other sections of the laws of Manu seem to sanction flesh-eating under certain circumstances, such as during religious ceremonies involving ritual animal sacrifices. But there are also references to using butter or flour shaped in the form of the animal that can be used as a substitute during such rituals. And G. Naganathan states in his booklet *Animal Welfare and Nature: Hindu Scriptural Perspectives*, "The condemnation of meat-eating has been thorough and unequivocal" (Mahabharata).[12]

In practice, some Hindus adhere, in varying degrees, to a vegetarian diet, and others do not.

A few branches of Sikhism also practice vegetarianism, including the Namdhari sect and the 3HO Golden Temple Movement. Sikhism is a mixture of Hindu and Islamic teachings, and most of the ten million Sikhs are not strict vegetarians. But Sikh scholar Swaran Singh Sanehi, in his book *Vegetarianism in Sikhism*, writes that "Sikh scriptures support vegetarianism fully," and that the religion's founder, Guru Nanak (1469–1538) "considered meat-eating improper."[13]

## Kindness to Animals

Animals are to be treated with kindness and compassion by Hindus, because humans and other creatures are all part of the same family.

According to Dr. Karan Singh, author of "The Hindu Declaration on Nature," "Animals have always received special care and consideration; numerous Hindu texts advise that all species should be treated as children":

> The evolution of life on this planet is symbolized by a series of divine incarnations beginning with fish, moving through amphibious forms and mammals, and then on into human incarnations. This view clearly holds that man did not spring fully formed to dominate the lesser lifeforms, but rather evolved out of these forms itself, and is therefore integrally linked to the whole of creation. This leads necessarily to a reverence for animal life.

And in his foreword to the booklet *Animal Welfare and Nature: Hindu Scriptural Perspectives*, Dr. Singh writes that "in the Hindu view of life, all creation is linked together by a golden thread":

> The seers of the Vedas, therefore, prayed for the welfare not only of the human race but for all living creatures, including animals, and indeed even for such apparently inanimate objects as trees and plants....
>
> The point that emerges is that animals are not to be looked upon as creatures to be cruelly exploited, but as partners with human beings in the spiritual adventure of living. Indeed, although hunting was also an old Hindu tradition, it is surely significant that in both our great epics, the *Ramayana* and the *Mahabharata*, tragedy should have been triggered by hunting episodes.[14]

Birds and animals kept as pets are supposed to be cared for particularly well by Hindus. They often "treat these pets as members of their family, and it is considered to be a pious and religious duty to tend and feed these pets," even before undertaking other duties.[15]

According to Professor S. S. Rama Rao Pappu, who has authored and edited several books on Hinduism, the Hindu doctrine of "unity of life" recognizes "the brotherhood of all living creatures":

> Hinduism recognizes that it is the same life principle which exists in all "life forms" from amoeba to man. The life forms do not differ in *kind* but only in the *degree* of evolution....
>
> Because of the "unity of life" doctrine in Hinduism, God does not show favoritism and neglect other forms of life. Humans alone are not God's chosen creatures....
>
> To the western religious precept, "Love thy neighbor," Hinduism adds, "and every living creature is thy neighbor."[16]

The great Indian leader Mahatma Gandhi (1869–1948), who led the struggle for independence from England, advocated kindness to animals.

He once stated, "The greatness of a nation and its moral progress can be judged by the way that its animals are treated."

Gandhi promoted vegetarianism and criticized the swamis who endorsed meat-eating. He taught that spiritual elevation entailed giving up pleasurable customs that caused others to suffer: "I do feel that spiritual progress does demand at some stage that we should cease to kill our fellow creatures for the satisfaction of our bodily wants. It ill becomes us to invoke in our daily prayers the blessings of God, the compassionate, if we in turn will not practice elementary compassion towards our fellow creatures." [17]

Gandhi has also been quoted as saying, "If the beasts had intelligent speech at their command, they would state a case against man that would stagger humanity."[18]

## The Sacredness of the Cow

In Hinduism, the cow is especially revered and even worshipped. Gandhi called the practice of venerating cows "the central fact of Hinduism, the one concrete belief common to all Hindus.... Protection of the cow means protection of the whole dumb creation of God."

Cows figure in an important way in two of the five major Hindu religious holidays. Janamastami, in August, is the birthday of Lord Krishna, who appeared five thousand years ago as a cow herder in the Indian village of Vrindaban. Krishna is the incarnation or earthly form of Vishnu, the supreme Lord of the World. Krishna demonstrated the necessity of protecting cows, and so is affectionately called Govinda, "one who gives pleasure to the cows."[19]

Today, Govinda is the central figure of renown for the International Society for Krishna Consciousness, popularly known as Hare Krishnas. They consider it "most sinful to kill and eat the flesh of these noble animals":

Vedic scriptures warn that the sinful human who eats the flesh of cows will be reborn and killed as many times as there are hairs on the body of the slaughtered animal. They also explain that the wars among humans directly result from the slaughter and consumption of innocent animals.[20]

Gopastami, falling in mid-November, is the day on which cows and bulls are brought into the temples for worship and to be honored as sacred members of society. Since cows provide milk and bulls plow the fields, these bovines have traditionally been appreciated as important parts of the agricultural society of India.[21]

In the past, the killing of cows has even been punished by the death penalty; and the conflict over the Moslem practice of sacrificing cows has caused rioting and conflict between the two groups.

Yet, paradoxically, the sacrificing of animals has always been, and still is, permitted and practiced by some castes of Hindus; for example, goats are sacrificed in Nepal. Some Hindus maintain that "in spirit, even the sacrificing of an animal is not really the killing of it.... The animal to be sacrificed is not considered to be an animal as such, but becomes a symbol." But this point is probably not fully appreciated by the animal being used.[22]

Hindu scholars say that Hinduism would, under certain circumstances, also approve *necessary* uses of animals in science if there were no alternatives and if the knowledge to be gained were important to improving the conditions of humankind. But the killing of animals for "luxury and fashion," such as to make fur coats, would not be condoned.[23]

### Reverence for Nature

In September, 1986, "The Hindu Declaration on Nature" was delivered by Dr. Karan Singh, president of Hindu Virat Samaj, in Assisi, Italy, summarizing the religion's view on protecting the environment, at the interfaith World Wildlife Conference on religion and nature.

The declaration begins by describing Hinduism's tradition of reverence for life:

> In the ancient spiritual traditions, man was looked upon as part of nature, linked by indissoluble spiritual and psychological bonds with the elements around him. This is very much marked in the Hindu tradition, probably the oldest living religious tradition in the world.... The Hindu viewpoint on nature ... is permeated by a reverence for life, and an awareness that the great forces of nature — the earth, the sky, the air, the water and fire — as well as various orders of life including plants and trees, forests and animals, are all bound to each other within the great rhythms of nature.[24]

In Hindu scriptures, forests and trees have always been considered especially sacred, the declaration states, and flowering trees are the subject of great reverence, often becoming a place of worship.

The declaration concludes that "centuries of rapacious exploitation of the environment have finally caught up with us, and a radically changed attitude toward nature is now not a question of spiritual merit or condescension, but of sheer survival:

> What is needed today is to remind ourselves that nature cannot be destroyed without humankind ultimately being destroyed itself.... This earth, so touchingly looked upon in the Hindu view as the Universal

Mother, has nurtured humankind up from the slime of the primeval ocean for billions of years. Let us declare our determination to halt the present slide toward destruction, to rediscover the ancient tradition of reverence for all life, and, even at this late hour, to reverse the suicidal course upon which we have embarked. Let us recall the ancient Hindu dictum: "The Earth is our mother, and we are all her children."[25]

## The Practice of Modern-Day Hinduism

Today, millions of Hindus in India conscientiously observe the tenets of their religion, adopting a life-style that includes following a vegetarian diet, showing compassion for other creatures, and respecting the natural environment. But many if not most Hindus pay little heed to the letter or the spirit of the admonitions of their faith, especially those intended to prevent and relieve the suffering of animals and the damaging of the environment.

Many Hindus willingly eat meat as long as someone else kills the animal; there is no shortage of slaughterhouses in India. Domestic animals and pets are often neglected, abused, and mistreated. An article by Ethel Mannin in the December 1961 edition of *The Ark* offers an explanation and analysis of the contradictory modern attitude of Easterners by one who has traveled widely in Japan, India, and Burma. Mannin observes that the Hindu and Buddhist "reverence for life" often manifests itself in a refusal to kill animals, but at the same time readily accepts the products of other people's killings. The refusal to put miserable and suffering animals, such as sick and aged cattle or unwanted puppies and kittens, out of their agony, because this would be taking life, results in "frightful cruelty" to animals and a concomitant indifference to suffering. This, she says, "makes a mockery of life as something to be valued, and a travesty of the much-vaunted 'spirituality of the East,' as opposed to 'Western materialism.'"[26]

The massive commercial exploitation of wildlife in India has had a devastating effect on the local ecology. Tens of thousands of monkeys have been taken from the wild (usually infants captured by shooting the mother out of a tree) and exported by animal traffickers for sale to medical researchers, mainly in the United States. (Fortunately, recent governments in India have somewhat restricted this trade.)

Also very damaging has been the massive commercial killing of snakes, lizards, and other reptiles in India for the Western fashion market, their skins to be made into belts, shoes, handbags, and other such goods. Snakes consume, and keep in check, the populations of rats, mice, and other potentially harmful rodents that eat grain, destroy crops, and contaminate food supplies. Thus, the current lack of interest in the

traditional reverence for life may be setting the stage for future massive starvation in the always overpopulated and food-scarce Indian
subcontinent.


## Animal Welfare in India Today

In the late 1980s, the largely inactive animal welfare movement in India
began to show some signs of revival. And there was no shortage of
problems to deal with. Some of these included the export of stray dogs
for meat, and the practice of capturing parakeets and other beautiful
exotic birds by blinding the leader of a flock and netting the others when
they came to its aid.

One of the most prominent figures in the country's environmental and animal protection movements has been Maneka Gandhi, the
widowed daughter-in-law of former Prime Minister Indira Gandhi. Although Maneka Gandhi is the sister-in-law of the recent Prime Minister
Rajiv Gandhi, she also serves as a leader of the nation's opposition party.

According to Maneka Gandhi, Hinduism has had little practical effect
in ameliorating the plight of India's animals. For example, slaughter of
food animals is still carried out in a cruel and primitive fashion:

> Most animals are brought to the city to be killed. They are under the stress
> of a 200 to 300 kilometer journey in trucks that do not accommodate
> animals. They break their legs before they arrive. They are left lying there
> without food and water for a couple of days. Then they kill them [by]
> slitting their throats and letting them bleed to death. Each animal takes 40
> minutes to die.

She points out that animal welfare "does not really exist in the culture we
have developed in the last couple of hundred years. As the population
increases, a certain hardness of heart also creeps in. Man in a panic has
no time for other species."

# Chapter 13 _____

# Jainism:
# Never Harm
# Any Living Creature

Of all the world's religions, none is more strict in its commitment to avoid harming living creatures than Jainism of India. The Jains' reverence for life is so strong that devout Jainist monks go to extreme lengths to avoid harming even insects and "lower" life forms such as mold and yeast. They sweep the path in front of them so as not to walk on insects and refrain from tilling the soil or brewing beverages. The Jainists truly live their religion, adopting a life-style intended to avoid killing any of the earth's other life forms. Yet, this has not prevented them from becoming some of India's most prosperous and successful citizens.

### The Founding of Jainism

Jainism came into being in India in the sixth century B.C.E. as an offshoot of Hinduism. It began as a reaction against the caste system, especially the claims of the Brahmins, the priestly class, to spiritual and social supremacy.

One of those who resisted the Brahmins' claim of superiority was a member of the nobility named Nataputta Vardhamana (599?–527? B.C.E.) who, as the founder of Jainism, came to be known as Mahavira, meaning "Hero" or "Great Man."[1] Said to be the son of a rajah, Mahavira was raised amid great luxury in the courts of ancient India. He led a princely life until he reached thirty years of age, at which time he decided to give away all of his treasures and earthly possessions. He left his wife and daughter, joined a community of monks, and then began to wander the countryside, naked, begging for food and refusing to greet or speak to anyone for twelve years. His purpose was to obtain release or deliverance (*moksha*) from the earthly cycle of birth, death, and rebirth by purifying his soul and practicing *ahimsa*.

The ancient Jainist documents recount the extreme lengths to which he went to avoid harming living creatures:

> Thoroughly knowing the earth-bodies and water-bodies and fire-bodies and wind-bodies, the lichens, seeds, and sprouts, he comprehended that they are, if narrowly inspected, imbued with life, and avoided to injure them. Walking, he meditated with his eyes fixed on a square space before him of the length of a man.... Looking a little sideward, looking a little behind, attentively looking on his path, [he walked so as not to step on any living thing].
>
> Many sorts of living beings gathered on his body, crawled about it and caused pain there. [But he exercised self-control so as not to scratch himself.] Without ceasing in his reflections, the Venerable One slowly wandered about, and, killing no creatures, he begged for his food.[2]

He carried a soft broom to gently sweep the path before him of insects to avoid crushing them. And he carefully examined his food for bugs, worms, eggs, cobwebs, mildew, sprouts, or any other living things, carefully removing any he found before consuming the food.[3]

During the thirteenth year of this quest, during a meditation, Mahavira at last achieved Nirvana, the state of release from the cycle of reincarnation through "victory" over the body and its desires. Afterward, he began to teach and convert people to his way of life, founding orders for monks and nuns without caste distinctions. He successfully carried on his work for thirty years, until his death at age seventy-two.[4]

## The Doctrines of Jainism

The Jainists go to great extremes to consider the rights of all living creatures. Mahavira believed that in order to be released from the cycle of birth, death, and rebirth, one must practice *ahimsa*, the doctrine of not harming any living thing. He would eat only leftover food prepared for someone else, so as to avoid being held accountable for taking the life of something. He carried a cloth to strain out any living beings and to hold over his mouth when talking to keep insects out of it. When outside, he would always examine and clear the ground before lying down to sleep or rest.[5]

Today, some Jainists still wear masks over their mouths and sweep the paths in front of them to avoid inhaling or crushing insects. They carefully inspect fruit that may contain worms, not out of distaste for worms, but because of their regard for life.[6]

The rules of *ahimsa* thus require that they eat only in daylight, to avoid ingesting bugs, and that they show care when traveling on a road and remove beings from the roadway. The Jainists believe that "all beings are fond of life; they like pleasure and hate pain, shun destruction and like to live, they long to live. To all, life is dear."[7]

The Jainists believe in the sacredness and indestructibility of souls, which are ranked according to their number of senses. The highest are those with five senses, and include gods, humans, and animals. Next came those with four senses — bees, butterflies, flies, and large insects. The third group, supposedly having no sight or hearing, comprises small insects and moths. Two-sensed beings are thought to have only taste and touch, and include shellfish, leeches, worms, and small creatures.

The last group, having only a sense of touch, is composed of trees, vegetables, lichens, seeds, "earth-bodies, wind-bodies, water-bodies, and fire-bodies." When freed from matter, these souls, in their pure state, rise to the top of the universe where, along with the other liberated souls, they are perfect and all-knowing, with infinite power and bliss.[8]

Among the vows taken by Jainists monks are pledges to "renounce all killing of living beings. . . . Nor shall myself kill living beings nor cause others to do it, nor consent to it." Several clauses of this vow specify how it is implemented by a *nirgrantha* (or ascetic). Besides being "careful in walk" and "careful in laying down utensils of begging, . . . a Nirgrantha eats and drinks after inspecting his food and drink. If a Nirgrantha would eat and drink without inspecting his food and drink, he might hurt and displace or injure or kill all sorts of living beings."[9]

Less rigorous rules apply to lay Jainists, including vows not to eat meat or engage in any work involving taking of life, and never knowingly to take the life of a sentient creature. The latter vow includes refraining from hunting, fishing, butchering, tilling the soil (because it disturbs insects and worms) and brewing (because it involves fermentation, a chemical reaction often induced by living organisms such as molds, yeast, bacteria, and enzymes).

## The Influence of the Jains

The Jains have always exerted a disproportionate influence on Indian society, considering that they represent less than 1 percent of the population, numbering from three to four million people, living mainly in the Bombay area.[10]

Because of their opposition to animal sacrifices, such practices are illegal in most Indian states, and vegetarianism is commonly practiced throughout the nation.

Animal sanctuaries, called *panjarapor*, can be found in every Jain village throughout India. Here, stray, injured, and unwanted animals, such as cows, camels, water buffalo, pigeons, and parrots, are cared for.[11]

One such hospice is the Charity Birds Hospital, located in a Jain temple complex in the heart of Old Delhi. A 1986 visitor was told by veterinarian Dr. R. K. Punshi that he treats, without charge, over 6,500 birds a year. One included a dazed vulture dropped off in a government limousine at the personal request of then Prime Minister Indira Gandhi, after it had been struck by her helicopter. "We let it rest a few hours and it recovered," said Dr. Punshi.

Describing the hospital's mission, he explained: "All that breathes is precious. Who is to say that the suffering of a sparrow is less worthy of solace than the pain of a man? The spark of life is no dimmer simply because it is encased in fur or feather."[12]

In a Bombay sanctuary, children come to pet the aging cattle that have been rescued from the streets, where they are often left to starve and suffer.[13]

Nor do the Jains neglect their fellow humans, and they have established schools, universities, and hospitals throughout India to help the poor and educate the population on a variety of subjects. At the Jainist schools, no meat-eating or biology experiments involving animals are allowed on campus.[14]

Jains frequent the animal markets of India, often buying up sheep, goats, and other creatures destined to be killed. Many Jains are able to do so, because they have achieved unusual financial success. As pointed out by filmmaker and author Michael Tobias, who has traveled throughout India producing television documentaries, "The Jains are remarkable for their ability to have made a modern success story out of ancient religious beliefs":

> The Jains today constitute one percent [or less] of the Indian population. Yet, by some estimates, their taxable income accounts for over fifty percent of India's total tax base. In addition, Jains contribute the overwhelming share of all Indian philanthropic donations. Their money comes from environmentally-sound, non-violent occupations....
>
> The Jains have found that non-violence pays off.... They have never taken up arms in their entire history. There is no record of Jain crime in modern India....
>
> Jainism is revolutionary, fiercely capitalistic, incredibly successful. Its success is expressly a function of its gentleness.[15]

The Jains have built some 863 temples throughout India, some of which are renowned for their elaborate and exquisite beauty and have become showplaces of Indian architecture.[16] No one may enter a Jain temple wearing leather or any other animal product.

Ironically, the magnificence of these structures built by Jainists, and their economic prosperity, are in sharp contrast with the ascetic early life of their founder. Yet, it is clear that of all the world's religions, the Jains without doubt go to the greatest lengths to live their faith's commitment of reverence for animals and nature.

_____

# Chapter 14

# Buddhism:
# Compassion
# for All Creatures

Buddhism, like Hinduism and Jainism, has as its main tenet the principle of *ahimsa*, "do not destroy life." Moreover, Buddhists are obliged to show compassion to all living creatures: "Compassion means to extend loving kindness to all beings, and it means that we should not kill or cause suffering to any sentient being. It means that we should relieve the suffering of other beings as much as we can."[1]

The views of Buddha, the religion's founder, are summed up in his statement, "The practice of religion involves, as the first principle, a loving compassionate heart for all creatures."[2] Buddha always stressed compassion; and in his Sermon on Loving Kind Compassion, he taught his disciples: "Be of a compassionate mind to all living beings and extend Loving kindness thus: May all living creatures and beings...be freed from sorrow! Be freed from suffering! and be happiness full!"[3]

A reverence for nature, especially trees, forests, and wildlife, is also an integral part of Buddhist philosophy, and Buddhism has exerted a positive influence in some countries in promoting conservation. But, as is the case with other religions, most Buddhists have been less than enthusiastic in following the traditions and injunctions of their faith.

Today, however, some Buddhists leaders are working to reawaken these traditions among their people and to encourage greater appreciation for protecting the environment. The success of these efforts could have far-reaching effects in determining the sustainability of human societies in many nations.

### The Founding and Spread of Buddhism

The founder of Buddhism was Siddartha Gautama (560?–483? B.C.E.), who was born into a wealthy family in northern India. Like Mahavira,

the founder of Jainism, Gautama abandoned a wife and child and renounced his wealthy life to wander the countryside under the most
primitive of conditions.

One day, after entering a grove and meditating at the foot of a tree,
which came to be known as the Bodhi (knowledge)-tree, he experienced
the ecstasy of Nirvana. From then on, he was known as the Buddha,
or the Enlightened One, and he quickly began to gain converts to his
religion.[4]

Buddhism spread rapidly throughout India and into Burma, Cambodia (Kampuchea), Ceylon (now Sri Lanka), China, Japan, Korea,
Mongolia, Siam (now Thailand), and Tibet. Buddhism became the state
religion of China in the fifth century C.E., but later nearly died out in its
mother country, India. Today, there are an estimated 300 to 600 million
Buddhists in the world; and the religion predominates in Burma, the Republic of Korea, Singapore, Sri Lanka, and Thailand. The religion also
has many adherents — in some cases a majority of the population — in
Taiwan, Outer Mongolia, and Nepal, as well as many in Cambodia, Laos,
and Vietnam, where communist governments discourage and suppress
the practice of religion.[5]

Buddhism contains so many different forms of beliefs and organizations that it, like Hinduism, should be considered not a *single* religion
but rather a *family* of them. Yet, there are certain tenets central to the
religion that are shared by all its various denominations. Chief among
these are the concepts of *ahimsa*, or reverence for life, and of the unity
and interrelatedness of all life forms.[6]

### Ahimsa ... Do Not Destroy Life

Of the precepts or injunctions prescribed for all Buddhist monks and lay
associates of the order, the first and most important is, "Refrain from
destroying life," the principle of *ahimsa*.[7]

A respected Tibetan scholar, Venerable Karma Gelek Yuthok, has
cited some stanzas from the Mahayana traditions about compassion for
living things: "Since the doctrine of Buddha specifies compassion, those
who take refuge in it should forsake harming the sentient beings with
a compassionate heart."[8] And the great Buddhist sage Tsongkhapa of
fourteenth-century Tibet taught: "The abandonment of harm to sentient beings is, to forsake all thoughts and deeds as — beating men or
beasts, binding with ropes, trapping and imprisonment, piercing the
noses, over burdening with loads beyond their strength, and similar
activities."[9]

Similarly, Dzogchen Patul Jigme Wangpo, in his volume called *The
Oral Transmission of Samandrabhadra*, writes: "As it has been said that

having taken refuge in The Doctrine, one should abandon harm to the living beings, the acts that are harmful to the other beings should not be done even in one's dreams.... Persevere with strong efforts to protect oneself from such acts."[10]

The world's foremost Buddhist leader, His Holiness Tenzin Gyatso, the fourteenth Dalai Lama (who has lived in exile since the Chinese takeover of Tibet in 1959), strongly advocates kindness to all animals. As he wrote in his book *A Human Approach to World Peace*,

> Whether they belong to more evolved species like humans, or simpler ones such as animals, all beings primarily seek peace, comfort and security. Life is as dear to a mute animal as it is to any human being; even the simplest insect strives for protection from dangers that threaten its life.
>
> Just as each one of us wants to live and does not wish to die, so it is with all other creatures in the universe, though their powers to effect this is a different matter.[11]

As the Dalai Lama told this writer in an interview, "Even ants and other insects will run away from danger.... They have intelligence and want to live, too. Why should we harm them?"[12]

In "The Buddhist Declaration on Nature," written in September, 1986, Nomgyal Rinpoche, the Abbot of Gyuto Tantric University, describes Buddhism as "rooted in genuine and unselfish compassion and love kindness that seeks to bring about light and happiness for all sentient beings":

> Buddhism is a religion of love, understanding and compassion, and committed toward the ideal of nonviolence. As such, it also attaches great importance to wild life and the protection of the environment on which every being in this world depends for survival.
>
> The simple underlying reason why beings other than humans need to be taken into account is that, like human beings, they too are sensitive to happiness and suffering; they too, just like the human species, primarily seek happiness and shun suffering. The fact that they may be incapable of communicating their feelings is no more an indication of apathy or insensibility to suffering or happiness than in the case of a person whose faculty of speech is impaired.[13]

Typifying much of the teachings of Buddhist scriptures, The *Dhammapada* (Verses of the law) states, "Whoever in seeking his own happiness inflicts pain on beings which also seek happiness, he shall find no happiness after death."[14]

## Compassion and Loving Kindness for All Creatures

Buddhism teaches that practicing *ahimsa* leads to a higher stage, that of compassion, altruism, and loving kindness. Of the latter, Buddha has said: "Making, all the time, a rich and extensive offering with all that can be found in the billions of worlds to the supreme noble beings, this merit cannot match one moment of loving kindness."[15] Another well-known teaching that exemplifies the central core of compassion in Buddhism is: "As a mother with her own life guards the life of her own child, let all embracing thoughts for all that lives be thine."[16] And Jiyu-Kennett-roshi has said:

> All things must be treated with utter respect as manifestations of the life force of Buddha, whether they be animal or human.... All creatures feel pain, grief, sorrow, joy, hunger, thirst; all creatures experience the cycle known as birth and death; it is natural and right for all creatures to want, and have the right, to live.[17]

Buddhist doctrine states that adherents "must not hate any being and cannot kill a living creature even in thought" and cites the Buddha as proclaiming, "A *bhikkhu* [monk] who has received ordination ought not intentionally to destroy the life of any living being down to a worm or an ant." The Buddha even ordered all monks not to travel during the rainy season in order to avoid crushing and harming plants and insects.[18]

Buddhists are not permitted to provide to others anything that "may be used to inflict injury on other living beings," such as weapons, nets, and poisons, nor to sell or transfer to others land where animals may be hunted or killed.[19]

Buddhists, of course, condemn killing for sport or pleasure. As one Buddhist publication says:

> Many thousands of living beings are killed each year by hunters and fishers. They consider it to be sport. If the animals and fish had guns and could protect themselves, it would be a different story. If there was an equal chance of the hunter or fisher being killed, it would no longer be "sport." ... They are gratifying their own ego without taking much chance of being hurt themselves.[20]

Buddhists also perceive that insensibility and cruelty toward animals, such as sport hunting, lead to similar treatment of humans. In the words of Nomgyal Rinpoche:

> Many have held up usefulness to human beings as the sole criterion for the evaluation of an animal's life. Upon closer examination, one discovers that this mode of evaluation of another's life and right to existence has

also been largely responsible for human indifference as well as cruelty to animals, not to speak of violence in today's world.

On sober reflection, one can find that there is a striking similarity between exterminating the life of a wild animal for fun, and terminating the life of an innocent fellow human being at the whim of a more capable and powerful person.

We should therefore be wary of justifying the right of any species to survive solely on the basis of its usefulness to human beings.[21]

Buddhism frowns on the eating of meat, and Buddha once said, "how can any faithful follower of the Buddha kill sentient life and eat the flesh?"

## Interrelatedness of All Life

Buddhists believe that all life forms are interrelated and part of a much larger unified life-force. Thus, to do harm to any part of this entity is to harm one's own self, and *all* life:

> In reality, there is only one life force in the universe. All of us are a part of this great Life Force. Whenever we cause suffering to any other being, we are causing suffering to this great Life Force. There is nothing that we do that affects only ourselves. The entire Universe is helped by our acts of compassion but is harmed by our acts of violence and unkindness.[22]

As Roger Corless, in *The Concern for Animals in Buddhism,* describes the cycle of birth, death, and rebirth that is a part of this unified life force:

> A Buddhist believes that he or she has been other than a human in the past and may be other than a human in the future. Thus, a Buddhist human is not intrinsically superior to any other sentient being; he feels as if all other beings are his relatives. In fact, since time, according to Buddhism, has no beginning, a Buddhist recognizes that he has been re-born an infinite number of times as every other sort of being, and that every other being has at one time or another been his mother, bringing him to birth and tenderly caring for him. Sentient beings, then, are sometimes called "mothers" and we seek to repay their kindness even if, at the moment, they happen to be our enemies.[23]

Traditional Buddhist stories, called jataka tales, describe the early births of Buddha, portraying him as such creatures as a lion, horse, dog, rabbit, swan, elephant, woodpecker, monkey, bull, ox, and parrot. In one such story, "The Hungry Tigress," Buddha, as a noble prince, encounters a starving tigress and her cubs. He is so moved by the suffering of the beasts that, in order to save them, he spontaneously offers his own body to them as food![24]

This concept of the cycle of existence and the kinship of all creatures, says Corless, leads to a reverence for all creatures:

> From this realization of the interconnectedness of all living beings in the web of cyclic existence comes the rationale for the first of the Five Precepts which are the foundation of Buddhist ethical conduct: not to harm sentient beings. This generally means that a Buddhist should not kill a sentient being, whether human or animal, and thus should not murder or eat meat. However, Buddhists can, under certain circumstances, go to war or kill in self-defense, and some Buddhists do eat meat.[25]

One explanation for meat-eating is offered by Corless, a rationale that would justify this for some Buddhists:

> On this basis, most Tibetan Buddhists eat meat. They do so because the altitude of the Tibetan mountains makes the growing of crops for human consumption difficult or impossible. So, the cattle eat what grass there is and the humans eat the cattle. But only as many cattle are killed as are strictly necessary. Hunting for sport is considered immoral, and Tibetans who move to more fertile lands, such as America, may become vegetarian. Buddhists in naturally lush countries such as Sri Lanka are more apt to be vegetarian, and Chinese Buddhists, especially the monks and nuns, regard meat eating as repellent to the Buddha and cite scriptural passages commending vegetarianism. Soybean curd (tofu) is thus known in China as "monks' food."[26]

Still, it is clear that Buddhist doctrines strongly discourage the eating of meat, and Buddha is said to have considered the desire to consume flesh foods as an "ignorant craving."

While there is not unanimity among all Buddhist sects concerning vegetarianism, the major denominations agree that Buddha forbade the eating of meat if one saw the creature being slaughtered; if one consented to its being killed; or if one knew the animal was being killed specifically for oneself. The prohibition covering these three conditions leaves open many others under which one might rationalize that meat could be eaten, and many Buddhists freely eat meat from animals that have not been slaughtered specifically for their sake.

Indeed, Buddhism's stress on *intention* over *consequences* provides a loophole, often taken advantage of, allowing the eating of meat that is not killed specifically for one's use. A typical instance of this is described by a traveler to Rangoon who tells of dining with "an eminent Buddhist" who refused to kill the huge cockroaches in his house, "declaring that Buddhists do not take life." He then proceeded to serve roast duck for dinner![27]

## Buddhism's Love for Nature

A reverence for the natural environment has always been one of the most important traditions of Buddhism. Stories of Buddha's early life are filled with natural imagery, especially of trees. According to Buddhist literature, he was born in a forest, in a grove of large-leafed sal trees. Legend has it that as the infant Buddha took his first seven steps, lotuses sprang up in their wake.[28] As a youth, he meditated in the shade of a jambo, a species of myrtle tree; and he later studied under a banyan tree. And Buddha achieved his enlightenment and Buddhahood under the spreading branches of the boddhi (the bo or peepul) tree (*Ficus religiosa*), the tree of knowledge that is considered sacred and special in both Buddhism and Hinduism. And a favorite story of Buddhist children is how Buddha as a child saved the life of a swan.[29]

In its early years, Buddhism showed a deep appreciation for the beauty and diversity of nature. The Buddhist faith has always stressed the necessity to avoid environmental pollution and the contamination of natural resources. According to Dr. Chatsumarn Kabilsingh, of Thammasat University in Bangkok, Thailand, "Centuries before contamination of the earth's water would be the widespread threat to human health that it is today, the Buddha set down rules forbidding pollution of water resources."[30]

Trees and forests are still accorded special respect by Buddhists. According to Dr. Kabilsingh:

Monks are forbidden to cut down trees, and know well the story of a monk long ago, who cut a tree's main branch. The spirit of the tree complained to Buddha, that by doing so, the monk had cut off his child's arm.

Another teaching relates that travelers, after having rested in the shade of a large banyan, on leaving began to cut down the tree. Their actions were condemned. The tree had given them shade, much like a friend, and to harm a friend is indeed an act of evil. . . . [31]

Such teachings remind Buddhists — monks and lay people alike — of the importance of showing respect for trees which provide food, shade and protection not only for people, but for all forest-dwellers.

The results of lack of respect for trees are clearly evident today. When large areas of forest are destroyed, erosion often follows, degrading watersheds, and ultimately making farming fruitless. Animal and plant species, losing their habitats, often disappear.[32]

Early Buddhist texts show an appreciation for the importance of maintaining wildlife habitat:

Among the beautiful expressions in Buddhist literature showing mutual relation and interdependence of humankind and wildlife, there was early on a realization that survival of certain species was in danger, and that losing such creatures diminishes the earth.

Scholars with the Pali Text Society, London, provide this particularly lovely translation of a stanza from the *Khuddakapatha:*

> Come back, O Tigers!, to the woods again, and let it not be leveled with the plains. For without you, the axe will lay it low. You, without it, forever homeless go.[33]

And the Buddhist Zen Master Ikkyu has stated, "The salvation of the birds and animals, oneself included — This is the object of religious practice."[34]

Although devout Buddhists are supposed to live on a diet of fruit, grains, and vegetables, they are also required to be careful not to prevent the growth of such foods. For example, they should be sure the fruit has had the seed removed before eating it.[35]

The *Jataka,* the elaborately narrated Birth Stories of Buddhism, are filled with paeans of praise for the beauty, richness, and diversity of nature. Volumes 4 and 5, in particular, celebrate forests, wildlife, and water. A place called the "Garden of Delight" is described as rich with trees, grass, flowers, rivers, and wildlife.[36]

But as with the eating of meat, Buddhist principles have not always corresponded with their practice. Yi-Fu Tuan, in an *American Scientist* article, "Our Treatment of the Environment in Ideal and Actuality," cites several such examples. Tuan asserts, for instance, that the Buddhists significantly contributed to the depletion of forests throughout much of Asia in order to build temples, causing over half of the deforestation in some areas.[37]

## Asoka: The King of Conservation and Compassion

There is a long Buddhist tradition of practicing, and not just preaching, kindness to animals. One of the most ardent advocates of Buddhism and its reverence for animal life was King Asoka the Great (c. 274–232 B.C.E.), one of the most renowned emperors in the history of India. Asoka gained the throne of Magadha in 273 B.C.E. and proceeded to conquer most of India and to add what is now Afghanistan and Baluchestan. But the misery and bloodshed caused by these conquests caused him great remorse; around 261 he publicly converted from Brahmanism (Hinduism) and became a zealous advocate of Buddhism. From then on, he worked not only to abolish war, but to do everything he could to protect animals.[38]

In order to show his "profound sorrow and regret" for the death and suffering he had caused, Asoka issued a series of edicts engraved upon rocks and pillars. These expressed his great sorrow and resolve to devote his reign to practicing the Buddhist concepts of peace, gentleness, and virtue. These principles were written in various dialects, and were spread throughout his dominion so that they could be read and studied by all his subjects.

The edicts instructed his people to live peacefully and avoid practicing violence, either on each other or against animals. Among the thirty-five edicts he issued in 256 B.C.E. were exhortations in favor of "gentleness toward living creatures" and the rule that "respect for living creatures must be firmly established." Asoka did away with the royal hunt, the traditional "sport" of royalty. Later, he reduced the palace's daily demand for meat to two peacocks and one antelope, and then abolished that amount.[39]

Asoka also issued decrees protecting wildlife throughout his kingdom. The killing of domestic animals for consumption was restricted, and certain animals, such as mothers with young or those under six months of age, could not be slaughtered. It was forbidden to burn forests or even chaff, which often contained living creatures; and on certain days — fifty-six in all — fish and game animals could not be taken. In addition, many types of wildlife were given protection from killing. Animal hospitals and roadside watering stations were established throughout the kingdom.[40]

## Buddhist Views and Actions on the Current Crisis

Religious beliefs and principles tend to lose much of their relevance unless they can be applied to appropriate situations and problems of contemporary society. And today there is a strong movement within Buddhism to improve the welfare of human society and the natural world by fighting the ongoing destruction of the environment.

As the Dalai Lama, the world's leading Buddhist spiritual leader, describes the current environmental crisis:

> As we all know, disregard for the natural inheritance of human beings has brought about the danger that now threatens the peace of the world, as well as the chance to live of endangered species.
>
> Such destruction of the environment and the life depending upon it is a result of ignorance, greed and disregard for the richness of all living things. This disregard is gaining great influence. If peace does not become a reality in the world and if the destruction of the environment continues as it does today, there is no doubt that future generations will inherit a dead world. . . . It is very important that we examine our responsibilities and our commitment to values, and think of the kind of world we are to bequeath to future generations.
>
> It is clear that this generation is at an important crossroad.

Various crises face the international community. The mass starvation of human beings and the extinction of species, . . . the continuing polluting of lakes, rivers and vast parts of the oceans, out of human ignorance and misunderstanding. There is a great danger that future generations will not know the natural habitat of animals; they may not know the forests and the animals which we of this generation know to be in danger of extinction.

We are the generation with the awareness of a great danger. We are the ones with the responsibility and the ability to take steps of concrete action, before it is too late.[41]

Dr. Nay Htun, a Buddhist and professor of environmental engineering, who serves as the Asia representative for the United Nations Environment Program, believes the Buddhist principles of conservation, if applied in time, could save the earth from disaster:

Compassion and tolerance toward all living beings; respect for all forms of life; harmony with nature rather than the arrogance to conquer it; responsible stewardship of nature for the benefit of present and future generations; less profligate use of resources — these are some of the fundamental attitudes and practices that need to be strengthened.

The Lord Buddha recognized these ethical principles and taught and practiced them Himself over two millennia ago. These principles apply even more today.[42]

And Abbot Rinpoche points out in "The Buddhist Declaration on Nature," protection of the environment is fundamental not only to Buddhism, but to the survival of all species, including humans:

People in the past were aware of this need for harmony between human beings and nature. They loved the environment. They revered it as the source of life and well being in the world. In my faraway country, I still remember what my parents said: they told us that various spirits and forces are dormant in the rivers, mountains, lakes and trees. Any harm done to them, they said, would result in drought, epidemics and sickness in human beings, and the loss of the fertility of the earth.

We regard our survival as an undeniable right. As co-inhabitants of this planet, other species too have this right for survival. . . . Human beings as well as other non-human sentient beings depend upon the environment as the ultimate source of life and well being.[43]

## Working to Apply Buddhist Principles

Several groups worldwide are working to apply Buddhist ideals to current problems facing animals and the environment. In the United States, a group founded by students of the Tassajara Zen Monastery, Buddhists Concerned for Animals, in San Francisco, works to educate people to:

see consideration of animals, and responsiveness to their suffering, as an integral part of religious practice. With unprecedented abuse and exploitation of animals in society today, we are joining together in our desire to end cruelty toward animals.

What BCA is trying to do is to nurture a wide sense of non-violence and an understanding which takes into consideration the intimate connectedness of people, plants, animals, and the life of the planet as a whole.[44]

The Zen Center in Rochester, New York, has also been active in promoting animal welfare, and its director, Roshi Philip Kapleau, has authored several articles and a book, *To Cherish All Life*, on the subject.[45]

An international organization, Buddhist Perception of Nature, is working to educate and influence the people and leaders of Asia to protect the remaining natural areas and wildlife there.[46]

In October 1985, Buddhist leaders from Thailand and Tibet announced they were joining forces to try to halt the destruction of the natural environment, calling on Buddhists everywhere to join the campaign. The project was organized by Nancy Nash, a distinguished American journalist and conservationist based in Hong Kong who founded and directs Buddhist Perception of Nature. These efforts have been endorsed and supported by the Dalai Lama and other Buddhist leaders worldwide. As the Tibetan coordinator Lodi G. Gyari put it, "Many of us feel that by doing our part of help save the world's biological resources, we are also helping promote world peace by reducing the stress brought on by destruction of the environment and disappearing resources."[47]

Buddhist perspectives have already been effective in influencing the policies of governments and populations of some Asian nations. For example, Sri Lanka has over 16 million people, 70 percent of whom are Buddhist and 20 percent Hindu. Although the nation is underdeveloped and overpopulated, it is still "a country of wildlife, a place where man and wildlife have lived together in a system of mutual tolerance for centuries."[48] According to Dr. Kabilsingh:

Buddhist teachings emphasize the importance of coexisting with nature, rather than conquering it. Devout Buddhists admire a conserving lifestyle, rather than one which is profligate.

The very core of Buddhism evolves around compassion, encouraging a better respect for and tolerance of every human being and living thing sharing the planet.

Wherever Buddhism is influential, studies will usually show some direct benefit for the natural world. In Sri Lanka, predominantly Buddhist, crowded by western standards, wildlife has not been virtually eliminated, as it has been in many parts of the world. The reason, according to researchers, is the country's largely religious and devout population.

Formal protection generally results from government action, but such actions, it is felt, would never have made much effect if they were not readily accepted by the people. Successful conservation there is based on deep philosophical convictions.[49]

In Thailand, Buddhist influence has helped conserve much of the native wildlife. Dr. Kabilsingh observes that the last remaining refuge for the nation's open-billed storks is Wat Phai Lom, a Buddhist temple near Bangkok:

Open-billed storks would be extinct in Thailand but for the fact their last remaining breeding ground is within the sanctuary of this temple.

Ecologists point out it is scientifically important to save this species of bird, whose sole diet is a local, rice-devouring species of snail. Without the storks, the snails would proliferate, then pesticides would be brought in, and an unnecessary, poisonous cycle would go into effect.

Buddhist precepts of personal and social conduct can take much of the credit for saving the open-billed stork in Thailand.... It is likely that, like the open-billed stork, much of what still survives of the natural world here is linked, in varying degrees, to the influence of Buddhism, the philosophy's focus on awareness, attitudes, and actions which should never harm, and ideally should actively help, all life on earth.[50]

In order to save the rainforests of northeast Thailand, Buddhist monks have begun "ordaining" trees, clothing them in the sacred orange robes of holy men in an effort to make the cutting of a tree tantamount to the unpardonable sin of killing a monk.

Until the Chinese invasion and takeover in 1950, Tibet was "a land where people and wildlife lived together in extraordinary harmony." According to Dr. Kabilsingh,

Many of our *Buddhist Perception of Nature* project's Tibetan research colleagues can point to the time, in living memory, when herds of wild blue sheep, yak, deer and flocks of migrating birds would travel with Tibetan nomads, or land in the midst of human settlements — apparently sensing they were safe. For the most part they were safe from harm, because the country was Buddhist.

The situation since the Chinese takeover has tragically changed, and Tibet is now described as "ecologically devastated" in many respects. In a special report for the U.N. Commission on Human Rights, it is noted that large areas are now deforested, and "a once flourishing wildlife seems to have been virtually wiped out."[51]

Still, there is tremendous potential for promoting conservation throughout Asia through a religiously oriented appeal. Indeed, the teachings of Buddhism, Dr. Kabilsingh points out, could be the salvation of our planet:

> Embodied in Buddhism is much ecologists and other conservation experts explain is urgently needed if destruction of the natural environment is to be halted, and life on earth as we know it is to continue.... That so much of the earth has already been destroyed, and destruction is actually increasing, is insupportable for Buddhists or people who feel a sense of responsibility for the condition of life on this planet now and for future generations.[52]

## Buddhism in Japan

Before the militarization and industrialization of Japanese society in the 1930s, Buddhism, Confucianism, and Shinto all exerted considerable influence over the Japanese people. These religions strive for harmony and cooperation between humans and nature, and the Japanese have traditionally been known as great lovers of nature. They are still renowned for their skill at planting and gardening, and, even in the most urban of settings, for bringing nature — plants and trees — into their homes.

As far back as 675 C.E., the Emperor Temmu Tenno limited the use of hunting devices and the consumption of meat from dogs, horses, cows, and monkeys. The following year, he commanded that certain provinces "let loose living things," a practice that continues throughout East Asia at ceremonial events.[53]

In his book *Japan*, Sir Edward Reed wrote that throughout the Japan of many decades ago, "the life of animals has always been held more or less sacred.... Neither Shintoism or Buddhism requiring or justifying the taking of the life of any creature for sacrifice."[54]

As then Japanese Prime Minister Yasuhiro Nakasone stated in an address to the United Nations at its fortieth anniversary session on October 23, 1985:

> We Japanese derive our beliefs and philosophy from traditions handed down by our ancestors over thousands of years, and from later influences of Confucianism and Buddhism. Basic to our philosophy is the concept that man is born by grace of the great universe.
>
> We Japanese generally believe that the great natural universe is our home, and that all living things should co-exist in harmony with the natural universe. We believe that all living things — humans, animals, trees, grasses — are essentially brothers and sisters.[55]

But such traditions and religious heritage have not prevented the modern, highly industrialized Japanese from becoming among the world's foremost polluters and destroyers of nature. In recent years, Japan has played a major role in wiping out vast populations of whales dolphins, seals, fish, and large areas of tropical rain forests throughout the world.

Prime Minister Nakasone's eloquent account of humankind's assault on the world's life-support systems also provided, unintendedly, an apt description of the activities of Japanese corporations:

> Our generation is recklessly destroying the natural environment which has evolved over the course of millions of years and is essential for our survival.
>
> Our soil, water, air, flora and fauna are being subjected to the most barbarian attack since the earth was created. This folly can only be called suicidal....
>
> Are we not destroying our environment on an unprecedented scale, and perhaps endangering the survival of all life on this planet? As a political leader, I cannot but feel a deep sense of responsibility for the situation I am witnessing.[56]

Much of the impetus for this abandonment of Buddhist principle stems from the post–World War II Western influence that has pervaded Japan. Previously, the killing of four-legged animals was frowned upon, and beef are rarely, if ever, eaten. But after the war, all this changed; and the Japanese were even encouraged by the American occupying forces to resurrect their whaling fleets and go out and help feed Japan. Thus, the impact of Westernization and the resulting lessening of Buddhist influence on these intelligent and industrious people have brought about tragic results for the world's wildlife and forests.

Yet, Buddhist principles are not entirely ignored, and even the Japanese whale killers maintain a sense of reverence for their victims, sometimes conducting ceremonies mourning their souls. For example, in late 1979, a Buddhist ceremony was held to pray for the souls of some sixteen thousand whales killed by the Japanese in the previous three years. In the Zen temple, the priests faced the altar and chanted prayers for the souls of the whales, after which the mourners — mainly crew members of the Japanese whaling ships — lighted sticks of incense. The Japanese Buddhists believe that whales, and other living creatures, have souls; and if one prays for the soul of a creature one has killed for food, it will move up to a higher level.[57]

Part of Japan's whaling culture involves legends of whalers being visited in their dreams by whales pleading for their lives, often pregnant or nursing females who offer to return and be captured if they can be temporarily spared to raise their calves. Whalers who ignored such dreams were said to have been punished severely, and this gave rise to the custom of conducting a burial ceremony for the fetus of a pregnant female. It would be wrapped in the jacket of the captain or harpoon gunner, buried and prayed for as at a human funeral, and a record of it would be inscribed in the books of a temple. Although this custom has been abandoned, in Japan's major whaling ports memorial services for whales are still held.[58]

Even the most hardened whale killers sometimes find they can no longer adapt to these seeming contradictions of Buddhist precepts. Akio Inai was a gunner on a Japanese whaling ship for some twenty-four years and killed over seven thousand whales. But one day he saw a mother whale risk death to return to the area where he was harpooning, to dive under and carry off her slow-moving calf. Afterward, he said, he could not fire his harpoon gun again.[59]

The coexistence of these contradictory Japanese impulses — a simultaneous desire both to revere and to exploit nature — has led to some remarkable ironies. In the late 1970s and early 1980s, Japanese fishermen on Iki Island made headlines around the world when they began regularly and brutally killing tens of thousands of dolphins, which they blamed for eating and depleting the once-abundant schools of fish around the island. (Most scientists said the actual causes of the reduction in fish populations were pollution and overfishing.)

This dolphin slaughter took place regularly for years, with the sea running red with the blood of stabbed cetaceans, despite the Islanders' insistence that they revered the very creatures they were killing. In the Buddhist and Shinto beliefs of the fishing villagers, to kill a dolphin is to court disaster. The Islanders even built shrines to honor the souls of the dead dolphins and of the fish they caught, believing that all life forms are sacred.[60] Yet, the killing continued for years, sparing neither pregnant nor nursing females or their calves, until protests from environmentalists and public opinion forced the slaughter to be ended or reduced.

In other ways, the traditional Buddhist teachings retain some influence in Japan, which is reflected by the low social status accorded those who do society's dirty work:

> In the East, generally, all who have to do with the slaughter of animals and the handling of their carcasses and hides are despised and made outcasts — even in modern Japan, that most progressive of Eastern countries. In Japan, such work is relegated to the *Etas*, the Japanese equivalent of India's untouchables. They live apart and no one would dream of intermarrying with them, ... though society is very happy to avail itself of their services, since they do work that the more "refined," more "ethical" people are not prepared to do for themselves.[61]

But perhaps the greatest abuse brought about by this hypocritical attitude is that of domestic animals in modern Japan, a situation vividly described by Ethel Mannin after a visit to the country:

Japanese cruelty to animals is heart-breaking. It is the cruelty of indifference, of total lack of imagination where animals are concerned: dogs tied
up under the verandas of houses and never off their chains — but never;
birds in tiny cages in which they cannot even stretch their wings — many
of them wild birds; cats which are never fed except for the fish bones and
scrapings of rice from the family plates, and which are always abandoned
when the family moves or goes on holiday; kittens taken to graveyards
and dumped there, because it would be unethical to have them painlessly
destroyed.

My Japanese host was incredulous when he learned that in my absence
a friend went to my London house every other day to feed my cat. "To feed
your cat?" he repeated, as though I had said something so extraordinary
he could not believe he had heard aright. He himself had a little dog
permanently tied up under the veranda surrounding the house; it subsisted
on leavings — mostly rice and fish-bones — from the family's plates.[62]

Yet, even in Japan, humanitarians and conservationists are hard at
work trying to conserve wildlife and help domestic animals. There is,
for instance, the Japanese Animal Welfare Society (JAWS), one of whose
strongest supporters has been Madame Fumihiko Togo, the charming
and influential wife of that country's ambassador to the United States
in the early 1980s. Each year, she had the embassy host a benefit tea
dance, the proceeds of which went to the Washington Humane Society,
the organization that does so much to help injured, sick, lost, homeless,
and abused animals in our nation's capital.

But conservationists have had scant impact in recent years on the
rapacious actions and policies of Japan, which continues to wreak havoc
on the world's ecosystems. The Japanese government would do well
to consider and implement the message of its former Prime Minister
Nakasone, given at his October 1985 address to the United Nations:

> If we are to preserve our irreplaceable Earth and ensure the survival of
> mankind, I believe we must create a new global ethic and devise systems
> to support it.
>
> Let us act today so that future historians can look back on the closing
> years of the Twentieth Century as the era when co-existence and mutual
> respect were achieved among all peoples for the first time and when men
> found a proper balance with nature....
>
> Thus I ask you to join me in a vow. Let us vow to work together so that,
> in the middle of the next century, when Halley's Comet completes another
> orbit and once again sweeps by our planet, our children and grandchildren
> will be able to look up at it and report that the Earth is one, and that
> mankind everywhere is co-existing in harmony and working for the well-
> being of all life on this verdant globe.[63]

*Chapter 15* _____

# Islam:
# Respect for Animals
# and Nature

There is not an animal on earth, nor a bird that flies on its wings, but they are communities like you.[1]

— Mohammed

The Moslem religion, in its laws and traditions, contains extremely strict prohibitions against cruelty to animals and destruction of nature and the natural environment. The Prophet Mohammed (570–632), the founder of the Moslem religion, taught that animals and natural resources, such as trees, should always be treated with reverence and respect. His teachings are recorded in the two most important documents of Islam, the Koran and the *Hadith*, which, together, constitute the original source of Islamic law (the *Shariah*). Both of these documents contain numerous laws and admonitions requiring that Muslims always show compassion to animals and respect for nature.

### The Koran's Humane Message

The most sacred and authoritative document in Islam is the Koran (in Arabic, *Qur'ān*) the holy scripture believed to contain divine revelations made by Allah to Mohammed. As John B. Noss, author of *Man's Religions*, puts it, "What is in the Qur'ān all orthodox Moslems accept for absolute truth; for it is the word of God himself."[2] In the Koran (*Qur'ān Majeed*), numerous injunctions to respect animals and nature are found, including the following:

No kind of beast is there on earth, nor fowl that flieth with its wings, but is a folk like you; then unto their Lord shall they be gathered.[3]

There is no moving creature on earth but God provides for its sustenance.[4]

249

And the earth — He has assigned it to all living creatures.[5]

And the earth — He spread it out for all living beings, with its fruits, blossom-bearing palms, husk-coated grains, and fragrant plants.[6]

In your own creation, as well as in the creation of all the animals pervading the earth, there are portents for those who believe.[7]

Seest thou not that it is God whose praises are celebrated by all beings in heaven and on earth, and by the birds with extended wings? Each one knows its prayer and psalm. And God is aware of what they do.[8]

Seest thou not that unto God pay adoration all things that are in the heavens and on earth — the sun, the moon, the stars, the mountains, the trees, the animals, and a large number among mankind? However, there are many human beings who do not, and deserve chastisement.[9]

Behold! Everything we have created is in due measure and proportion.[10] And the earth — we have spread out its expanse and cast on it mountains in stable equilibrium, and caused life of every kind to grow on it, justly weighed.[11]

Do not spread corruption on earth, after it has been put in order.[12]

And the Koran calls the superstitious practice of the pagans of slitting the ears of animals "devilish acts."[13]

### The Compassionate "Traditions" of Mohammed

A strong tradition of compassion toward animals is also found in the *Hadith*, the collected "traditions" of the prophet Mohammed. He has said, "It behooves you to treat the animals gently"[14] and stated that "verily, there are rewards for our doing good to dumb animals."[15]

The *Hadith* also tells us that "all creatures are like a family of God; and He loves the most those who are the most beneficent to His family."[16] And "Whoever is kind to the creatures of God, is kind to himself."[17] Once, when on a trip, Mohammed scolded his companions who had taken two fledglings of a bird called *hammara*, saying, "Who has injured the feelings of this bird? Return them to her." Another time, he made a man who had robbed a nest restore the eggs to it.[18]

Another *Hadith* (or tradition) of Mohammed says that giving food and drink to animals "are among those virtuous gestures which draw us one step nearer to God." And it is said that "everyone who shows clemency, even towards a mere bird under the knife, will find God's clemency towards him on Doomsday."[19]

## Rewards and Punishments for Treatment of Animals

Mohammed often spoke of the rewards and punishments one would receive according to his treatment of animals. He once said to his companions he had seen a vision of a woman being punished in hell because she had starved a cat to death.[20] Other of his statements include the following from the Koran:

> There is a meritorious reward [*Thawab*] for every act of charity and kindness to every living creature.[21]

> A good deed done to an animal is as meritorious as a good deed done to a human being, while an act of cruelty to an animal is as bad as an act of cruelty to a human being.[22]

> He who takes pity even on a sparrow and spares its life, God will be merciful to him on the Day of Judgment.[23]

> There is no man who kills even a sparrow, or anything smaller, without a justifiable cause, but God will question him about it.[24]

The *Hadith* tells of the punishment one is likely to receive if one curses animals:

> A woman riding a she-camel, being annoyed with her mount, cursed it. God's messenger [Mohammed], let him be blessed and saved, heard this curse. "Take her that is on the back of this camel," he said, "and put her on the earth, for she is accursed." Then he ordered the she-camel to be unloaded and to be sent back so as to punish its rider.[25]

It is also recorded that Mohammed once classified needless killing of animals as one of the seven deadly sins. Saying, "Avoid the seven abominations," he cited as one of the sins the verse from the Koran, "And kill not a living creature, which Allah has made sacrosanct, except for a justifiable reason."[26]

## Mercy to Beasts of Burden

Mohammed took special pity on beasts of burden, used so extensively in Moslem countries, and required that they be treated kindly. He forbade the beating of animals and branding, striking, or painting them on the face. When he saw a donkey who had been branded on the face, he exclaimed, "May Allah condemn the one who branded it."[27] He has been quoted as saying, "The curse of God be upon him who exceedingly punishes any animal," and "whoever has a horse and treats it well, will be treated well by God."[28]

Mohammed showed concern for beasts of burden on other occasions as well, telling his followers, "Do not use the backs of your beasts as pulpits (i.e., dismount for talking and business), for God has only made them subject to you in order that they may bring you to a town you could only otherwise reach by fatigue of body."[29]

Mohammed is also recorded as saying some beasts of burden were better than their riders:

> Do not ride such animals unless they enjoy perfect health. When leaving them after riding, make sure of their state of well-being. Do not use them like easy chairs or pulpits during your speeches on highways or market-places. Verily, there exist among the ridden ones some who are indeed better than their riders, and who praise their Lord more worthily.[30]

On one occasion, when asked why he was wiping his horse's face with his gown, Mohammed replied, "Last night I had a reprimand from Allah regarding my horse for having neglected him."[31] Another time, upon seeing a man riding upon a lean and sickly camel, he said, "Fear God in these dumb animals, and ride them when they are fit to be ridden, and let them go free when it is right that they should rest[32] [or, free them from work while they are still in good health]."[33] Mohammed ordered that horses be treated with special care, saying: "Do not clip the forelock of a horse, for a decency is attached to its forelock; nor its mane, for it protects it; or its tail, for it is its fly-flap."[34]

Mohammed also banned ritualistic abuse of working animals, according to the English Arabic scholar, David Samuel Margoliouth (1858–1940):

> Foolish acts of cruelty which were connected with old superstitions were swept away by him. No more was a dead man's camel to be tied to his tomb to perish of thirst and hunger. No more was the evil eye to be propitiated by the bleeding of a certain portion of the herd. No more was the rain to be conjured by tying burning torches to the tails of oxen.[35]

### Condemnation of Blood Sports

Mohammed repeatedly prohibited sports and amusements involving harm to animals. According to B. A. Masri, an expert authority on Islamic law, "All kinds of animal fights are strictly forbidden in Islam"; and he cites the injunction, "God's messenger forbade inciting animals to fight each other."[36] It is also forbidden for a Muslim to eat the meat of animals that die in public fights, such as at bullfights.[37] Other laws and traditions cited by Masri include the following prohibitions by Mohammed:

He condemned those who take up anything alive as a mere sport.[38]

He forbade blood-sports, as the bedouins used to do.[39]

He forbade using a living creature as a target and condemned those who do so.[40]

He reprimanded some children who were shooting arrows at a ram, saying "Do not maim the poor beast."[41]

He declared the meat of a bird or animal set up and shot at, "*Mujaththema,*" as carrion and unlawful to eat.[42]

Mohammed even condemned caging creatures and called it "a great sin for a man to imprison those animals which are in his power."[43]

Mohammed is said to have stated that "one who kills even a sparrow or anything smaller without a justifiable reason will be answerable to Allah." When he was asked what would be a proper reason, he responded, "To kill for food — not to kill and discard it."[44] In the *Ahadith,* it is told that a companion of Mohammed once saved a hen from being shot:

Ibn 'Umar happened to pass by a party of men who had tied a hen and were shooting arrows at it. When they saw Ibn 'Umar coming, they scampered off. Ibn 'Umar angrily remarked: "Who has done it? Verily! Allah's Messenger has invoked a curse upon one who does this kind of thing."[45]

Muslim literature reports that the Prophet Mohammed forbade the commercial trade in wild animal pelts by banning their use in the following laws found in the *Ahadith:*

The Holy Prophet Muhammad prohibited the use of skins of wild animals.

The Holy Prophet forbade the skins of wild animals being used as floor-coverings.

The Holy Prophet said: "Do not ride on saddles made of silk or leopard skins."[46]

## Islam Requires Humane Slaughter

Mohammed did not forbid killing animals for food, but required that it be done as humanely as possible, saying: "If you must kill, kill without torture."[47] His views are summarized in this statement:

Allah Who is Blessed and Exalted, has prescribed benevolence towards everything and has ordained that everything be done the right way; so, when you must kill a living being, do it the proper way — when you slaughter an animal, use the best method and sharpen your knife so as to cause it as little pain as possible.[48]

Mohammed also stated that one could not keep an animal waiting to be slaughtered[49] and could not kill it while it was tied and bound.[50] He also declared, "Do not deal hastily with a being before it is stone dead";[51] and stated: "Whatever is cut off an animal while it is still alive [al-muthla] is carrion and unlawful [haram] to eat."[52] In order to ensure that no suffering is caused to any animal "with even a flicker of life in it," Mohammed forbade any assault on its body, such as skinning or slicing, until it was cold.[53]

Mohammed once said to a man who was sharpening his knife in the presence of an animal about to be slaughtered: "Do you intend inflicting death on the animal twice — once by sharpening the knife within its sight, and once by cutting its throat?"[54]

And the Imam Hazrat Ali ibn Abi Talib (600?–661) — the fourth caliph (656–61) and the son-in-law of Mohammed — has stated "on the authority of the Holy Prophet": "Do not slaughter an animal in the presence of other animals."[55]

Hazrat 'Umar ibn al-Khattab, the second caliph (634 or 635–644), once saw a man sharpening his knife while holding down a sheep with his foot on its face and chased the man away. Another time he saw a man refusing to give a sheep water to drink before it was slaughtered. He flogged this man too, and made him give water to the sheep.[56] He often said one must "give time to a slaughtered animal, before starting to flay it, till it is dead cold."[57]

According to B. A. Masri, "Many other Muslim authorities have also given juristic opinions (Fatawah) to the same effect that, after slaughter, time should be given for the rigor mortis to set in before cutting up the carcass."[58]

Even though animal sacrifices are still commonly practiced in Moslem countries, the Koran (22:37) offers a better alternative to slaughtering animals: "Their flesh will never reach Allah, nor yet their blood — but your devotion and piety will reach him."[59]

## Islamic Laws Protecting the Environment

The Muslim reverence for the environment has been eloquently summarized in the "Muslim Declaration on Nature." Delivered at the World Wildlife Conference in September, 1986 in Assisi, Italy, by Dr. Abdullah Omar Nasseef, secretary general of the Muslim World League, the statement makes it clear that the earth is not humankind's to abuse:

The essence of Islamic teaching is that the entire universe is God's creation. Allah makes the waters flow upon the earth, upholds the heavens, makes the rain fall, and keeps the boundaries between day and night. The whole of the rich and wonderful universe belongs to God, its maker.

The Muslim obligation to take care of nature is stressed by Dr. Nasseef, who writes that humans should be "responsible trustees of Gods' gifts and bounty ... ":

responsible for maintaining the unity of His creation, the integrity of the earth, its flora and fauna, its wildlife and natural environment.

For the Muslim, mankind's role on earth is that of a *khalifa*, or trustee of God. We are God's stewards and agents on Earth. We are not masters of this Earth; it does not belong to us to do what we wish. It belongs to God and He has entrusted us with its safekeeping.

According to Islamic law, Dr. Nasseef says, humans will be answerable to God for their treatment of the creation:

The *Khalifa* is answerable for his/her actions, for the way in which he/she uses or abuses the trust of God. Islam teaches us that we have been created by God and that we will return to God for judgment. ... The *Khalifa* will render an account of how he treated the trust of God on the Day of Reckoning.[60]

The importance of nature protection is also discussed in a 1983 booklet, *Islamic Principles for the Conservation of the Natural Environment*, written by four scholars in the Department of Islamic Studies (including the chairman) at King Abdul Aziz University in Jeddah, Saudi Arabia. Under the heading "Legislative Rules of Islamic Law," the document states that "protection, conservation, and development of the environment and natural resources is a mandatory religious duty to which every Muslim should be committed":

This commitment emanates from the individual's responsibility before God to protect himself and his community.

Any deliberate or intentional damage to the natural environment and resources is a kind of mischief or corruption that is forbidden by Islam. It is rather a kind of detestable impudence which every Muslim should shun, and which every ruler or supporter should prohibit. ... "He who does not show concern for the interest and good of all Muslims is not a Muslim."[61]

This publication describes how Islamic law requires that we not use up our natural resources, but save them for our children:

Man should not abuse, misuse, or distort the natural resources, as each generation is entitled to benefit from them, but is not entitled to own them permanently.... Nor should he use natural resources irrationally or in such a way as to destroy living resources or spoil their habitats and food bases.... We should not sacrifice the coming generations for the sake of any doubtful material or economic benefit for the contemporary generation.[62]

Concerning wildlife, "Islam emphasizes all measures for the survival and perpetuation of these creatures so that they can fully perform the functions assigned to them, for He considers them living communities, exactly like mankind. God says, 'There is not an animal (that lives) on earth, nor a being that flies on its wings, but [forms part of] communities like you.'" Even insects come under these protective rules:

Also the Prophet (God bless him and grant him peace) has rightly shown us, through his commandments and teachings, how to rear and conserve these creatures. An ant once stung one of the Prophets who then ordered a whole colony of ants to be burned down in retaliation. God taught him in rebuke, "Thou hast destroyed a whole nation that celebrates God's praise for an ant that stung thee."[63]

And a community has the right to protect itself from pollution:

The State has the right to forbid any action, whether temporary or permanent, that may lead to or result in damage or mischief. No one is entitled to stop or even spoil the community's sustainable use of any of the basic elements or resources of the environment. This applies to air pollution by smoke, and exhaust from factories and cars. It equally applies to water pollution through destruction of public wells, or the dumping of toxic materials into them to render them unsuitable or unfit for use.[64]

The booklet goes on to say that "development projects should be designed to achieve all objectives for the overall welfare of all mankind without causing any damage to nature, the environment...and the natural resources," adding that:

Developmental actions and projects undertaken in one country should not lead to or result in any kind of damage, harm, or degradation in the natural environment of another country. Private or local progress should not be achieved at the expense of others, or through damage or anything that leads to damage to others.[65]

The environmental ethics of Islam provide a practical guide to their implementation; and over the centuries, many Islamic scholars and jurists have developed rules and laws to protect nature and natural resources. Great emphasis has been placed on preserving forests, water, and grazing land. The *Shariah* (Muslim law) contains strict rules designed to protect the environment, such as *hima*, preserves set up for the protection of forests and wildlife. There are also *haram* zones, areas where development is prohibited in order to preserve nature. In the thirteenth century, the classical Muslim jurist Izz ad-Din ibn Abd as-Salam even formulated a legal bill of rights for animals![66]

### The Tradition of Reverence for Nature

Mohammed's reverence for nature is reflected in his teachings on the virtue of planting trees:

> Whoever plants a tree and diligently looks after it until it matures and bears fruit is rewarded. Each time a Moslem planteth a tree or soweth a seed, the fruit of this plant that a bird, a man, or a beast shall eat, shall be credited to his account as an alms (or, as charity).[67]
>
> Even when the world is coming to an end "on doomsday, if any one of you has a palm-shoot in hand, he should plant it."[68] The world is green and beautiful, and God has appointed you his stewards over it.[69]

Thus, protection of the natural environment is a tradition handed down directly from Mohammed himself.

The Koran tells us that the earth's natural resources are for animals as well as humans: "And we send down pure water from the clouds, that we may give life thereby, by watering the parched earth, and slake the thirst of those we have created — both the animals and the human beings in multitude."[70]

Some Moslems apparently took these injunctions quite seriously. Gazelles were considered sacred animals by some Arab communities, such as at Mecca and Tabala. According to *The Paper Ark* by Bill Clark, the Harith tribe would wash and bury with a formal ceremony any dead gazelle they found, and then go into mourning for an entire week.[71]

### Muslim Lore on Kindness

Much of the Moslem tradition on kindness to animals was influenced and recorded by the Egyptian jurist and naturalist Kamal al-Din al Damiri (1344?–1405). In his book *Life of Animals*, he set down many stories of the teachings and acts of Moslem holy men concerning animals. There is, for example, the story of a stray cat that would give its food to a blind feline companion, and thus inspired a sheik to consecrate himself to the Lord.[72] Moslem lore also tells of a suffering cat who was helped by a man, and it was this act of compassion that caused him to be forgiven his sins by the Lord.[73]

In another story, a "black slave boy" gives his meager lunch to a hungry stray dog he has taken pity on. This is seen by a wealthy landowner who is so moved, he buys the slave, frees him, and gives him an entire palm grove. Another tale recounts how a faithful dog helps bring to justice the killer of his master.[74]

The blind Arabic poet and philosopher Abu al-Ala al-Maarri (973– 1057), whose writings exerted a profound influence on many generations of Moslems, taught reverence for all animals. He once said that one should not slay any living creature and that it was better to spare a flea than to give alms to the poor.[75]

In *Past and Future Ethics*, by M. A. R. Tuker, the following statement is attributed to Mohammed:

> Truly, there are rewards for our doing good to dumb animals, and giving them water to drink. An adulteress was forgiven who passed by a dog at a well, for the dog was holding out his tongue for thirst, which was near killing him; and the woman took off her boot and tied it to the end of her garment and gave him to drink, and she was forgiven for that act [adultery].[76]

A similar story is recorded of a man filling his shoe with water for a thirsty dog.[77]

There is a tale related by an eighth-century Moslem historian of two Moslems who witnessed an ostrich swallow some jewels and then were themselves accused of committing the crime. They allowed themselves to be beaten severely as thieves rather than reveal what had happened and have the ostrich killed.[78]

## Islam Prohibits Vivisection

The foremost authority in the Western world on Islamic teachings on animals is the aforementioned Al-Hafiz Basheer Ahmad Masri, an expert on the Koran who has been active in animal welfare work for almost half a century. A Sunni Muslim who is the retired imam of the Shah Jehan Mosque in Surrey, England, Masri began his work for animals as far back as 1944 in the British African colony of Tanganyika (now Tanzania). His title "Al-Hafiz" is used by someone who knows the entire Koran by heart.[79]

Masri has written numerous papers and articles on Islam and animals, which have provided much of the material for this chapter. He is also the author of a definitive book on the subject, *Islamic Concern for Animals*, published in England by the Athene Trust, which works "to promote harmony between animals, the natural world, and man."[80] Masri summarizes the theme of his book as follows: "According to the spirit and overall teachings of Islam, causing avoidable pain and suffering to the defenseless and innocent creatures of God is not justifiable under any circumstances."[81]

In his article "Islam and Experiments on Animals" in *International Animal Action* magazine, Masri has set forth a detailed and documented case against vivisection, pointing out that:

> Many of the experiments that are being done on animals in the name of scientific research and education are not really necessary and are sheer cruelty. Such experiments are a contradiction in terms of the Islamic teachings.... According to Islam, all life is sacrosanct and has a right of protection and preservation.

Masri argues that instead of animals "being cut to pieces, organ by organ, just for the students to look at their anatomical structures," the students could instead learn by "using charts, pictures, photographs, dummies, or the corpses of animals that have died their natural death."

> There is no doubt that the Islamic prohibition against the cutting or injuring of live animals, especially when it results in pain, suffering and disfigurement, does apply to modern vivisection in science.... In the Traditions (Ahadith) and the Qur'ān Majeed... we find expressed the principle that any interference with the body of a live animal, which causes pain or disfigurement, is contrary to the Islamic precepts.

Masri does not condemn *all* research on animals, but would sanction it only under very limited circumstances:

> Some research on animals may yet be justified, given the Traditions of Islam, only if the laboratory animals are not caused pain or disfigurement, and only if human beings or other animals would benefit because of the research. The most important of all considerations is to decide whether the experiment is really necessary and that there is no alternative for it. It needs be repeated that the basic point to understand about using animals in science is that the same moral, ethical and legal codes should apply to the treatment of animals as are being applied to humans.[82]

Masri also condemns factory farming as a violation of Islamic precepts:

> In cases where farm animals are reared under inhumane conditions, there are numerous analogous precepts in the Islamic Law forbidding such

kinds of cruelty and declaring the flesh of such animals as unlawful to eat (*Harām*).

Even the battery hens and their eggs . . . even trading in them or their by-products would be unlawful. Verse 63, Chapter 5 of the Qur'ān *Majeed* forbids any kind of food procured by dishonest means.[83]

### The Status of Animals in Today's Moslem World

The humane precepts of Islam are remarkable considering the seeming harshness of many of its laws toward human misconduct, such as cutting off the hand of a thief or stoning to death an adulteress. It should be kept in mind that the early faith of Islam was a product of the mentality of warlike tribes, whose culture had to reflect and adapt to the harsh conditions of life in the desert, where survival itself was often difficult.

In many ways, the Moslem creed considers animals in a utilitarian way, to be used by humans for food, clothing, and beasts of burden, and to be sacrificed in submission to Allah. But the Moslem religion, and the teachings of Mohammed in particular, set a clear limit beyond which we should not go in using animals, forbidding the use of unnecessary abuse, overwork, or cruelty to creatures whose faithful and invaluable service has made possible a way of life in that part of the world.

As *Islamic Principles for Conservation* . . . puts it, Islam looks at animals in two ways:

- As living creatures in themselves attesting to God's wisdom and omnipotence;

- As creatures subjected in the service of man and playing a vital part in the development of this world.[84]

In practice, it is sometimes difficult to reconcile these two views; and it is seldom that animals are given the benefit to this ambiguity.

Anyone who has ever visited or lived in a Moslem country knows that animals in those areas of the world are hardly treated with the compassion and respect required by Islamic law. Indeed, observers are often shocked by the scenes of animal suffering so commonly seen in the Moslem world — overloaded donkeys being whipped and beaten, stray dogs and cats being starved and kicked, sheep being sacrificed in the streets. Little regard is shown for the environment, and even critically endangered species of wildlife are avidly hunted.

Alas, as with Christianity, Judaism, and others of the world's major religions, most present-day Moslems largely ignore or are unaware of their great Islamic tradition of reverence for animals and nature.

# The Baha'i Faith: Loving-Kindness to Every Creature

The Baha'i religion has a long tradition of advocating respect for animals and nature.

The faith began as an offshoot of the Shiite branch of Islam, in Persia (Iran), where it is considered a heresy and is now outlawed and its adherents cruelly persecuted. There are some five million members of the Baha'i faith in twenty thousand Baha'i communities in over 150 countries throughout the world, with one of the most active communities being in the United States.

The founder of the Baha'i faith, Baha'u'llah ("Glory of God," 1817–92), has taught that all religions should unite and that the human race is one under God. Animals and nature are seen as part of the unity of the earth and the universe.[1]

Robert A. White, in an article in the *Journal of Baha'i Studies*, writes that

> all the central figures of the Baha'i Faith had a fond love and a strongly expressed need for contact with the beauty of Nature and the countryside. ...Knowing of Baha'u'llah's love for plants, many of the Baha'is who traveled from Iran to visit him...brought plants with them, refusing to drink the little water they carried across the desert, saving it for the plants.[2]

A January 1990 treatise in the "Baha'i National Review" in the *American Baha'i* set forth the faith's fundamental principles on conservation. Among these are the following:

> Nature is held in high regard. Baha'u'llah states that the contemplation of nature creates an awareness of the "signs" and "tokens" of God and constitutes proof of His existence. Thus:
> ...Every time I lift up mine eyes unto Thy heaven, I call to mind Thy highness and Thy loftiness, and Thine incomparable glory and greatness;

261

and every time I turn my gaze to Thine earth, I am made to recognize the evidences of Thy power and the tokens of Thy bounty. And when I behold the sea, I find that it speaketh to me of Thy majesty, and of the potency of Thy might, and of Thy sovereignty and Thy grandeur. And at whatever time I contemplate the mountains, I am led to discover the ensigns of Thy victory and the standards of Thine omnipotence.

Nature reflects the "names and attributes of God." It is the expression of "God's Will . . . in . . . the contingent world." Baha'u'llah writes:

Say: Nature in its essence is the embodiment of My Name, the Maker, the Creator. Nature is God's Will and is its expression in and through the contingent world. It is a dispensation of Providence ordained by the Ordainer, the All-Wise.[3]

Abdu'l-Baha (1844–1921), the founder's eldest son and successor, has indicated that although humans occupy a station that is "higher and nobler" than nature and are "rulers over nature's sphere and province," nature is nevertheless accorded respect and reference. He has said that "the Lord of all mankind hath fashioned this human realm to be a Garden of Eden, an earthly paradise." And Robert White observes, "To continue to assert the extreme degree of independence and 'false sense of omnipotence' given us by our mastery of Nature now threatens to destroy all life." He quotes Baha'u'llah as saying,

Not a single atom in the entire universe can be found which doth not declare the evidences of His might, which doth not glorify His holy name. . . . So perfect and comprehensive is His creation that no mind nor heart, however keen or pure, can ever grasp the nature of the most insignificant of His creatures.[4]

As another Baha'i publication puts it, "For Baha'is, there follows an implicit understanding that nature is to be respected and protected, as a divine trust for which we are answerable."[5]

The Baha'i Publishing Trust's "Conservation of the Earth's Resources" says,

Traditional respect for nature, born of intimate contact with her power and immediate reliance on her bounties, has virtually disappeared. Its place has been taken by materialistic and exploitative philosophies which have given rise to the economic and political systems that are driving our planet to ruin.[6]

Compassionate treatment of animals is another fundamental tenet of Baha'ism. Baha'u'llah has called for humans to "show kindness to animals," and has written: "Look not upon the creatures of God except with the eye of kindliness and of mercy, for Our loving providence hath pervaded all created things."[7] Abdu'l-Baha has writtenthat "tenderness and loving-kindness (to animals) are basic principles of God's heavenly kingdom":

> Briefly, it is not only their fellow human beings that the beloved of God must treat with mercy and compassion, rather must they show forth the utmost loving-kindness to every living creature. For in all physical respects, and where the animal spirit is concerned, the selfsame feelings are shared by animal and man.... What difference is there when it cometh to physical sensations? The feelings are one and the same, whether you inflict pain on man or beast. There is no difference here whatever. And indeed ye do worse to harm an animal, for man hath a language, he can lodge a complaint.... But the hapless beast is mute, able neither to express its hurt nor take its case to the authorities.... Therefore is it essential that ye show forth the utmost consideration to the animal, and that ye be even kinder to him than to your fellow-man.

Abdu'l-Baha also understood the importance of humane education to a child's character: "Train your children from their earliest days to be infinitely tender and loving to animals. If an animal be sick, let the children try to heal it, if it be hungry, let them feed it, if thirsty, let them quench its thirst, if weary, let them see that it rests."[8]

Although the eating of meat is not banned, it is strongly discouraged by such Baha'i writings as the following:

> Regarding the eating of animal flesh and abstinence therefrom . . . he [man] is not in need of meat, nor is he obliged to eat it. Even without eating meat he would live with the utmost vigor and energy.... Truly, the killing of animals and the eating of their meat is somewhat contrary to pity and compassion, and if one can content oneself with cereals, fruit, oil and nuts, such as pistachios, almonds and so on, it would undoubtedly be better and more pleasing.[9]

Baha'is are called upon by their faith to "make conservation of the environment an integral part of their ongoing activities." Today, the Baha'i International Community's Office of the Environment is active across the globe and has initiated tree planting and protection projects and other training, educational, and conservation programs in over thirty countries.[10]

These activities embody the Baha'is reverential feelings toward nature, which Robert White thus summarizes: "An attitude of awe and gratitude towards the earth is part of attaining spiritual humility.... The human soul is refreshed and revitalized by contact with the beauty, mystery, and grandeur of nature."[11]

# Notes

## Chapter 1 / The Bible's Message of Conservation and Kindness to Animals

1. From a sermon on Love Canal by James N. Brewster, minister of St. Paul's United Methodist Church, Niagara Falls, N.Y., "The Search for a New Bowl and Salt," in *Pro-Earth*, edited by Nadine Hundertmark (New York: Friendship Press, 1985), 58–59

2. Elijah D. Buckner, *The Immortality of Animals* (Philadelphia: George Jacobs, 1903), 38.

## Chapter 2 / Animal Sacrifices: Condemned by the Prophets

1. See, for example, Exodus 21:17, 22:17–19, 31:14–15, 35:2; Leviticus 20:9–10, 13–16, 22–27; Numbers 1:51, 3:10, 38, 15:32–36, 18:7; Deuteronomy 13:5–6, 10–17, 17:3–8, 12, 21:18–21, 22:22–27.

2. See Exodus 23:29–33; Numbers 31:7–9, 15–17, 32–35; 33:33, 50–53; Deuteronomy 7:2–5, 20:10–19; Joshua 6:17–21, 8:24–25; Judges 1:4–18, 25–35, 9:45–54, 12:6; 1 Samuel 15:8, 32–33.

3. See Genesis 24; Exodus 21:2–3, 6–16, 20–27; Leviticus 25:39–46; Deuteronomy 15:17, 21:10–14, 23:15–16; Nehemiah 5:5, 7:66; Jeremiah 22:13–23.

4. Philip Pick, "Judaism and the Vegetarian," *Vegetarian World* (Los Angeles) 2, no. 8 (1976): 6.

5. J. H. Hertz, editor, *The Pentateuch and Haftorahs* (London: Soncino Press, 1958), 560.

6. Ibid., 804.

7. Ibid., 201.

8. Philip Pick, "Judaism and the Vegetarian."

9. J. H. Hertz, *The Pentateuch and Haftorahs*, 518.

10. Ibid., 410–11.

11. See *The Living Bible, Paraphrased* (Wheaton, Ill.: Tyndale House, 1971), 464.

12. Dudley Giehl, *Vegetarianism: A Way of Life* (New York: Harper & Row, 1979), 163.

13. V. A. Holmes-Gore, *These We Have Not Loved* (Wheaton, Ill.: Theosophical Press, 1946), 12–13.

14. Alfred Edersheim, *The Temple: Its Ministry and Services as They Were at the Time of Jesus Christ*, rev. ed. (Boston: Ira Bradley, 1881), 111.

15. Ibid., 100; see also, V. A. Holmes-Gore, *These We Have Not Loved*, 12–13; and Alfred Edersheim, *Life and Times of Jesus*, 1:369–70.

16. *Washington Post,* January 25, 1980, A-18.

17. "Police Seize Animals Prepared for Sacrifice by Cult in the Bronx," *New York Times,* June 8, 1980; Scott Harris, "Sacrifices: Religious Groups Fear Animal Protection Law Would Destroy Rituals," *Los Angeles Times,* reprinted in *Ann Arbor (Michigan) News,* October 9, 1988, B1, 6.

## Chapter 3 / The Early Christian Saints: Compassion and Love for Animals

1. William Edward Hartpole Lecky, *History of European Morals,* vol. 2, chap. 4 (New York: Arno Viers, 1975), 168, 171.

2. Ibid., 161.

3. Andrew Linzey, "Christianity and the Rights of Animals," *The Animals' Voice* magazine (Los Angeles), August 1989, 45.

4. C. W. Hume, *The Status of Animals in the Christian Religion* (London: Universities Federation for Animal Welfare, 1957), 26.

5. Kathe Geist, "Friends in the Wilderness," *Christian Science Monitor,* February 9, 1976, 28.

6. C. W. Hume, *The Status of Animals in the Christian Religion,* 54.

7. John Chrysostom, Homily xxxix, 35, on the Epistle to Romans, as quoted in the Catena Graeca. See Hume, ibid., 21; Charles D. Niven, *History of the Humane Movement* (New York: Transatlantic Arts, 1967), 26.

8. Niven, ibid., 27; *The Animal Stewardship* 1, no. 6, "Reverence for Life" (Los Angeles), July 1974, 4.

9. Ambrose Agius, *The Ark* (London, Catholic Study Circle for Animal Welfare), 103–4.

10. Ibid., 14.

11. Ambrose Agius, *God's Animals* (London: Catholic Study for Animal Welfare, 1970), 54.

12. Ibid.

13. Ambrose Agius, *The Ark,* 104.

14. Ambrose Agius, *God's Animals,* 54.

15. W. E. H. Lecky, *History of European Morals* (New York: Arno Viers, 1975), 2:170–71.

16. Ambrose Agius, *God's Animals,* 54.

17. F. L. Gross, editor, *The Oxford Dictionary of the Christian Church* (London: Oxford University Press, 1957), 558–59.

18. *The Book of Saints,* 5th ed., compiled by the Benedictine Monks of St. Augustine's Abbey, Ramsgate (New York: Thomas Crowell, 1966), 315.

19. W. E. H. Lecky, *History of European Morals,* 170–71.

20. Ibid., 169.

21. Ibid., 169–70.

22. Ibid.

23. Ibid.; *Webster's Biographical Dictionary* (Springfield, Mass.: G. & C. Merriam, 1976), 1135.

24. W. E. H. Lecky, *History of European Morals,* 169.

25.  Ibid.; *Webster's Biographical Dictionary*, 739 and 495.

26.  W. E. H. Lecky, *History of European Morals*, 170.

27.  Ibid.

28.  *Webster's Biographical Dictionary*, 52.

29.  W. E. H. Lecky, *History of European Morals*, 172.

30.  Ambrose Agius, *God's Animals*, 52.

31.  Barry H. Lopez, *Of Wolves and Men* (New York: Charles Scribner's Sons, 1978).

32.  Ambrose Agius, *God's Animals*, 44.

33.  *Webster's Biographical Dictionary*, 157.

34.  Ibid., 1152.

35.  Ambrose Agius, *God's Animals*, 51.

36.  Richard Power, "Pagan Survivals," *The Ark* (London: Catholic Study Circle for Animal Welfare, Christmas 1979), 13.

37.  The Rev. Kevin Daley, Speech at the Annual General Meeting, Catholic Study Circle for Animal Welfare (CSCAW), November 4, 1969, Dublin, Ireland; published by the CSCAW, London.

38.  Ibid.

39.  Ambrose Agius, *God's Animals*, 52.

40.  La Marquise de Rambures, *L'Eglise et la pitié envers les animaux* (Paris: Crepin-Leblond, 1908), 274–75. (English translation Burns and Oates, London, 1908); as quoted by Agius, ibid., 47.

41.  La Marquise de Rambures, ibid., 22; as quoted by Agius, ibid., 46.

42.  La Marquise de Rambures, ibid., 37; as quoted by Agius, ibid., 48.

43.  La Marquise de Rambures, ibid., 123; as quoted by Agius, ibid., 53.

44.  Alban Butler, *Lives of the Saints*, rev. and supplemented by Reverend Herbert Thurston and Donald Attwater (New York: P. J. Kenedy and Sons), 120; as quoted by Agius, ibid., 54–55.

45.  La Marquise de Rambures, *L'Eglise et la pitié envers les animaux*, 269; as quoted in Ambrose Agius, God's Animals, 51.

46.  *Webster's Biographical Dictionary*, 741.

47.  Alban Butler, *Lives of the Saints*, 372; as quoted by Ambrose Agius, God's Animals, 53.

48.  Butler, ibid., 362; as quoted by Agius, ibid.

49.  Butler, ibid., 24; as quoted by Agius, ibid., 53.

50.  Gerald Carson, *Men, Beasts, and Gods* (New York: Charles Scribner's Sons, 1972), 21.

51.  St. Francis of Assisi, *The Little Flowers of St. Francis* (New York: E. P. Dutton, 1951), 36–54.

52.  Michael W. Fox, *Saint Francis of Assisi, Animals, and Nature* (Washington, D.C.: The Humane Society of the United States, 1989), part 1.

53.  W. E. H. Lecky, *History of European Morals*, 172; Barry Lopez, *Of Wolves and Men*, 212.

54.  Lecky, ibid.

55.  Michael W. Fox, *Saint Francis of Assisi, Animals, and Nature*, part 1.

56.  Brochure of the National Catholic Society for Animal Welfare, 1959.

57.  Ambrose Agius, *The Ark*, 104.

58. Thomas of Celano, *Saint Francis of Assisi*, translated from the Latin by Placid Hermann (Chicago: Franciscan Herald Press, 1983); as cited in Michael Fox, *Saint Francis of Assisi, Animals, and Nature*, part 1.

59. C. W. Hume, *The Status of Animals in the Christian Religion*, 27.

60. Ibid.

61. Ambrose Agius, *God's Animals*, 49.

62. Ibid., 47.

63. Ibid.

64. Ibid., 52.

65. W. E. H. Lecky, *History of European Morals*, 172.

66. Ibid., 169.

67. John Ryan, *Irish Monasticism, Origins and Early Developments* (Ithaca: N.Y.: Cornell University Press, 1972), 129.

68. Ambrose Agius, *God's Animals*, 45.

69. Ibid.; W. E. H. Lecky, *History of European Morals*, 161.

## Chapter 4 / The Middle Ages and the Renaissance: The Church Sanctions Cruelty to Animals

1. *Webster's Biographical Dictionary* (Springfield, Mass.: G. & C. Merriam, 1976), 570.

2. Barry Holstun Lopez, *Of Wolves and Men* (New York: Charles Scribner's Sons, 1978).

3. Ibid., 213–17.

4. Ibid., 215.

5. See, for example, Genesis 1:30, Job 12:11, and Ecclesiastes 3:18–21.

6. C. W. Hume, *The Status of Animals in the Christian Religion* (London: Universities Federation for Animal Welfare, 1957), 184.

7. Ibid., 29.

8. Ibid.

9. Thomas Aquinas, "Whether It Is Unlawful to Kill Any Living Things," *Summa Theologica*, part II, question 64, article 1; as cited in C. W. Hume, *The Status of Animals in the Christian Religion*.

10. Thomas Aquinas, "Whether Irrational Creatures Also Ought to Be Loved Out of Charity," *Summa Theologica*, part II, question 25, article 3; as cited in Hume, ibid.

11. Jean Gautier, *Un prêtre se penche sur la vie animale* (Paris: Crepin-Leblond, 1958); English translation, *A Priest Reflects on Animal Life* (New York: Kennedy & Sons, 1957), 97; as cited in Ambrose Agius, *God's Animals* (London: Catholic Study Circle for Animal Welfare, 1970), 10.

12. *Webster's Biographical Dictionary*, 56; Jacques Maritain, *St. Thomas Aquinas* (New York: Sheed and Ward); as cited by Charles D. Niven, *History of the Humane Movement* (New York: Transatlantic Arts, 1967), 34–36.

13. C. W. Hume, *The Status of Animals in the Christian Religion*, 23; Gerald Carson, *Men Beasts, and Gods* (New York: Charles Scribner's Sons, 1972), 20.

14. James George Frazer, *The New Golden Bough*, edited by Theodor H. Gaster (New York: S. G. Phillips, 1959), 646.

15. Barbara W. Tuchman, *A Distant Mirror* (New York: Alfred A. Knopf, 1978), 92, 119.

16. James George Frazer, *The New Golden Bough*, 642–47.

17. Andrew Linzey, "Christianity and the Rights of Animals," *The Animals' Voice* (Los Angeles), August 1989, 44.

18. Gerald Carson, *Men, Beasts, and Gods*, 17.

19. Barry Lopez, *Of Wolves and Men*.

20. Ibid., 225.

21. Ibid., 238.

22. Ibid., 219, 239–40.

23. Ibid., 241.

24. Ibid., 150.

25. E. MacCurdy, *The Mind of Leonardo da Vinci* (London: Jonathan Cape, 1928), 173, 177, 182, 194; as cited by Charles D. Niven, *History of the Humane Movement*, 39.

26. Michel de Montaigne, "Essays," *Encyclopaedia Britannica Great Books* (Chicago, 1952), 25:206–9.

27. Martin Luther, *Luther's Works*, Jaroslav Pelikan, ed. (St. Louis: Concordia, 1955), 9:220; Gerald E. Jones, "Concern for Animals in Five American Churches," dissertation, Brigham Young University, 1972, University Microfilms, 300 N. Zeeb Rd., Ann Arbor, MI 48106, no. 72-23-190.

28. W. E. H. Lecky, *History of European Morals*, vol. 2, chap. 4 (New York: Arno Viers, 1975), 173.

29. Dix Harwood, *Love for Animals* (New York, 1928), 145–46; Gerald E. Jones, "Concern for Animals in Five American Churches."

30. Joseph Wood Krutch, *The World of Animals* (New York: Simon & Schuster, 1961) 19, 25.

31. René Descartes, *Philosophical Letters*, translated and edited by Anthony Kenny (Oxford University Press, 1970).

32. C. W. Hume, *The Status of Animals in the Christian Religion*, 32.

33. Joseph Wood Krutch, *The World of Animals*, 25.

34. C. W. Hume, *The Status of Animals in the Christian Religion*, 57, 181; Ambrose Agius, *God's Animals*, 88; Raphael Brown (author of *Fifty Animal Stories of St. Francis*), letter to Christine Stevens, president, Animal Welfare Institute, Washington, D.C., January 20, 1959.

35. Ibid.; *American Ecclesiastical Review* (Philadelphia) 11 (1894): 42–45, as cited by Brown, ibid.

## Chapter 5 / Changing the "Animal Hell of Merry England"

1. E. S. Turner, *All Heaven in a Rage* (New York: St. Martin's Press, 1965), 55–56.

2. Ibid., 61; Joseph Strutt, *The Sports and Pasttimes of the People of England*

(London, 1831), 283; as cited in Gerald Carson, *Men, Beasts, and Gods* (New York: Charles Scribner's Sons, 1972), 45.

3. W. E. H. Lecky, *History of European Morals* (New York: Arno Viers, 1975), 164.

4. E. S. Turner, *All Heaven in a Rage*, 56–57.

5. Ibid., 116; Charles D. Niven, *History of the Humane Movement* (New York: Transatlantic Arts, 1967), 43; Edward G. Fairholme and Wellesley Pain, *A Century of Work for Animals: The History of the R.S.P.C.A. 1824–1924* (New York: E. P. Dutton, 1924), 16.

6. Fairholme and Pain, ibid.

7. W. E. H. Lecky, *History of European Morals*, 175 (fn.); Gerald E. Jones, dissertation, Brigham Young University, 1972, University Microfilms, 300 N. Zeeb Rd., Ann Arbor, MI 48106, no. 72-23-190, 12.

8. Ibid.

9. Charles D. Niven, *History of the Humane Movement*, 50; E. S. Turner, *All Heaven in a Rage*, 112–18, Gerald Carson, *Men, Beasts, and Gods*, 46.

10. Carson, ibid., 45.

11. Ibid., 23.

12. Ibid.

13. Charles D. Niven, *History of the Humane Movement*, 111.

14. Fairholme and Pain, *A Century of Work for Animals*, 16.

15. *Webster's Biographical Dictionary* (Springfield, Mass.: G. & C. Merriam, 1976), 1051; Gerald E. Jones, "Concern for Animals in Five American Churches."

16. Thomas More, *Utopia* (New York: Collier, 1910), 200–201; as cited in Jones, ibid., 8.

17. *Webster's Biographical Dictionary*, 1240

18. Joseph Wood Krutch, *The World of Animals* (New York: Simon & Schuster, 1961), 23.

19. Ibid.; Gerald E. Jones, "Concern for Animals in Five American Churches," 12.

20. George F. Will, "The Subversive Pope," *Newsweek* October 15, 1979, 140.

21. Fairholme and Pain, *A Century of Work for Animals*, 4–5.

22. Scott Smith, "Human History and Theology," *Vegetarian World* (Los Angeles) 2, no. 10 (1977): 7; John Wesley, *Sermons on Several Occasions* (New York: J. Soule and T. Mason, 1818), 2:167.

23. Wesley, ibid., 113, 167–69.

24. *Webster's Biographical Dictionary*, 222.

25. Fairholme and Pain, *A Century of Work for Animals*, 4.

26. Joseph Butler, *The Analogy of Religion* (Philadelphia: J. B. Lippincott, 1882), 87–88; Gerald E. Jones, "Concern for Animals in Five American Churches," 18.

27. John Hildrop, *Free Thoughts on the Brute Creation* (London, 1754); as cited by Dix Harwood, *Love for Animals* (New York, 1928), 149–51.

28. Fairholme and Pain, *A Century of Work for Animals*, 7–8; Francis H. Rowley, *Our Dumb Animals*, as cited by C. Richard Calore, "The Clergy Speak for Animals," *Voice of the Voiceless* (Los Angeles), n.d., 10.

29. Fairholme and Pain, ibid., 8–9.

30. Ibid., 7.

31. Ibid., 12; Jeremy Bentham, *An Introduction to the Principles of Morals and Legislation* (London, 1780), 310–11; as cited in Emily Stewart Leavitt, *Animals and Their Legal Rights* (Washington, D.C.: Animal Welfare Institute, 1968 [revised 1970]), 9–10; Jeremy Bentham, *The Works of Jeremy Bentham* (New York: Russell and Russell, 1962), 562; as cited in Gerald E. Jones, "Concern for Animals in Five American Churches," 12.

32. Charles Niven, *History of the Humane Movement*, 54–55.

33. Laurence Sterne, *The Life and Opinions of Tristram Shandy* (New York, 1950), 115.

34. Fairholme and Pain, *A Century of Work for Animals*, 11.

35. Ibid., 6.

36. Ibid., 11–12.

37. Joseph Wood Krutch, *The World of Animals*, 22.

38. Fairholme and Pain, *A Century of Work for Animals*, 19, 22; E. S. Turner, *All Heaven in a Rage*, 119–28.

39. Turner, ibid., 120.

40. Ibid., 119–28; Emily Stewart Leavitt, *Animals and Their Legal Rights*, 11.

41. Turner, ibid., 125–28; Leavitt, ibid., 11–12, 24–26.

42. Turner, ibid.; Leavitt, ibid.

43. Charles Niven, *History of the Humane Movement*, 62–63; Fairholme and Pain, *A Century of Work for Animals*, 45; W. E. H. Lecky, *History of European Morals*, 176–77 (fn.).

44. Fairholme and Pain, ibid., 73–74.

45. Ibid., 15, 83–84; E. S. Turner, *All Heaven in a Rage*, 120–30; Gerald Carson, *Men, Beasts, and Gods*, 47; C. Richard Calore, *The Clergy Speak for Animals*, 6; V. A. Holmes-Gore, *These We Have Not Loved* (Wheaton, Ill.: Theosophical Press, 1946), 18.

46. Gerald Carson, *Men, Beasts, and Gods*, 53–56; E. S. Turner, *All Heaven in a Rage*, 129–30; Andrew Linzey, "Christianity and the Rights of Animals," *The Animals' Voice* (Los Angeles), August 1989, 45.

47. C. Richard Galore, *The Clergy Speak for Animals*, 7.

48. Gerald Carson, *Men, Beasts, and Gods*, 47.

49. Samuel Eliot Morrison, *Builders of the Bay Colony* (New York: Houghton-Mifflin, 1930), 232.

50. John G. Wood, *Man and Beast, Here and Hereafter* (London, 1874); *Webster's Biographical Dictionary*, 1594; Emily Stewart Leavitt, *Animals and Their Legal Rights*, 9; Gerald E. Jones, "Concern for Animals in Five American Churches," 21.

51. John Paul Fox, *Animals, Cruelty, and Kindness* (Salt Lake City, 1979), 29, 34.

52. *Animal Rights and Human Obligations*, edited by Tom Regan and Peter Singer (Englewood Cliffs, N.J.: Prentice-Hall, 1976), 72–73, 78–80.

## Chapter 6 / The Settling of America:
## Religious Reverence, and Hatred, for Animals

1. John Robbins, *Diet for a New America* (Walpole, N.H.: Stillpoint, 1987).

2. Emily Stewart Leavitt, *Animals and Their Legal Rights* (Washington, D.C.: Animal Welfare Institute, 1970), 13.

3. Ibid., 13–14.

4. Ibid.

5. Samuel Eliot Morrison, *Builders of the Bay Colony* (New York: Houghton Mifflin, 1930), 232 (fn).

6. Barry Holstun Lopez, *Of Wolves and Men* (New York: Charles Scribner's Sons, 1978), 170–72.

7. Ibid., 142.

8. Ibid.

9. Michael Bean, *The Evolution of National Wildlife Law* (Washington, D.C.: Council on Environmental Quality, 1977), 89; William F. Sigler, *Wildlife Law Enforcement* (Dubuque, Ia.: William C. Brown), 4.

10. Jacqueline Froelich, "A Christian Ecologist's Response to Native American Presence and Spirituality," *Christian Ecology*, Proceedings of the First North American Conference on Christianity and Ecology (NACCE), edited by Frederick W. Krueger (San Francisco: NACCE, 1988), 77.

11. John H. Hess, "French Anthropologist . . . Deplores 20th Century," *New York Times*, December 31, 1969; as cited in Gerald Carson, *Men, Beasts, and Gods* (New York: Charles Scribner's Sons, 1972), 182.

12. Michael Frome, *American Forests*, July 1970, 3.

13. Hope Ryden, *God's Dog* (New York: Coward, McCann, and Geoghegan, 1975), 14–15.

14. "Wild, Wild World of Animals," Time-Life Television, WJLA-TV, Washington, D.C., November 4, 1979.

15. Barry Lopez, *Of Wolves and Men*, 90–91.

16. Ibid.

17. James E. Carroll, "Responsibility and Dominion," in "The Clergy Speak for Animals," *Voice of the Voiceless*, edited by C. Richard Calore (Los Angeles), n.d., 8–9.

18. John C. Ewers, *The Horse in the Blackfoot Indian Culture* (Washington, D.C.: Smithsonian Institution, U.S. Government Printing Office, 1955), 374.

19. Ibid.

20. "This Earth Is Sacred," *Environmental Action Magazine* (Washington, D.C.), November 11, 1972, 7; "This Land Is Sacred to Us," *Pro-Earth*, edited by Nadine Hundertmark (New York: Friendship Press, 1985), 3.

21. John Paul Fox, *Animals, Cruelty, and Kindness* (Salt Lake City, 1979), 3.

22. T. C. McLuhan, *Touch the Earth* (Toronto: New Press, 1971), 6.

23. Ellen Bernstein, *The Trees' Birthday* (Philadelphia: Turtle River Press, 1988), 8–b.

24. David Sterling, "Earth Day, 1990," Winona, Minn., April 1990.

25. Associated Press, "Spiritual Heads Face Deteriorating World," *Atlanta Journal and Constitution* January 13, 1990, B-10.

26. Oren Lyons, "Global Threat Can Unite Humanity," *Daybreak* (Highland, Md.), Summer 1988.

27. William J. Haskett, *Shakerism Unmasked: or, The History of the Shakers* (Pittsfield, 1828), 173.

28. Brochure of American Horse Protection Association, Washington, D.C.; Edward Deeming Andrews, *The People Called Shakers* (New York: Dover, 1963), 120.

29. Anna White and Leila S. Taylor, *Shakerism: Its Meaning and Message*, North Family of Shakers, by Fred J. Heer, Columbus, Ohio, 1904; Gerald E. Jones, "Concern for Animals in Five American Churches," dissertation, Brigham Young University, 1972, University Microfilms, 300 N. Zeeb Rd., Ann Arbor, MI 48106, no. 72-23-190, 45.

30. Edward D. Andrews, *The People Called Shakers*, 284; Gerald E. Jones, "Concern for Animals in Five American Churches," 50.

31. Paulina Bates, *The Divine Book of Holy and Eternal Wisdom*, United Society, called Shakers, Canterbury, N.H., 1849, 413–14; Jones, ibid.

32. Michael Frome, *American Forests*, 3

33. Lynn Riddle, "Shaker Village Buoyed by New Blood," *New York Times*, August 28, 1988, 15; Associated Press, "Shaker's Death Mourned as Sect's Numbers Dwindle," *Atlanta Journal and Constitution* June 18, 1988, 14-D.

34. Howard Williams, *The Ethics of Diet* (London: F. Pitman, 1883), 258–60; Gerald E. Jones, "Concern for Animals in Five American Churches," 32; Bernard Uni, "Vegetarian Roots," *Vegetarian Times*, April 1990, 52–57.

35. John Woolman, *The Journal of John Woolman* (New York: P. F. Collier and Son, 1909), 170–73.

36. Francis H. Rowley, *The Humane Idea* (Boston: American Humane Society, 1912), 37.

37. Ibid., 36.

38. Frances E. Clark, ed., *Poetry's Plea for Animals* (Boston: Lothrop, Lee, and Shepard, 1972), 273–81.

39. Ibid., 259–62, 286–88.

40. Agnes Carr, *The Animals and Birds Redeemed from Death (Their Eternal Glory)* (San Francisco: Filmer Brothers, 1953), 43.

41. Ibid.; C. Richard Calore, "Humane Ministers of the 19th Century," *Voice of the Voiceless* (Los Angeles), n.d.

42. Stephen Fox, *John Muir and His Legacy* (Boston: Little, Brown, 1981).

43. John Muir, *Journal*; as cited in Cleveland Amory, *Man Kind? Our Incredible War on Wildlife* (New York: Harper & Row, 1974), 77–78.

44. Nathaniel P. Reed, Former Assistant Secretary of the Interior, address to the Sierra Club's 1981 Annual Meeting, San Francisco, May 2, 1981.

45. Richard Cartwright Austin, *Baptized into Wilderness: A Christian Perspective on John Muir* (Atlanta: John Knox Press, 1987), 8–9.

46. Ibid.

47. Ibid., 51.

48. Ibid., 42.

49. Ibid., 2–3, 90.

50. Emily Stewart Leavitt, *Animals and Their Legal Rights*, 15–17.

51. Ibid.

52. Zulma Steele, *Angel in Top Hat* (New York, 1942), 35; as cited in Gerald Carson, *Men, Beasts, and Gods*, 95–120.

53. Carson, ibid.; Emily Stewart Leavitt, *Animals and Their Legal Rights*, 17–21.

54. Carson, ibid., 54, 103; William Alan Swallow, *Quality of Mercy: History of the Humane Movement in the United States* (Boston, 1963), 158–60.

55. Gerald E. Jones, "Concern for Animals in Five American Churches," 28.

56. Emily Stewart Leavitt, *Animals and Their Legal Rights*, 135–37.

57. Francis H. Rowley, *The Humane Idea*, 65.

58. Emily Stewart Leavitt, *Animals and Their Legal Rights*, 136–37.


## Chapter 7 / The Catholic Church:
## From Hostility, to Indifference, to Concern


1. W. E. H. Lecky *History of European Morals, from Augustine to Charlemagne* (New York: Arno Viers, 1975).

2. Desmond Morris, *The Human Zoo* (New York, 1969), 76.

3. Anna Kingsford, *The Credo of Christendom*, 239; as cited in V. A. Holmes-Gore, *These We Have Not Loved* (Wheaton, Ill.: Theosophical Press, 1946), 20.

4. Emily Stewart Leavitt, *Animals and Their Legal Rights* (Washington, D.C.: Animal Welfare Institute, 1970), 8; Basil Wrighton, "Justice and the Animals," *The Ark* (London, Catholic Study Circle for Animal Welfare), April 1952.

5. Basil Wrighton, "Cruelty and Sport," *The Ark*, April 1961; *Animal Rights and Human Obligations*, edited by Tom Regan and Peter Singer (Englewood Cliffs, N.J.: Prentice Hall, 1976), 179.

6. Basil Wrighton, "Cruelty and Sport," above note 5.

7. C. W. Hume, *The Status of Animals in the Christian Religion* (London: Universities Federation for Animal Welfare, 1957), 181.

8. Emily Stewart Leavitt, *Animals and Their Legal Rights*, 9.

9. *The Oxford Dictionary of Quotations*, 2nd ed. (London: Oxford University Press, 1955), 254.

10. Ambrose Agius, *God's Animals* (London: Catholic Study Circle for Animal Welfare, 1970), 90.

11. Jean Gautier, *Un prêtre et son chien* (A priest and his dog) (Paris, Crepin-Leblond), 104; as cited in C. W. Hume, *The Status of Animals in the Christian Religion*, 55.

12. Hume, ibid.

13. Ambrose Agius, *God's Animals*, 8.

14. Ibid., 5, 8; *The Shepherd's Crook*, Good Shepherd Shelter, Cobble Hall, Vancouver Island, British Columbia, Canada, April 1966, 1.

15. *The Ark*.

16. Ambrose Agius, "The Catholic Study Circle for Animal Welfare," brochure of CSCAW, London.

17. *The Ark*, December 1961

18. Kevin Daley, "On the Christian Responsibility for the Whole of Creation," *The Ark*, 1969.

19. Ambrose Agius, *God's Animals*, 113.

20. *The Shepherd's Crook*, 9–11.

21. Ambrose Agius, *God's Animals*, 106–7.

22. Ibid., 3.

23. "This Side of Heaven," *The National Observer* (Washington, D.C.), September 16, 1968.

24. Associated Press, "Sparrow's Death Enrages Britons," *Times Herald* (Port Huron, Mich.), August 12, 1979.

25. "Nun Defies Church on Animal Home," *New York Times*, May, 5, 1965; Associated Press, "Nuns Defy New Order to Close B.C. Shelter," *Tacoma News Tribune* August 25, 1965.

26. Helen Jones, president, International Society for Animal Rights, Clark's Summit, Pa.

27. "Priest Asks Humane Treatment Law Protecting Animals in Experiments," *Religious News Service*, Washington, D.C., October 2, 1962; William H. Hendrix, "Churches Spark Anti-Cruelty Drive," *Newark (N.J.) Star-Ledger*, August 16, 1968.

28. J. Barrie Shepherd, "Theology for Ecology," *Catholic World* (New York), July 1970, 172–75.

29. *Voice of the Voiceless*, P.O. Box 17403, Foy Station, Los Angeles, CA 90017.

30. Colman McCarthy, "Papal Specifics," *Washington Post*, September 30, 1979, G-5.

31. International Network for Religion and Animals, 2913 Woodstock Ave., Silver Spring, MD 20910.

32. North American Conference on Religion and Ecology, 5 Thomas Circle N.W., Washington, DC 20005.

33. Andrew Linzey, "Christianity and the Rights of Animals," *The Animals' Voice* (Los Angeles), August 1989, 43.

34. Patrice Greanville, "Animal Intelligencer," *Animals' Agenda*, November 1986, 26.

35. Colman McCarthy, *Washington Post*, December 25, 1988.

36. Ambrose Agius, *God's Animals*, 58.

37. Gerald Carson, *Men, Beasts, and Gods* (New York: Charles Scribner's Sons, 1972), 16–17.

38. Charles D. Niven, *History of the Humane Movement* (New York: Transatlantic Arts, 1967), 32.

39. Cleveland Amory, "The Terrible Truth Behind the Moment of," *Holiday*, October 1969, 79.

40. Ambrose Agius, *God's Animals*, 82–90.

41. "The Catholic Church, an Opponent of Bull-Fighting," *The Ark*, Autumn 1964; Ambrose Agius, *God's Animals*, 89.

42. Agius, ibid.

43. "The Catholic Church, an Opponent of Bull-Fighting."

44. Ambrose Agius, *God's Animals*, 88–89; C. W. Hume, *The Status of Animals in the Christian Religion*, 76, 181; Raphael Brown (author of *Fifty Animal Stories*

*of St. Francis*), letter to Christine Stevens, Animal Welfare Institute, Washington, D.C., January 20, 1959.

45. Brown, ibid.; Charles D. Niven, *History of the Humane Movement*, 44; "The Catholic Church, an Opponent of Bull-Fighting."

46. Ambrose Agius, *God's Animals*, 90.

47. Basil Wrighton, "Cruelty and Sport," *The Ark*.

48. Ambrose Agius, *God's Animals*, 54.

49. Ibid., 107; Ambrose Agius, "The Popes and Animal Welfare," Catholic Study Circle for Animal Welfare, London.

50. James J. Quinn, S.J., "A Proper Respect for Men and Animals," *U.S. Catholic*, June 1965; as cited in Gerald Carson, *Men, Beasts, and Gods*, 41; Justus George Lawler, "Do Animals Have Rights?" *Jubilee* (New York), November 1965, 37.

51. Brochure, National Catholic Society for Animal Welfare (now the International Society for Animal Rights), Clark's Summit, Pa., 1959.

52. Eric H. Hansen, editorial, *Our Dumb Animals*, February 1958.

53. *The Shepherd's Crook*, 1.

54. *L'Osservatore Romano*, March 29, 1982, 9; as cited in Andrew Linzey, *Christianity and the Rights of Animals* (New York: Crossroad, 1987), 155–56.

55. "Pope: Protecting Nature is a Christian Duty," *Atlanta Constitution*, July 13, 1987.

56. "Postscripts," *Wall Street Journal*, November 17, 1989, A11; "Il Santo Padre ai Participanti alla XXV Conferenza Generale della F.A.O.," distributed by International Network for Religion and Animals, Silver Spring, Md.

57. Clyde Haberman, "John Paul Rebukes Lands That Foster Environment Crisis," *New York Times*, December 6, 1989; Associated Press, "Pope Lashes Out at Environmental Degradation," *Atlanta Constitution*, December 6, 1989.

58. Clyde Haberman, "Pope Challenges Rich Nations to Start Sharing," *New York Times*, May 10, 1990, A9; Nancy Nusser, "Capitalism's Toll on Poor Prompts Pope to Demand End to Economic Justice," *Atlanta Constitution*, May 10, 1990.

59. "Peripatetic Pope," *Atlanta Constitution*, January 1990, A-2.

60. "The Population Challenge," Zero Population Growth, Washington, D.C.; "State of the World Population," United Nations Population Fund; as cited in "The World's Population," *Wall Street Journal*, May 15, 1990, A21; and in Paul Lewis, "U.N. Says World Population Will Reach 6.25 Billion by Year 2000," *New York Times*, May 15, 1990.

61. Russell E. Train, former administrator, U.S. Environmental Protection Agency, remarks before the North American Conference on Religion and Ecology, "Caring for Creation Conference," Washington, D.C., May 18, 1990.

62. Ari L. Goldman, "Focus on Earth Day Should Be on Man, Cardinal Cautions," *New York Times*, April 23, 1990, A14.

63. James Clad, "The Fragile Forests, Church Pastoral Letter protests against Despoliation," *Far Eastern Economic Review*, February 25, 1988.

## Chapter 8 / The Protestant Churches: Addressing the Ecological Reformation

1. John Robbins, *Diet for a New America* (Walpole, N.H.: Stillpoint, 1987), 20.

2. V. A. Holmes-Gore, *These We Have Not Loved* (Wheaton, Ill.: Theosophical Press, 1946).

3. Robert McConnell Hatch, "Conservation: A Challenge to the Churches," *Appalachia* (Boston, Appalachian Mountain Club), June 1968.

4. Ibid.

5. Frederick L. Thomsen, "Why People Are Cruel to Animals, part 1, *Report to Humanitarians*, no. 22, Humane Information Services, St. Petersburg, Fla., December 1972, 1.

6. C. Richard Calore, "Foreword," "The Clergy Speak for Animals," *Voice of the Voiceless* (Los Angeles), n.d., 2.

7. Russell E. Train, Remarks before the North American Conference on Religion and Ecology, "Caring for Creation" Conference, Washington, D.C., May 18, 1990.

8. "The NACCE Proceedings: Book Announcement," North American Conference on Christianity and Ecology, San Francisco, 1990; Melvin A. Schmidt, "God So Loved the World," Bluffton, Ohio, March 23, 1990.

9. Charles D. Niven *History of the Humane Movement* (New York: Transatlantic Arts, 1967), 12.

10. Melvin Schmidt, "God So Loved the World."

11. Nathaniel P. Reed, address to Sierra Club's Annual Meeting, San Francisco, May 2, 1981.

12. Ron Wolf, "New Voice in the Wilderness," *Rocky Mountain*, March/April 1981.

13. John A. Hoyt, "Making Earth Our Home," *HSUS News* (Washington, D.C., Humane Society of the United States), Spring 1990.

14. Lynn White, Jr., "The Historical Roots of our Ecological Crisis," *Science* 155, no. 3767 (March 10, 1967): 1205.

15. Ibid.

16. Ibid., 1206.

17. Joseph Wood Krutch, *The World of Animals* (New York: Simon & Schuster, 1961), 21.

18. Edward B. Fiske, "Religion: The Link between Faith and Ecology," *New York Times*, January 21, 1970.

19. Arnold J. Toynbee "The Genesis of Pollution," *Horizon* (New York: American Heritage), Summer 1973, 7.

20. Laura Sessions Stepp, "Modern Garden of Eden Endangered," *Washington Post*, May 16, 1990, A8.

21. Tom Regan, "Religion and Animal Rights," *The Animals' Voice* (Los Angeles), August 1989, 104–5.

22. Tom Regan, "The Promise and Challenge of Religion," *The Animals' Voice*, August 1989, 42.

23. René Dubos, *A God Within* (New York: Charles Scribner's Sons, 1972), 158–59.

24. Vincent Rossi, "Theocentrism: The Cornerstone of Christian Ecology," *Christian Ecology*, North American Conference on Christianity and Ecology, San Francisco, 1988, 27.

25. Lynn White, Jr., "The Historical Roots of our Ecological Crisis," 1205.

26. C. Richard Calore, *The Clergy Speak for Animals*, 8–9.

27. Andree Hickok, "Bless, O Lord, This Thy Creature," *Yankee*, October 1966, 30.

28. Robert McConnell Hatch, "Cornerstones for a Conservation Ethic," *Atlantic Naturalist*, April–June 1967, 155.

29. Robert McConnell Hatch, "Conservation: A Challenge to the Churches," 22.

30. Ibid., 23.

31. Ibid., 23–24.

32. "Caring for Creation Conference Catalyzes New Environmental Coalition," North American Conference on Religion and Ecology, Washington, D.C., June 1990.

33. Mary Baker Eddy, *Science and Health with Key to the Scriptures*, Allison V. Stewart, for the Trustees under the will of Mary Baker Eddy, Boston, 1917, 514–15.

34. Erwin D. Canham, "Dominion Not Despoilment," *Christian Science Sentinel*, May 1, 1971, as quoted in *Cleansing Man's Environment* (Boston: Christian Science Publishing Society, 1972), 2.

35. C. W., Hume, *The Status of Animals in the Christian Religion* (London: Universities Federation for Animal Welfare, 1957), 59.

36. "Christian Faith and Practice," 1959, not further identified.

37. *The Oxford Dictionary of Quotations*, 2nd ed. (New York: Oxford University Press, 1955), 232.

38. Ellen G. White, *Counsel on Diet and Foods* (Takoma Park, Md.: Review and Herald Publishing Association, n.d.), 81.

39. Ellen G. White, *Ministry of Healing* (Takoma Park, Md.: Review and Herald Publishing Association, n.d.), 315.

40. "What Is Man Doing to the Earth?," "Saving the Earth from Ruin," *The Watchtower* (Brooklyn, N.Y.: Watchtower Bible and Tract Society of New York), July 1, 1990, 4–5.

41. "Who Will Inherit the Earth?," *Awake!* (Brooklyn, N.Y.: Watchtower Bible and Tract Society of New York), January 22, 1989, 3.

42. For an extensive description of Mormon teachings on animals, see Gerald E. Jones and Scott Smith, *Animals and the Gospel*, Millennial Productions (2455 Calle Roble, Thousand Oaks, CA 91360), 1980, $3; Gerald E. Jones, "Concern for Animals in Five American Churches," dissertation, Brigham Young University, 1972, University Microfilms, 300 N. Zeeb Rd., Ann Arbor, MI 48106, no. 72-23-190; John Paul Fox, *Animals, Cruelty, and Kindness* (Salt Lake City, 1979), 5, 14–15, 24, 31.

43. Fox, ibid., 4.

44. Scott Smith, personal communication, 1982, 1990.

45. John Paul Fox, *Animals, Cruelty, and Kindness*, 21–22, 30

46. Ibid., 23

47. Scott Smith, "Religion and Food: The Mormons," *Vegetarian World* 11, no. 6 (1976): 13.

48. Gerald E. Jones and Scott Smith, *Animals and the Gospel*; Scott Smith, personal communication, May 21, 1990; letter from Scott Smith, Thousand Oaks, Calif., to Lewis Regenstein, July 23, 1990.

49. Billy Graham, "My Answer," *Detroit Free Press*, June 11, 1975.

50. Ibid. (undated), 1975.

51. Ralph L. Williams, Billy Graham Evangelistic Association, Minneapolis, Minn., June 27, 1975.

52. "NACRE's Executive Summary," North American Conference on Religion and Ecology, Washington, D.C., May 1990.

53. Lloyd Putnam, *Enlarging Our Religion* (Denver, Colo.: American Humane Association, 1957).

54. Richard Koenig, "Can We Save Mother Earth?" *Lutheran Witness*, May 1970.

55. Robert M. Hatch, "Conservation: A Challenge to the Churches."

56. Laurie Johnston "People," *New York Times*, October 7, 1975.

57. "Bless Animals, Curse Hunters," Associated Press, *Oakland (Michigan) Press*, October 4, 1975.

58. C. Richard Calore, "The Clergy Speak for Animals," 5.

59. Ann Cottrell Free, *Animals, Nature, and Albert Schweitzer* (Washington, D.C.: Humane Society of the United States, n.d.).

60. Rachel Carson, *Silent Spring* (New York: Crest Paperback, 1962), vii.

61. "Man in His Living Environment," Report of a Working Party of the Board for Social Responsibility of the Church of England, London, 1970, 24–25; as cited in Andrew Linzey, *Christianity and the Rights of Animals* (New York: Crossroad, 1987), 151.

62. *Man and Nature*, edited by Hugh Montefiore (London: Collins, 1975), 67–68; as cited in Linzey, ibid., 151–52.

63. *RSPCA Today* (London), no. 22 (July 1977): 1, as cited in Linzey, ibid., 152.

64. "General Synod Report of Proceedings, November 1977," vol. 12, no. 3 (London, 1977), 10; as cited in Linzey, ibid.

65. "Statement by the Archbishop of Canterbury on Animal Welfare Matters," Lambeth Palace, London, January 1981, 12–2; as cited by Linzey, ibid., 154–55.

66. Linzey, ibid., 107.

67. Chris Lawson, *Some Quaker Thoughts on Animal Welfare* (London: Quaker Social Responsibility and Education, 1985), 4; as cited in Linzey, ibid., 155.

68. C. W. Hume, *The Status of Animals in the Christian Religion*, 58.

69. "Church and Nation," Report to the General Assembly of the Church of Scotland, 1978; as cited in Andrew Linzey, *Christianity and the Rights of Animals*, 153.

70. C. W. Hume, *The Status of Animals in the Christian Religion*, 58.

71. Ibid.

72. "A Methodist Statement on the Treatment of Animals," adopted by the Methodist Conference, London, 1980, 3; as cited in Andrew Linzey, *Christianity and the Rights of Animals*, 153–54.

73. Jürgen Moltmann, "Reconciliation with Nature," distributed by North American Conference on Religion and Ecology (NACRE), Washington, D.C.

74. Jürgen Moltmann, "Human Rights and Rights of Nature," NACRE, International Conference on Caring for Creation, Washington, D.C., May 15–17, 1990.

75. Ambrose Agius, *God's Animals* (London: Catholic Study Circle for Animal Welfare [CSCAW], 1970).

76. Andrew Linzey, *Christianity and the Rights of Animals*, 63.

77. *The Ark*, Catholic Study Circle for Animal Welfare, London, England.

78. Colman McCarthy, "When the Peaceable Kingdom?" *Washington Post*, December 25, 1988.

79. Russell Train, "Caring for Creation."

## Chapter 9 / The 1980s: A Revolution in Environmental Theology

1. Edward B. Fiske, "Religion: The Link between Faith and Ecology," *New York Times*, January 4, 1970.

2. Ibid.

3. "Church Energy Kit," Energy Education Project, National Council of Churches, New York.

4. "Commitments for Energy Conservation," Interfaith Coalition on Energy, Washington, D.C.

5. *Energy and Ethics*, Energy Education Project, National Council of Churches, New York, 1979, 33–34.

6. Ibid., 4–7.

7. "101 Ways to Help Save the Earth," Greenhouse Crisis Foundation and the Eco-Justice Working Group of the National Council of Churches of Christ, Washington, D.C., 1990.

8. Wes Granberg-Michaelson, "At the Dawn of the New Creation: A Theology of the Environment," *Sojourners* (Washington, D.C.), November 1981.

9. Vincent Rossi, "The Eleventh Commandment: Toward an Ethic of Ecology," *Epiphany Journal* (San Francisco), 1981.

10. Andrew Linzey, "The Place of Animals in Creation: A Christian View," *Animal Sacrifices*, edited by Tom Regan (Philadelphia: Temple University Press, 1986), 116.

11. Andrew Linzey, "Christianity and the Rights of Animals," *The Animals' Voice* (Los Angeles), August 1989, 44–45.

12. Andrew Linzey, *Christianity and the Rights of Animals* (New York: Crossroad, 1987).

13. Ibid., 148–49.

14. Letter from Frederick W. Krueger, North American Conference on Christianity and Ecology (NACCE), San Francisco, June 1, 1987.

15. "Prospectus," NACCE, San Francisco, 1987.

16. Thomas C. Fox, "Coalition Draws Belated Church into Ecostruggle," *National Catholic Reporter*, September 4, 1987.

17. Ibid.

18. Thomas Berry, "Christianity and Ecology: A Critique and a Proposed Statement," NACCE, San Francisco, 1987.

19. Ibid.

20. David Haenke, "Bioregionalism: The Natural Lines of Creation," *Christian Ecology: Building an Environmental Ethic for the Twenty-First Century*, Proceedings of the First North American Conference on Christianity and Ecology, edited by Frederick W. Krueger, San Francisco, 1988, 54.

21. Wendell Berry, "God and Country," *Christian Ecology*; Charmayne Denlinger Brubaker, "Greed and Ignorance Keep Us from Responsible Living," Mennonite Central Committee News Service, September 4, 1987.

22. Hans Schwarz, "Toward a Christian Ecological Consciousness," NACCE, 1987; and excerpted in *Christian Ecology*, 12–14.

23. Calvin B. DeWitt, "A Sustainable Earth: Religion and Ecology in the Western Hemisphere," a paper prepared for the Only One Earth Forum, May 14–15, 1987, AuSable Institute of Environmental Studies, Mancelona, Mich.; Calvin B. DeWitt, "Responding to Creation's Degradation: Scientific, Scriptural, and Spiritual Foundations," August 1987, NACCE, San Francisco.

24. "Prospectus," NACCE.

25. "Stewardship Embraces Conservation," *USA Today*, February 28, 1990.

26. "Liberation of Life," Report from the Consultation of the Sub-Unit on Church & Society of the World Council of Churches, Geneva, held in Annecy, France, September 10–16, 1988.

27. Ibid.

28. Ibid.

29. Ibid.

30. Tom Regan, "Religion and Animal Rights," *The Animals' Voice*, August 1989, 24–27, 104–6.

31. Letter from Rev. Dr. Freda Rajotte, program secretary, World Council of Churches, Geneva, April 26, 1990.

32. "Chronicle," *New York Times*, March 8, 1990, B24; David Clark Scott, "To Save Earth, Ideals Must Change," *Christian Science Monitor*, March 23, 1990; James L. Franklin, "Biologist Asks Christians to Support Animal Rights," *Boston Globe*, July 14, 1979.

33. *Orthodoxy and the Ecological Crisis* (Gland, Switzerland: Ecumenical Patriarchate, World Wide Fund for Nature International, 1990).

34. "Preserving and Cherishing the Earth," an Appeal for Joint Commitment in Science and Religion; Statement of Scientists, Response of Religious Leaders; received from Carl Sagan, Cornell University, Ithaca, N.Y..

35. Jim Castelli, "Worshippers Join Fight to Save the Earth," *USA Today*, February 28, 1990.

36. "Southern Baptists Place New Emphasis on Earth Care," *Firmament: The Quarterly of Christian Ecology* (San Francisco, North American Conference on Christianity and Ecology), Summer 1990, 11.

37. "The Valdez Principles: Religions Invest in Corporate Responsibility,"

*Sabbath Newsletter* (New York, United Nations Environment Program), June 1990, 3.

38. Ibid.

39. "Shining the Light on Animal Creation," Christian Concern for Animals Committee of the Connecticut Conference of the United Church of Christ, Hartford, Conn., 1990.

40. Jim Castelli, "Worshippers Join Fight to Save the Earth."

41. "What on Earth Can I Do?" *The Christophers*, New York (undated).

42. *Sabbath Newsletter*, 1 and 4.

43. Ibid., 4.

44. Ibid., 3.

45. *Animal*, the Magazine of Ministries for Animals (Berkeley, Calif.), Spring/Summer 1988.

46. Frances Arnetta, "Questions Christians (and Others) Should Ask about Animals . . . and Some Answers," Christians Helping Animals and People, Inc., Selden, N.Y.

47. "What on Earth Can I Do?"

48. Melvin A. Schmidt, "God So Loved the World: Telling the Salvation Story as if the Earth Mattered," Bluffton, Ohio, March 23, 1990.

49. Jim Castelli, "Worshippers Join Fight to Save the Earth."

50. Press releases and other material from North American Conference on Religion and Ecology, Washington, D.C., May 1990.

51. Michael W. Fox, presentation at "Caring for Creation Conference," May 1990.

52. "Center for Respect of Life and Environment," brochure, Humane Society of the United States, 2100 L Street N.W., Washington, D.C. 20037.

53. "Replenish the Earth," Interfaith Council for the Protection of Animals and Nature, 4290 Raintree Lane, N.W., Atlanta, GA 30327.

54. "Network News," International Network for Religion and Animals, 2913 Woodstock Ave., Silver Spring, MD 20910, Winter 1990.

55. Personal communication, April 1990.

56. Jim Castelli, "Worshippers Join Fight to Save the Earth."

57. "Christians Grow to 1.75 Billion during 1980's," *Atlanta Constitution*, June 23, 1990, C5. (Most estimates place the number of Eastern Orthodox at 250 million.)

58. Les Ann Kirkland, "Church Activism to Stop Toxic Pollution," *Christian Ecology*, 105–6.

59. Albert Fritsch, statement, *Christian Ecology*, 5.

## Chapter 10 / The Religious Basis for Vegetarianism

1. See, for example, Amos 6:4; Isaiah 7:21–22, 22:13–14; Ezekiel 47:12; Jeremiah 7:16, 21, 16:13, 19; Joel 2:19; Psalm 5:6–10, 50:9–10, 13; Proverbs 23:20–21.

2. William Morris, ed., *The American Heritage Dictionary of the English Lan-*

*guage* (New York: Houghton-Mifflin, 1969), 563 and 876; John B. Noss, *Man's Religions* (New York: Macmillan, 1966), 632.

3. H. Williams, *The Ethic of Diet* (London: F. Pitman, 1883), chaps. 7, 8, and 10; as cited in Keith Akers, *A Vegetarian Sourcebook* (New York: G. P. Putnam's Sons, 1983), 179–80; Dudley Giehl, *Vegetarianism: A Way of Life* (New York: Harper & Row, 1979), 162–63, 174; Steven Rosen, *Food for the Spirit* (New York: Bala Books, 1987), 18–20.

4. Rosen, ibid.

5. Ibid.

6. Jerome, "Against Jovinianus," *Nicene and Post-Nicene Fathers* (New York: Christian Literature, 1895), 6:392–94.

7. Steven Rosen, *Food for the Spirit*, 19.

8. G. G. Coulton, *Inquisition and Liberty* (Peter Smith, 1969), 74; *Heresies of the High Middle Ages*, edited and translated by Walter L. Wakefield and Austin P. Evans (New York: Columbia University Press, 1969), 480; as cited in Dudley Giehl, *Vegetarianism: A Way of Life*, 168.

9. William Paley, *The Principles of Moral and Political Philosophy* (New York: Harper & Brothers, 1849), 283–84; as cited in Giehl, ibid., 60–61.

10. Basil Wrighton, "The Golden Age Must Return: A Catholic's Views on Vegetarianism," *British Vegetarian*, November–December 1965.

11. Steven Rosen, *Food for the Spirit*, 19.

12. Marvyn G. Hardinge, "Vegetarianism: A New Concept?," *Vegetarianism, Life, and Health*, National Health Journal (Washington, D.C.: Review and Herald Publishing Association, 1973), 8; William Metcalfe, *Out of the Clouds, into the Light* (Philadelphia: J. B. Lippincott, 1872), 8–9; Bernard Unti, "Vegetarian Roots," *Vegetarian Times*, April 1990, 52–57.

13. Mary Baker Eddy, *Science and Health with Key to the Scriptures*, Allison V. Stewart, for the Trustees under the will of Mary Baker Eddy, Boston, 1917, 514.

14. Steven Rosen, "Critics Praise . . . " in *Food for the Spirit*.

15. Keith Akers, *A Vegetarian Sourcebook*.

16. John B. Noss, *Man's Religions*, 636–38.

17. *Jesus Was a Vegetarian — Why Aren't You?* (Imlaystown, N.J.: Edenite Society, 1977); *The Humane Gospel of Jesus*.

18. John Robbins, *Diet for a New America* (Walpole, N.J.: Stillpoint, 1987); John Robbins, "Realities, 1989" (Santa Cruz, Calif.: EarthSave Foundation, 1989); "Intense Confinement," *Close-Up Report* (Washington, D.C.: Humane Society of the United States, February 1990); "War on the Environment," Fund Facts (New York: Fund for Animals, 1990); Frances Moore Lappé, *Diet for a Small Planet* (New York: Ballantine Books, 1982).

## Chapter 11 / Judaism: The Jewish Tradition of Kindness

1. "Animals, Cruelty to," *Encyclopedia Judaica* (Jerusalem: Keter, 1974), 6–7.

2. Slavonic Enoch 59:5; Testament of Zebulun 5:1; as cited in "Animals, Protection of," *Universal Jewish Encyclopedia* (New York, 1939), 1:330.

3. J. H. Hertz, ed., *The Pentateuch and Haftorahs* (London: Soncino Press, 1958).

4. Nathan Ausufel, *The Book of Jewish Knowledge* (New York: Crown, 1964), 6.

5. Richard Schwartz, "Judaism and Animal Rights," distributed by CHAI (Concern for Helping Animals in Israel), Alexandria, Va.

6. Rabbi Solomon Ganzfried, *Code of Jewish Law* (New York: Hebrew Publishing Company, 1961), book 4, chap. 191, 84; as cited by Richard H. Schwartz, *Judaism and Vegetarianism* (Smithtown, N.Y.: Exposition Press, 1982), 12.

7. Steven Rosen, *Food for the Spirit* (New York: Bala Books, 1987), 43; Nathan Ausufel, *The Book of Jewish Knowledge.*

8. "A Vision of Vegetarianism and Peace," edited by Rabbi David Hacohen, P.O. Box 64119, Highlands North, Johannesburg, South Africa; as cited in "Jewish Humane Education; Backup Material for 10 Lessons," CHAI (Concern for Helping Animals in Israel), Alexandria, Va.

9. "Jewish Humane Education," ibid.

10. W. E. H. Lecky, *History of European Morals, from Augustus to Charlemagne (1869)* (New York: Arno Viers, 1975), 167 (fn.).

11. Jacob S. Raisin, *Popular Studies in Judaism.*

12. "Man's Place in Nature," *Blessing and Praise: A Book of Meditation and Prayers* (Cincinnati: Central Conference of American Rabbis, 1923), 161.

13. Ibid., 162.

14. Ibid., 163.

15. J. H. Hertz, *The Pentateuch and Haftorahs*, 755; *Authorized Prayer Book*, 290, as cited in Ellen Bernstein, *The Trees' Birthday* (Philadelphia: Turtle River Press, 1988).

16. *Tanhuma*, Deuteronomy *end.*; as cited by Rabbi Barry Freundel, Kesher Israel Congregation, Washington, D.C., "The Earth Is the Lord's: How Jewish Tradition Views Our Relationship and Our Responsibility to the Environment," *Jewish Action*, Summer 1990, 24–25.

17. David Geffen, "New Year of the Trees," *Southern Israelite* (now *Atlanta Jewish Times*), February 1, 1980, 5.

18. Ibid.

19. Gemera Baba Bathra, Baba Kamma 82b, as cited in Barry Freundel, "The Earth Is the Lord's," 22–23.

20. Koheleth Rabbah, 7:28; as cited in Barry Freundel, 22

21. Ellen Bernstein, "The Earth's Seder," *Reform*, March 1989.

22. David Geffen, "New Year of the Trees"; Barry Freundel, "The Earth Is the Lord's," 22–24.

23. Freundel, ibid.

24. "Covenant for Conservation," Interfaith Coalition on Energy, Washington, D.C., 1978.

25. Arthur Hertzberg, "The Jewish Declaration on Nature" and "The Jewish Celebration," statements presented at World Wildlife Conference, Assisi, Italy, September 1986; distributed by the International Network for Religion and Animals, Silver Spring, Md.

26. J. H. Hertz, *The Pentateuch and Haftorahs*, 854

27. Ibid.

28. Barry Freundel, "The Earth Is the Lord's."

29. *Universal Jewish Encyclopedia,* 326.

30. Ibid.

31. Arthur Hertzberg, "The Jewish Declaration on Nature."

32. Sidney J. Jacobs, "Who Shall Live? Who Shall Die?" *Animals' Agenda* (Monroe, Conn.), October 1989, 26.

33. J. H. Hertz, *The Pentateuch and Haftorahs,* 29–30.

34. Ibid., 83.

35. Ibid., 298.

36. Ibid., 532.

37. Ibid., 672–73.

38. *Encyclopedia Judaica.*

39. Arthur Hertzberg, "The Jewish Declaration on Nature."

40. *Encyclopedia Judaica.*

41. *Universal Jewish Encyclopedia,* 326.

42. Ibid.

43. Ellen Bernstein, *The Trees' Birthday,* 5a.

44. *Code of Jewish Law.*

45. "Jewish Humane Education."

46. Arthur Hertzberg, "The Jewish Declaration on Nature."

47. "Jewish Humane Education."

48. Ibid.

49. Alfred J. Kolatch, *The Jewish Book of Why* (Middle Village, N.Y.: Jonathan David, 1981).

50. "Jewish Humane Education."

51. Alfred Kolatch, *The Jewish Book of Why.*

52. Ibid.

53. James A. Rimbach, "The Judeo-Christian Tradition and the Human/ Animal Bond," *International Journal for the Study of Animal Problems* (Washington, D.C., Humane Society of the United States), July/September 1982, 198–207.

54. J. H. Hertz, *The Pentateuch and Haftorahs,* 767.

55. Ibid.

56. Richard H. Schwartz, "Vegetarianism Is Good for Us," *Jewish Spectator* (Santa Monica, Calif.), Summer 1980, 54–56.

57. *Code of Jewish Law,* 84.

58. J. H. Hertz, *The Pentateuch and Haftorahs,* 854.

59. Richard Schwartz, "Vegetarianism Is Good for Us."

60. *Encyclopedia Judaica,* 6; Philip Pick, "Let Us Show Compassion...", *Vegetarian World* (Los Angeles) 2, no. 8 (1976): 5–6.

61. Ibid.

62. Maimonides, Yad, Shabbat 21:9–10, as referenced in *Encyclopedia Judaica,* 6.

63. "Jewish Humane Education."

64. "Judaism Condemns White Veal," *Agscene* (Compassion in World Farming), United Kingdom, August/September 1988, 16.

65. J. H. Hertz, *The Pentateuch and Haftorahs*, 855.

66. Ibid.

67. Gerald Carson, *Men, Beasts, and Gods* (New York: Charles Scribner's Sons, 1972), 209.

68. Ellen Bernstein, "Panel Questions Kosher Slaughter Practices," *Atlanta Jewish Times*, March 17, 1989, 18–A.

69. Nina Natelson, "Where Are the Jewish Voices in the Fight for Animal Rights?" *Detroit Jewish News*, September 23, 1988.

70. Ellen Bernstein, "Panel Questions Kosher Slaughter Practices."

71. Ibid.

72. Nina Natelson, "Where Are the Jewish Voices in the Fight for Animal Rights?"

73. Sidney J. Jacobs "A Jewish Voice for Animals," *The Animals' Voice* (Los Angeles), August 1989, 48–49.

74. Ibid.; Sidney J. Jacobs, "Who Shall Live? Who Shall Die?" 31.

75. Arthur Hertzberg, "The Jewish Declaration on Nature"; *Encyclopedia Judaica*.

76. Dennis Prager, *The Nine Questions People Ask about Judaism* (New York: Simon & Schuster, 1981).

77. Simon Glazer, *Guide to Judaism* (New York: Hebrew Publishing Company, 1971).

78. Dudley Giehl, *Vegetarianism as a Way of Life* (New York: Harper & Row, 1979), 77–78.

79. Ibid.

80. Ibid.

81. *Encyclopedia Judaica*.

82. Richard Schwartz, "Vegetarianism Is Good for Us."

83. *Universal Jewish Encyclopedia*, 327, 330.

84. Ibid.

85. Richard Schwartz "Vegetarianism Is Good for Us."

86. Dudley Giehl, *Vegetarianism as a Way of Life*, 78.

87. Ibid., 142–43.

88. Sidney Jacobs, "Who Shall Live? Who Shall Die?" 33; Richard Schwartz, *Judaism and Vegetarianism*.

89. Richard Schwartz, "Vegetarianism Is Good for Us."

90. "A Vision of Vegetarianism and Peace," edited by Rabbi David Hacohen, P.O. Box 64119, Highlands North, Johannesburg, South Africa; as cited in "Jewish Humane Education; Backup Material for 10 Lessons," CHAI (Concern for Helping Animals in Israel), Alexandria, Va.

91. Sidney Jacobs, "Who Shall Live? Who Shall Die?" 32.

92. "Jewish Vegetarians," P.O. Box 1463, Baltimore, MD 21203.

93. Roberta Kalechofsky, "Philip Pick...," *Animals' Agenda* (Monroe, Conn.), October 1989, 30; Ben Gallob, "Jewish Vegetarianism: A Growing Movement," *Atlanta Jewish Times*, April 3, 1987, 27.

94. Kalechofsky, ibid.; Gallob, ibid.

95. Ben Gallob, ibid.

96. Roberta Kalechofsky, Micah Publications, 255 Humphrey St., Marblehead, MA 01945.

97. Roberta Kalechofsky, "Haggadah for the Liberated Lamb," Micah Publications, Marblehead, Mass.

98. J. H. Hertz, *The Pentateuch and Haftorahs*, 213.

99. Richard Schwartz, "Biblical Stories and Legends from the Jewish Tradition Related to Compassion for Animals," excerpts from *Judaism and Vegetarianism*, by Richard Schwartz; distributed by CHAI.

100. J. H. Hertz, *The Pentateuch and Haftorahs*, 854.

101. Richard Schwartz, "Biblical Stories and Legends from the Jewish Tradition."

102. Ibid.

103. Ibid.; S. Y. Agnon, *Days of Awe* (Jerusalem: Schocken, 1939); as cited in "Jewish Humane Education."

104. Ben Ami, quoted by Joe Green, *The Jewish Vegetarian Tradition*, 19–20; as cited in "Jewish Humane Education."

105. David Rimbach, "The Judeo-Christian Tradition and the Human/Animal Bond," 203.

106. Martin Buber, "Tales of the Hasidim," 1:249; as cited in "Jewish Humane Education"; Richard Schwartz, "Biblical Stories and Legends from the Jewish Tradition."

107. "Jewish Humane Education."

108. Ibid.

109. Roberta Kalechofsky, "Haggadah for the Liberated Lamb," 9.

110. Albert Vorspan, *The Crisis of Ecology: Judaism and the Environment* (New York: Union of American Hebrew Congregations, 1970).

111. *Jewish Spectator* (New York), June 1969.

112. Arthur Hertzberg, "The Jewish Declaration on Nature."

113. "What Are We Doing?" Jewish Theological Seminary of America, *New York Times*, October 5, 1989.

114. *The Union Prayerbook for Jewish Worship* (New York: Central Conference of American Rabbis, 1973,, part 2, 10.

115. Ibid., 23–24.

116. Ibid., 41.

117. Ibid., 42.

118. Ibid., 54.

119. Roberta Kalechofsky, "Haggadah for the Liberated Lamb."

120. *The Union Prayerbook*, 128, 190, 194, 251, 298–99, 347.

121. *Gates of Repentance: The New Union Prayerbook for the Days of Awe* (New York: Central Conference of American Rabbis, 1978), 83, 92, 181, 299–301, 366.

122. Ibid., 367.

123. Ibid., 329.

124. *High Holiday Prayerbook*, compiled by Rabbi Morris Silverman (Hartford, Conn.: Prayer Book Press, 1956), 212, 230, 253, 462.

125. Marianne Bernhard, "Sacred Books Buried by Synagogues," *Washington Post*, May 2, 1980, C-16.

126. Roger Caras, "The Promised Land: Israel for Biblical Beasts," *International Wildlife* (National Wildlife Federation), May–June 1973.

127. Ibid.

128. Raphael Rothstein, "General Yoffe's Biggest Battle," *Audubon Magazine* (New York), March 1972; Bertram B. Johansson, "Modern 'Ark' to Save Biblical Animals," *Christian Science Monitor*, December 12, 1973; "Noah's Park," *Time*, August 28, 1972.

129. Ibid.; Martin Zucker, "Biblical Animals of the Holy Land," *Animal Kingdom*, March 1972.

130. Ibid.; Terence Smith, "Israel Preserving Animals of Bible," *New York Times*, November 29, 1972.

131. Yossi Leshem, "Air Space Co-Existence Is Not Only for the Birds!" *Israel: Land and Nature* (quarterly journal of the Society for the Protection of Nature in Israel, Tel Aviv), Winter 1985–86, 89–90.

132. CHAI, P.O. Box 3341, Alexandria, VA 22302.

133. "What Are Conditions for Animals in Israel?," CHAI; "Chai Lights," Winter 1985–86; and other CHAI material.

134. Nina Natelson, "Where Are the Jewish Voices in the Fight for Animal Rights?"

135. "Update on Reports of IDF's Use of Dogs as Walking Explosives," CHAI, 1989.

136. Letter to CHAI members, CHAI, 1990.

137. Roberta Kalechofsky, Jews for Animal Rights, 255 Humphrey St., Marblehead, MA 01945.

138. Shomrei Adamah, Church Rd. and Greenwood Ave., Wyncote, PA 19095.

139. Ellen Bernstein, "The Earth's Seder," *Reform Magazine*, March 1989.

140. Virginia Bourquardez, International Network for Religion and Animals (INRA), 2913 Woodstock Ave., Silver Spring, MD 20910.

141. Interfaith Council for the Protection of Animals and Nature, 4290 Raintree Lane, N.W., Atlanta, GA 30327.

## Chapter 12 / Hinduism: The Kinship of All Creatures

1. John Walters, *The Essence of Buddhism* (New York: Thomas Y. Crowell, 1964), 10; Agnes Carr, *The Animals and Birds Redeemed from Death (Their Eternal Glory)* (San Francisco: Filmer Brothers, 1953), 45; Durg Chauhan, "Animals and Ahimsa: The Hindu Perspective," *INROADS* (International Network for Religion and Animals, P.O. Box 1335, North Wales, PA 19454), Summer/Fall 1990, 2.

2. G. Naganathan, *Animal Welfare and Nature: Hindu Scriptural Perspectives*, Center for Respect of Life and Environment, 2100 L Street, N.W., Washington, D.C., 1989.

3. Agnes Carr, *The Animals and Birds Redeemed from Death*; Marie Dreyfus, *Crimes against Creation* (Trowbridge, Wiltshire, England: Massey, n.d.), 164.

4. John B. Noss, *Man's Religions* (New York: Macmillan, 1966), 122–23.

5. Agnes Carr, *The Animals and Birds Redeemed from Death*; Marie Dreyfus, *Crimes against Creation*, 153–63.

6. *The Thirteen Principal Upanishads*, translated by R. E. Hume (London: Oxford University Press, 1934), 233.

7. Basil Wrighton, "Animals in the Other Religions," *The Ark* (London, Catholic Study Circle for Animal Welfare), April 1968; Marie Dreyfus, *Crimes against Creation*, 153, 163.

8. *The Laws of Manu*, vol. 25 of *Sacred Books of the East*, trans. George Buhler (Oxford: Clarendon, 1886), 484, 496–98; Edward Westermark, *The Origins and Development of Moral Ideas* (London: Macmillan, 1917), 497; Dreyfus, ibid.

9. Ibid.

10. John Noss, *Man's Religions*.

11. *Laws of Manu*, chap. 5, sec. 48, as cited in Dudley Giehl, *Vegetarianism: A Way of Life* (New York: Harper & Row, 1979), 170–71; Basil Wrighton, "Animals in the Other Religions."

12. Ibid.; G. Naganathan, *Animal Welfare and Nature: Hindu Scriptural Perspectives*, 15.

13. Steven Rosen, *Food for the Spirit* (New York: Bala Books, 1987), 73.

14. Karan Singh, "The Hindu Declaration on Nature," Assisi, Italy, September 29, 1986; distributed by the International Network for Religion and Animals, Silver Spring, Maryland; "Foreword," G. Naganathan, *Animal Welfare and Nature: Hindu Scriptural Perspectives*.

15. Basant Kumar Lal, Magadh University, "Hindu Perspective on the Use of Animals in Science," 5, distributed by the World Society for the Protection of Animals, Boston.

16. S. S. Rama Rao Pappu, "Unity of Life in Hinduism," *The Animals' Voice* (Los Angeles), August 1989, 52–54.

17. Mohandas K. Gandhi, *The Moral Basis of Vegetarianism*, compiled by R. K. Prabhu (Navajivan Publishing House, 1959), 20; as cited in Dudley Giehl, *Vegetarianism: A Way of Life*, 161; Agnes Carr, *The Animals and Birds Redeemed from Death*, 45.

18. John Paul Fox, *Animals, Cruelty, and Kindness* (Salt Lake City, 1979).

19. John B. Noss, *Man's Religions*.

20. Mahatma Dass, "Krishna Consciousness," *The Animals' Voice*, 54–55.

21. John B. Noss, *Man's Religions*.

22. Basant Kumar Lal, "Hindu Perspective on the Use of Animals in Science."

23. Ibid.

24. Karan Singh, "The Hindu Declaration on Nature."

25. Ibid.

26. Ethel Mannin, "The Eastern Attitude toward Animals," *The Ark*, December 1961, 110–13.

## Chapter 13 / Jainism: Never Harm Any Living Creature

1. John B. Noss, *Man's Religions* (New York: Macmillan, 1966), 154.

2. Ibid.

3. Ibid., 156.

4. Ibid., 168.

5. Ibid., 155–56, 165; Eleanor N. Schwartz, "A Reluctant Burden," Travel Section, *New York Times*, March 12, 1989, 39.

6. Edward Westermark, *The Origin and Development of Moral Ideas* (London: Macmillan, 1917), 497–89.

7. Christopher Chapple, "Noninjury to Animals: Jaina and Buddhist Perspectives," *Animal Sacrifices*, edited by Tom Regan (Philadelphia: Temple University Press, 1986), 216.

8. John B. Noss, *Man's Religions*, 159–60.

9. *The Gaina Sutras*, vol. 22 of *Sacred Books of the East*, translated by Hermann Jacobi (Oxford: Clarendon, 1884), 202–3; John Noss, *Man's Religions*, 161.

10. Noss, ibid., 168; Christopher Chapple, "Noninjury to Animals: Jaina and Buddhist Perspectives," 217.

11. Michael Tobias, "Ahimsa," *The Animals' Voice* (Los Angeles), August 1989, 57.

12. "Saint Francis of India Runs Free Hospital for Birds," *Boston Globe*, reprinted in *Atlanta Journal and Constitution*, November 27, 1986, 55A.

13. Michael Tobias, "Ahimsa," 57.

14. Ibid., 56–57; Dudley Giehl, *Vegetarianism: A Way of Life* (New York: Harper & Row, 1979), 173.

15. Tobias, ibid.

16. Eleanor Schwartz, "A Reluctant Burden."

## Chapter 14 / Buddhism: Compassion for All Creatures

1. T. W. Rhys Davids, *Buddhism*, 1878, 139, 160; as cited in V. A. Holmes-Gore, *These We Have Not Loved* (Wheaton, Ill.: Theosophical Press, 1946), 6.

2. Ibid.

3. Rev. Iru Price (Shik Po Chih), "Compassion," Humanitarian Literature Distribution Service, San Francisco.

4. John B. Noss, *Man's Religions* (New York: Macmillan, 1966), 175–76.

5. Nancy Nash, "Buddhist Perception of Nature: A New Perspective for Conservation of Nature," Hong Kong, 1985.

6. John Noss, *Man's Religions*, 196.

7. Ibid., 177.

8. Tsongkhapa, "Great Expositions on the Gradual Path"; as cited in Chatsumarn Kabilsingh, "How Buddhism Can Help Protect Nature," *Tree of Life: Buddhism and Protection of Nature* (Hong Kong: Buddhist Perception of Nature, 1987), 11.

9. Tsongkhapa, ibid.

10. Chatsumarn Kabilsingh, "How Buddhism Can Help Protect Nature," 11.

11. Normita Thongtham, "Saving Nature through Buddhism," *Bangkok Post*, November 5, 1985; "Saving Nature through Buddhism," *Nation*, October 31, 1985.

12. Interview with Dalai Lama, Atlanta, Ga., September 19, 1987.

13. Venerable Lungrig Nomgyal Rinpoche, "The Buddhist Declaration on Nature," Assisi, Italy, September 29, 1986.

14. Basil Wrighton, "Animals in the Other Religions," *The Ark* (London: Catholic Study Circle for Animal Welfare), April 1968.

15. *Samadhiraja Sutra*, vol. 2, Dege version; as cited by Chatsumarn Kabilsingh, "How Buddhism Can Help Protect Nature," 11–12.

16. *Khunddakapatha* (London: Pali Text Society, 1960); as cited by Kabilsingh, ibid.

17. "The Practice of Non-Injury," Buddhists Concerned for Animals, San Francisco.

18. Christopher Chapple, "Noninjury to Animals: Jaina and Buddhist Perspectives," *Animal Sacrifices*, edited by Tom Regan (Philadelphia: Temple University Press, 1986), 221.

19. Ibid.

20. Iru Price, "Compassion."

21. "The Buddhist Declaration on Nature."

22. Iru Price, "Compassion."

23. Roger Corless, *The Concern for Animals in Buddhism*, International Network for Religion and Animals, Silver Spring, Md.

24. Rafe Martin, "Buddhism and Animals, *The Animals' Voice* (Los Angeles), August 1989, 55.

25. Roger Corless, *The Concern for Animals in Buddhism*.

26. Ibid.

27. Basil Wrighton, "Animals in the Other Religions"; Ethel Mannin, "The Eastern Attitude toward Animals," *The Ark*, December 1961, 110–13.

28. Chatsumarn Kabilsingh, "How Buddhism Can Help Protect Nature," 14.

29. Ibid.

30. "Buddhist Perception of Nature," brochure by the 1987 Rolex Awards, Hong Kong, 1987.

31. Pacittiya, Bhutagama Vagga, *Thai Tripitaka*, 2:347; as cited in Chatsumarn Kabilsingh, "How Buddhism Can Help Protect Nature," 10.

32. Kabilsingh, ibid.

33. Ibid., 13–14.

34. "Newsletter" Buddhists Concerned for Animals, San Francisco, Winter 1986–87, 3.

35. Chatsumarn Kabilsingh, "How Buddhism Can Help Protect Nature," 11.

36. Ibid., 14–15.

37. Yi-Fu Tuan, "Our Treatment of the Environment in Ideal and Actuality," *American Scientist*, no. 58 (1970): 248; as cited in René Dubos, *A God Within* (New York: Charles Scribner's Sons, 1972), 160.

38. John B. Noss, *Man's Religions*, 199–200.

39. Ibid.

40. Ibid.; Basil Wrighton, "Animals in the Other Religions."

41. "The Buddhist Declaration on Nature."

42. Nay Htun, "The State of the Environment Today: The Needs for Tomorrow," *Tree of Life*, 19, 29.

43. "The Buddhist Declaration on Nature."

44. "The Practice of Non-Injury."

45. Christopher Chapple, "Noninjury to Animals: Jaina and Buddhist Perspectives," 231.

46. Nancy Nash, "Buddhist Perception of Nature: A New Perspective for Conservation of Nature."

47. "Saving Nature through Buddhism," *The Nation.*

48. Nancy Nash, "Buddhist Perception of Nature: A New Perspective for Conservation of Nature," 12.

49. P. Moyle and F. R. Senanayke, *Tigerpaper,* U.N. Food and Agriculture Organization, October 1980; as cited in Chatsumarn Kabilsingh, "How Buddhism Can Help Protect Nature," 8.

50. Kabilsingh, ibid., 7.

51. *Tibet: The Facts* (London: Scientific Buddhist Association, 1984); as cited in Kabilsingh, ibid., 8.

52. Kabilsingh, ibid., 8, 15.

53. Christopher Chapple, "Noninjury to Animals: Jaina and Buddhist Perspectives," 225.

54. Edward Westermark, *The Origins and Development of Moral Ideas* (London: Macmillan, 1917), 500.

55. *Tree of Life,* 16.

56. Ibid.

57. "Japanese Whalers Solemnly Mourn the Creatures They Have Dispatched," *Baltimore Sun,* November 12, 1979.

58. Ibid.

59. Ibid.

60. *Island on the Edge,* movie produced and filmed by Hardy Jones, Sausalito, Calif., 1979.

61. Ethel Mannin, "The Eastern Attitude toward Animals."

62. Ibid.

63. *Tree of Life,* 16.

## Chapter 15 / Islam: Respect for Animals and Nature

1. Sura 6, aya 38; as cited in Abou Bakr Ahmed Ba Kader, Abdul Latif Tawfik El Shirazy Al Sabbagh, Mohammed Al Sayyed Al Glenid, and Movel Yousef Samarrai Izzidien, *Islamic Principles for the Conservation of the Natural Environment* (Gland, Switzerland, and the Kingdom of Saudi Arabia: International Union for the Conservation of Nature and Natural Resources, 1983), 17.

2. John B. Noss, *Man's Religions* (New York: Macmillan, 1966), 714.

3. Qur'an Majeed, Sura VI; as cited by Guy Delon, in report distributed by the Animal Welfare Institute, Washington, D.C.

4. Qur'an Majeed 11:6; as cited in Al-Hafiz B. A. Masri, "Synopsis of Islamic Teachings on Animal Rights," distributed by International Network for Religion and Animals, Silver Spring, Md.

5. Qur'an Majeed 55:10–12; as cited by Masri, ibid.

6. Ibid.

7. Qur'an Majeed 45:4; as cited in Masri, ibid.

8. Qur'an Majeed 24:41; as cited in Masri, ibid.

9. Qur'an Majeed 22:18; as cited in Masri, ibid.

10. Qur'an Majeed 54:49; as cited in Masri, ibid.

11. Qur'an Majeed 15:19; as cited in Masri, ibid.

12. Qur'an Majeed 7:56; as cited in Masri, ibid.

13. Qur'an Majeed 5:103 and 4:118, 119; as cited in Masri, ibid.

14. Masri, ibid.

15. Basil Wrighton, "Animals in the Other Religions," *The Ark* (London, Catholic Study Circle for Animal Welfare), April 1968.

16. *Hadith Mishkat*, 3:1392; as cited in B. A. Masri, "Synopsis of Islamic Teachings on Animal Rights."

17. *Hadith Bukari*; as cited in Masri, ibid.

18. *Hadith Muslim* and Awn, 2658; as cited in Masri, ibid.

19. Guy Delon, superintendent of the American Fondouk, Fez, Morocco; from the Animal Welfare Institute, Washington, D.C.

20. *Hadith Bukhari*, 4:337; as cited in B. A. Masri, "Synopsis of Islamic Teachings on Animal Rights."

21. *Hadith Awn*, 7, 222:2533; as cited in Masri, ibid.

22. *Hadith Mishkat*, book 6, chap. 7, 8:178; as cited in Masri, ibid.

23. Cf. *Al-Tabarani*; as cited in Masri, ibid..

24. *Hadith Al-Nasai*, 7, 206; as cited in Masri, ibid.

25. Guy Delon, in report distributed by the Animal Welfare Institute, Washington, D.C.

26. Al-Hafiz B. A. Masri, "Excerpts from the Islamic Teachings on Animal Welfare," World Society for the Protection of Animals, London.

27. Ibid.; Guy Delon, in report distributed by the Animal Welfare Institute, Washington, D.C.

28. Delon, ibid.

29. *Hadith Awn*, 7, 235:2550; as cited in B. A. Masri, "Synopsis of Islamic Teachings on Animal Rights"; Basil Wrighton, "Animals in the Other Religions."

30. *Hadith Awn*, 7, 221:2532; as cited in Masri, ibid.; Guy Delon, in report distributed by the Animal Welfare Institute, Washington, D.C.

31. Al-Hafiz B. A. Masri, *Islamic Concern for Animals* (Petersfield, Hants., England: Athene Trust, 1987).

32. Basil Wrighton, "Animals in the Other Religions."

33. B. A. Masri, "Excerpts from the Islamic Teachings on Animal Welfare."

34. *Hadith Awn*, 7, 216 and 217:2525; as cited in B. A. Masri, "Synopsis of Islamic Teachings on Animal Rights."

35. V. A. Holmes-Gore, *These We Have Not Loved* (Wheaton, Ill.: Theosophical Press, 1946), 6–7.

36. *Riyad as-Salihin* of Imam Nawawi; English translation: London: Curzon Press, 1975, 271, Hadith no. 1606; as cited in B. A. Masri, "Islam and Experiments on Animals," *International Animal Action*, no. 18 (1987): 10.

37. Masri, ibid.

38. *Hadith Muslim*, 3:1958; as cited in B. A. Masri, "Synopsis of Islamic Teachings on Animal Rights."

39. *Hadith Awn*, 8, 15:2803; as cited in Masri, ibid.

40. *Ahadith Bukhari and Muslim*, 3:1957; as cited in Masri, ibid.

41. *Hadith Al-Nasai*, 7:238; as cited in Masri, ibid.

42. *Hadith Tirmidhi*, chap. *Al-At'imah*, 1473; as cited in Masri, ibid.

43. B. A. Masri, "Excerpts from the Islamic Teachings on Animal Welfare."

44. Ibid.

45. B. A. Masri, "Islam and Experiments on Animals."

46. Ibid.

47. *Hadith La Taqtolu bi-l-Iza'a*; as cited in B. A. Masri, "Synopsis of Islamic Teachings on Animal Rights."

48. *Hadith Muslim*, 2:156; as cited in Masri, ibid.

49. *Hadith Muslim*, 10:739; as cited in Masri, ibid.

50. *Hadith Sahih Muslim-Kitab-us-Said*, 1079; as cited in Masri, ibid.

51. *Kitab Al-Maqanna*, 3:542; as cited in Masri, ibid.

52. *Hadith Tirmidhi*, 1480; as cited in Masri, ibid.

53. B. A. Masri, "Islam and Experiments on Animals."

54. *Al Fruo Min-al-Kafi Lil Kulini*, 6:230; as cited in B. A. Masri, "Synopsis of Islamic Teachings on Animal Rights."

55. Al-Mahli, 7:457; as cited in Masri, ibid.

56. *Badae Al-Sanae*, 6:2811; as cited in Masri, ibid.

57. Al-Mahli, 7:457; as cited in Masri, ibid.

58. Kitab al-Nil wa Shifa al-Alib, 4:460; as cited in B. A. Masri, "Islam and Experiments on Animals."

59. B. A. Masri, "Excerpts from the Islamic Teachings on Animal Welfare."

60. Abdullah Omar Nasseef, "The Muslim Declaration on Nature," Assisi, Italy, September 29, 1986; distributed by the International Network for Religion and Animals, Silver Spring, Md.

61. *Islamic Principles for the Conservation of the Natural Environment*, 20.

62. Ibid., 13, 24.

63. Ibid., 16–17.

64. Ibid., 22.

65. Ibid., 24.

66. "The Muslim Declaration on Nature."

67. Guy Delon, in report distributed by the Animal Welfare Institute, Washington, D.C.

68. *Hadith Musnad of Ahmad*, 5:440 and 3:114; as cited in B. A. Masri, "Synopsis of Islamic Teachings on Animal Rights."

69. "The Muslim Declaration on Nature."

70. Qur'an Majeed 25:48–49; as cited in B. A. Masri, *Islamic Concern for Animals*, reviewed by Brian Klug, "Network News," International Network for Religion and Animals, Silver Spring, Md., no. 6, Winter 1988.

71. Bill Clark, *The Paper Ark* (New York: Everest House, 1979), 60.

72. Guy Delon, in report distributed by the Animal Welfare Institute, Washington, D.C.

73. Ibid.

74. Ibid.

75. R. A. Nicholson, *A Literary History of the Arabs* (Cambridge, England, 1930), 323; as cited in Basil Wrighton, "Animals in the Other Religions."

76. M. A. R. Tuker, *Past and Future Ethics*, 182; as cited in V. A. Holmes-Gore, *These We Have Not Loved*, 7.

77. Guy Delon, in report distributed by the Animal Welfare Institute, Washington, D.C.

78. Dudley Giehl, *Vegetarianism: A Way of Life* (New York: Harper & Row, 1979), 173–74.

79. Brian Klug, "Network News," International Network for Religion and Animals, Silver Spring, Md., no. 6, Winter 1988.

80. Ibid.

81. Ibid.

82. B. A. Masri, "Islam and Experiments on Animals."

83. B. A. Masri, "A Glimpse of Islam on Animals," *The Animals' Voice* (Los Angeles, Compassion for Animals Foundation), August 1989, 50–51.

84. *Islamic Principles for the Conservation of the Natural Environment*, 17.

## Chapter 16 / The Baha'i Faith: Loving-kindness to Every Creature

1. "The Baha'i Statement on Nature," Introduction, Baha'i International Community, Office of Public Information, *Baha'i History Calendar*, Baha'i Distribution Hawaii, Honolulu, Hawaii, 1989; brochure by the Office of the Environment, Baha'i International Community, New York, December, 1989.

2. Robert A. White, "Spiritual Foundations for an Ecologically Sustainable Society," *Journal of Baha'i Studies*, February 1, 1989.

3. "Conservation of the Earth's Resources," "Baha'i National Review," *American Baha'i*, January 1990, 9–12.

4. Robert White, "Spiritual Foundations for an Ecologically Sustainable Society."

5. "The Baha'i Statement on Nature."

6. "Conservation of the Earth's Resources," Baha'i Publishing Trust of the United Kingdom, 1990; from David Sterling, "Earth Day, 1990," Winona, Minn., April 1990.

7. "The Baha'i Statement on Nature."

8. "Conservation of the Earth's Resources," "Baha'i National Review," *The American Baha'i*.

9. Ibid.

10. "Brochure."

11. Robert White, "Spiritual Foundations for an Ecologically Sustainable Society."

# Index